literature media
information systems

Critical Voices in Art, Theory and Culture
A series edited by Saul Ostrow

Now Available

Seams: Art as a Philosophical Context
Essays by Stephen Melville
Edited and Introduced by Jeremy Gilbert-Rolfe

Capacity: History, the World, and the Self in Contemporary Art and Criticism
Essays by Thomas McEvilley
Commentary by G. Roger Denson

Media Research: Technology, Art, Communication
Essays by Marshall McLuhan
Edited and with a Commentary by Michel A. Moos

Literature, Media, Information Systems
Essays by Friedrich A. Kittler
Edited and Introduced by John Johnston

Forthcoming Titles

England and Its Aesthetes: Biography and Taste
Essays by John Ruskin, Walter Pater, and Adrian Stokes
Commentary by David Carrier

The Wake of Art: Criticism, Philosophy, and the Ends of Taste
Essays by Arthur C. Danto
Commentary by Gregg Horowitz and Tom Huhn

Beauty Is Nowhere: Ethical Issues in Art and Design
Edited and Introduced by Richard Roth and Susan King Roth

Difference/Indifference: Musings on Postmodernism,
Marcel Duchamp and John Cage 1973–1997
Introduction, Essays, Interviews and Performances by Moira Roth
Commentary by Jonathan D. Katz

Music/Ideology: Resisting the Aesthetic
Edited and with an Introduction by Adam Krims
Commentary by Henry Klumpenhouwer

The Myths of Postmodern Theory
Essays by Nicholas Zurbrugg
Commentary by Warren Burt

This book is part of a series. The publisher will accept continuation orders which may be cancelled at any time and which provide for automatic billing and shipping of each title in the series upon publication. Please write for details.

friedrich
a. kittler

essays

literature
media

information systems

edited and
introduced

john
johnston

G+B
ARTS

Australia · Canada · China · France · Germany · India · Japan · Luxembourg · Malaysia
The Netherlands · Russia · Singapore · Switzerland · Thailand · United Kingdom INTERNATIONAL

Amsteldijk 166
1st Floor
1079 LH Amsterdam
The Netherlands

British Library Cataloguing in Publication Data

Kittler, Friedrich A.
  Literature, media, information systems : essays. -
  (Critical voices in art, theory and culture)
  1. Technology - Social aspects   2. Technology in literature
  3. Mass media and literature
  I. Title   II. Johnston, John
  306.4'6

ISBN 90-5701-071-2

CONTENTS

*C*ritical Voices in Art, Theory and Culture is a response to the changing perspectives that have resulted from the continuing application of structural and poststructural methodologies and interpretations to the cultural sphere. From the ongoing processes of deconstruction and reorganization of the traditional canon, new forms of speculative, intellectual inquiry and academic practices have emerged which are premised on the realization that insights into differing aspects of the disciplines that make up this realm are best provided by an interdisciplinary approach that follows a discursive rather than a dialectic model.

In recognition of these changes, and of the view that the histories and practices that form our present circumstances are in turn transformed by the social, economic, and political requirements of our lives, this series will publish not only those authors who already are prominent in their field, or those who are now emerging—but also those writers who had previously been acknowledged, then passed over, only now to become relevant once more. This multigenerational approach will give many writers an opportunity to analyze and reevaluate the position of those thinkers who have influenced their own practices, or to present responses to the themes and writings that are significant to their own research.

In emphasizing dialogue, self-reflective critiques, and exegesis, the *Critical Voices* series not only acknowledges the deterritorialized nature of our present intellectual environment, but also extends the challenge to the traditional supremacy of the authorial voice by literally relocating it within a discursive network. This approach to texts breaks with the current practice of speaking of multiplicity, while continuing to construct a singularly linear vision of discourse that retains the characteristics of dialectics. In an age when subjects are conceived of as acting upon one another, each within the context of its own history and without contradiction, the ideal of a totalizing system does not seem to suffice. I have come to realize that the near collapse of the endeavor to produce homogeneous terms, practices, and histories—once thought to be an essential aspect of defining the practices of art, theory, and culture—reopened each of these subjects to new interpretations and methods.

My intent as editor of *Critical Voices in Art, Theory and Culture* is to make available to our readers heterogeneous texts that provide a view that looks ahead to new and differing approaches, and back toward those views that make the dialogues and debates developing within the areas of cultural studies, art history, and critical theory possible and necessary. In this manner we hope to contribute to the expanding map not only of the borderlands of modernism, but also of those newly opened territories now identified with postmodernism.

Saul Ostrow

Friedrich Kittler: The Passage from
Network to Narrative

his collection of Friedrich A. Kittler's essays along with John Johnston's invaluable commentary make available for the first time not only previously untranslated[1] texts, but also an overview and analysis of the significance of Kittler's work in communications theory as well as literature. On the basis of the postulate that literature best records media's effect both psychologically and heuristically, Kittler's research focuses on what technology inscribes upon us and how we in turn reproduce its narratives of self-identity and otherness.

If you are wondering why you haven't heard of Friedrich Kittler before this, it is because knowing about him is the exception to the rule, even though he has a growing reputation in Comparative Literature departments in the United States and among those who are concerned with technology's continuing effect on our cultural outlook as well as our daily lives. This reputation is based on the few texts that have been circulated through such magazines as *1-800*, or those which can be found on the Internet.[2] Until working on this volume, the only work of Professor Kittler's I was familiar with was the publication of a portion of the introduction to "Gramophone, Film, Typewriter."[3] While this text demonstrated the complexity of Kittler's analysis and the breadth of knowledge he brings to bear on his subject, neither context nor indication of the broader implications of his work were supplied.

Kittler, a professor at the Institute for Aesthetics at Humboldt University in Berlin, is the author of seven books[4] and more than one hundred articles of literary and media criticism. Following the work of Marshall McLuhan, Kittler informs his understanding of media and literature with a Paul Virilio-like interest in technologies'

relations to the wars that produce them. Tracing the origins of the
Internet and fiber optics to the military's need for media that would
survive nuclear detonations, Kittler finds greater significance in the
fact that this new communications network connected computers
rather than human beings. The implication of this for Kittler is
twofold: first, that information and communication had gained their
autonomy, and second, that we are now moving toward becoming
the *object* of technological developments that were once secreted
within our body. In this schema, technology, which Marshall
McLuhan theorized was the extension of our bodies into the world,
now becomes the object of technology literally modifying and transforming the body that had given rise to it. Though this is rarely if ever
expressed outside of science fiction, it is seemingly a process that can
only be understood in the most mechanistic or prosthetic manner.
Kittler is not stimulated by the notion that we are becoming cyborgs,
but instead by the subtler issues of how we conceptually become
reflections of our information systems.

This problem of our being absorbed into our own technology is,
for Kittler, not a humanist one; instead his primary concern is how
this may effect *how* and *what* comes to be represented, psychologically as well as culturally. In turn, Kittler proposes the idea that our
ability to interpret such texts is largely the result of historically determined communication systems. As John Johnston points out, these
"discourse networks are the subject of representation as well as the
mechanism of its changing meaning." In other words, the media
creates the means of *representation*—its subject and content—and
these are also the product of their storage medium's (the means of
preservation and *reproduction*) effect on the author and audience alike.
This, too, is in keeping with Marshall McLuhan's view that technology as an extension of our bodies and senses caused changes in our
perception and conception of the social. While this holds true—
from Gutenberg's invention of the printing press to the advent of
telecommunications—what Kittler brings to this equation is the
idea that this relationship is being inverted. He foresees the day
when we will be technology's product—if we aren't already.

Kittler finds the record of this transformation of ours discourse
networks inscribed in literature. Those of us who grew up with
Dracula (the movie—not the novel) would never have guessed that

this quintessential gothic tale of an "undead" aristocrat feeding on the blood and vitality of an emerging middle class of doctors, lawyers, real estate agents, and secretaries might record the changes being wrought by the fragmentation of the data stream's flow by the late-nineteenth-century technologies originally intended for that same data's storage.

In Kittler's reading of Bram Stoker's novel, Dracula is defeated by the ability of those on the side of good to retrieve and correlate the necessary information concerning Dracula's movements. This information is recorded in a network of data storage made up of newspapers, phonograph records, and stenographic notes. Kittler finds attached in such benign inventions a malevolent text in which the flow of information in the process of telling a story records the encroachment and transformation of what had previously been deemed the body's territory. Understanding this, he speculates what effect the melding together of these various media through digitalization may eventually have; perhaps it will not only erase the very notion of medium all together, but also that of the body.

Skilled in reading the signs of media's encroachment as well as mapping the course of the progress of humanity's integration into the very technologies that we imagine we have invented, Kittler predicts the result will be a loss of the body and its extensions, such as language—both written and spoken. Through this process the "natural," or what was once thought of as natural, is not absorbed; rather, it is dissolved, for it is only the residue of the voice, the word, our image or gesture that is now preserved, undifferentiated from one to the other. Everywhere Kittler turns he finds the message of modernism, which is a history of the fragmentation of the data stream and in turn of our self-image and identity.

In recognizing literature's capacity to give representation to the changing epistemologies induced by technology, Kittler now focuses on the price to be paid for the services that computing renders. For him the most obvious aspect is that the commands of the applications we use command *us*. This reshaping of behavior—nearly invisible to us—lurks behind the promise of an interactive, virtual reality. The inaccessibility of the computer's operating system, which commands and reacts to our actions at the keyboard, or the click of a mouse, mirrors, according to Kittler, the bureaucratic structures that we navigate daily. As Johnston points out, he perceives in this the fulfillment of the Hegelian dream of reality someday being nothing more than the product of a universal medium. The difference is that, for Hegel, this medium was to be history, whereas, for us, it just might be the computer's operating system. Digital processing as a universal medium capable of not only storing images, sound, motion, and text but also of doing calculation marks not only the reunification of the data stream but also its transformation as well.

In his commentary Johnston defines both the parameters and consequences of this epistemological transformation. The new system (or perhaps it is only an interim one) of digital media, while doing away with medial differences, does maintain certain continuities through the random generation of psychological and neurological effects. Beyond this, these systems dissolve our ability to differentiate, on the level of natural and artificial, between such effects and those of the theoretical import of information theory and cybernetics. The fact is that such a transformation can only be recognized and accounted for retrospectively. Given the damned-if-you-do, damned-if-you-don't nature of this situation, anyone who is presently writing finds himself trapped in the nether state of recording, either consciously or unconsciously, the demise of one system, or of its having become the tool of another. The irony of this is not missed by Johnston, for he raises the question then of how this analyses impacts on Kittler's own endeavors as well as those of any other author. Yet in this scenario, all is not lost: The possibility exists that our new discourse network will be capable of not just recording the displacement of modernism's constructs but also of forming the background against which this new episteme will be foregrounded. Johnston perceives that this possibility, evident in Kittler's ability to articulate this situation, has the effect of "extending and contesting the best of twentieth-century theory on technology" as well as recontextualizing French poststructuralism.

Saul Ostrow

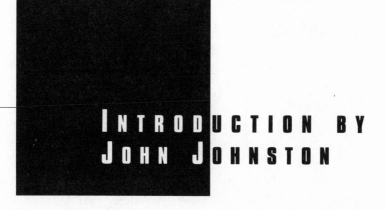

INTRODUCTION BY JOHN JOHNSTON

Friedrich Kittler: Media Theory
After Poststructuralism

Friedrich Kittler: Media Theory After Poststructuralism

John Johnston

Fiber Optic Networks: Connecting Up the "Present"

This volume presents a selection of recent essays by Friedrich Kittler that focus on the multiple relations between twentieth-century technical media and literature, psychoanalysis, war, and computer technology. These essays consolidate Kittler's previous research by considering new material, and extend it by confronting the information technologies that characterize our *fin de millenium*.

"Media determine our situation [*Lage*], which (nevertheless, or for that very reason) merits a description." So Kittler begins the preface to *Grammophon Film Typewriter* (1986), his detailed account of the technological separation and storage of the data stream brought about by the new media of phonograph, film, and typewriter at the beginning of the twentieth century.[1] In the very first chapter, however, Kittler envisions a point, not too distant as the century draws to an end, when the very difference that media make will be subsumed and cancelled—not in the *Geist* of Hegelian *Aufhebung*, but in the digital numbers of an electronic feedback loop:

> The general digitalization of information and channels erases the difference between individual media. Sound and image, voice and text have become mere effects on the surface, or, to put it better, the interface for the consumer. . . . In computers everything becomes number: imageless, soundless, wordless quantity. And if the optical fiber network reduces all formerly separate data flows to one standardized digital series of numbers, any medium can be translated into another. With numbers nothing is impossible. Modulation, transformation, synchronization; delay, memory, transposition; scrambling, scanning, mapping—a total connection of all media on a digital base erases the notion of the medium itself. Instead of hooking

> up technologies to people, absolute knowledge can run as an endless
> loop. (infra, 31)

With the full deployment of fiber optic cables and computer technology, what we call our "sense perception" devolves to a "dependent
variable" worked out between engineers and sales people. What
passes for "reality"—i.e., the meaningful mixing of words and
images—will only hold together until the separation of media that
defines our modernity has ended. Meanwhile, however, there are still
media, and today's technological standard can be described in terms
of "partially connected media systems."

Any flight on a commercial jet airliner will illustrate. Whereas
the crew are connected to radar screens, diode displays, radio beacons and nonpublic channels, the passengers are encased in a "multi-
media embryonic sack" in which in-flight movies, microwave cuisine,
and Muzak all serve to screen out the "real background: noise, night,
and the cold of an unlivable outside" (infra, 32). No doubt Kittler
chooses this example not only because the jet is a site where densely
connected media still remain separate according to technological
standard, frequency, user allocation and interface, but also because
the different positions of address in this conglomerate of communication systems point to an evident discrepancy in technical expertise.
In other words, for Kittler today's "situation" is defined by the inven-
tors and the technicians who understand the technology and how it
"constructs our sense perception" on the one hand, and the end-
users and consumers increasingly dependent on it who are kept distanced and ignorant by an array of user-friendly devices on the other.

Kittler's comments on American cyberculture in a recent interview reveal a growing apprehension and dismay in this regard:

> In America there seems to be greater loyalty to industrial achievement
> [than there is in Europe]; there's a morality that dictates that one should
> not hack or patch or copy. The result, it seems to me, is that one is that
> much more hopelessly surrendered to the industrially determined
> products while their foam packing turned to the outside sells as
> cyberspace ideology. I looked at a few issues of *Mondo 2000* in this
> light. So there's one guru or prophet who writes the programs, and
> everyone else is a consumer who doesn't intervene in the process in
> any serious way, especially not at the level of hardware, but just lets it
> run until it has built up a largely literary science fiction phantasm on top
> of itself.[2]

On one side, the secrecy and cynicism of a military/postindustrial elite increasingly dependent upon inaccessible machine "intelligence," on the other a wide-eyed (and commercially useful) utopianism and technical ignorance. Yet, despite these flanking obstacles, Kittler insists that our present "situation" can be identified, that is, recognized and understood.

DN 2000

Is the present "situation" still fully recognizable in relation to the "discourse network of 1900"? In *Discourse Networks 1800/1900* (1985), Kittler sets apart and contrasts two distinct "discourse networks"—that of nineteenth-century romanticism and that of early twentieth-century modernism. At first, literature appears to serve as a privileged example. But an essential strategy of this earlier work is to demonstrate how the intelligibility and consequent meaning of literary texts is always and only possible because its discourse is embedded in and operates as part of a specific discourse network comprised of other discourses contemporaneous with it, pedagogy and philosophy in 1800, psychophysics and psychoanalysis in 1900. Thus, notions about what an author is, what makes a text literary, and what defines the activities of reading and writing are all historically determined aspects of a larger communication system. Literature, consequently, "whatever its subjects and topics may be," can be treated as a form of data processing; literary texts receive and store, process and transmit information in a way "not structurally different from computers."[3] Methodologically, literary texts constitute a "discourse on discourse," a reflection on the very hardware of cultural data processing and its historical variables.[4] At the same time, these texts cannot be read as an autonomous discourse. In the absence of any universal reference, literature requires the support of other discourses—scientific and/or institutional—in order to "make a so-called sense."[5]

With the invention of new storage and transmission media, which Kittler explores more fully in *Grammophon Film Typewriter*, discourse analysis alone can no longer suffice, and literary criticism can no longer ignore the materiality of its objects. Before the twentieth century, written texts provided the central archive for the storage of all cultural data, a monopoly enshrined in the discourse network of

1800. As the translation of a silent and wordless nature, language was invested with spiritual powers whose thematization provided the basis of romantic poetry and hermeneutics. This synthesis dissolves with the invention of the film and the phonograph, which record and store optical and aural data automatically with superhuman precision, and the typewriter, which mechanically removes writing from the sensuous continuity of the hand's movement, and frees it from the double domination of eye and consciousness. Around 1900, with the separations and discontinuities these new technical media bring about, writing becomes merely one medium among others, and visible as such. It emerges, not out of nature, but against a background "noise" that Nietzsche sensed behind his back at the writing desk and that psychophysics studied. A literature of books and authors soon gives way to intransitive writing, or the "writing down of delirium," since the latter "coincides with what sciences and the media were doing."[6]

Things change once again with the invention of the computer, heralded by Alan Turing's Universal Machine of 1936. For Kittler, it is not at all fortuitous that it was also Turing who decrypted the Enigma code which had allowed German tanks, submarines, and dive bombers to communicate, thus turning the tide of the Second World War in the Allies' favor. Just as Kittler follows Marshall McLuhan (though showing contrarily that media precisely prohibit understanding), he also follows Paul Virilio in pointing out how modern communications and the entertainment industry are by-products of war and the exigencies of military strategy and logistics.[7] Thanks to the military need for a communications system that could survive nuclear detonations, today we have fiber optic cables and a new medium called the Internet, which, as is widely known, grew out of ARPANET, a decentralized control network for intercontinental ballistic missiles.

What the new communications network connects, of course, are computers, which add a third capacity to the early twentieth-century media of storage and transmission perfected in the First and Second World Wars. That capacity is calculation, which allows the translation of any medium into any other through the digitalization of all information. If the historical synchronicity of film, phonograph, and typewriter in the early twentieth century separated the data flows of optics, acoustics and writing and rendered them autonomous, current electronic technologies are bringing them back together; in the future a total connection of all media on a digital base will erase the very notion of a medium. In the meantime, we live among "partially connected media systems." Subjects of computer technology, our fate is now readable in the architecture of the Intel microprocessor chip.

Which brings us back to the question posed earlier: Is a new discourse network, "DN 2000," already looming on the event horizon? Kittler acknowledges that his own work "has become part of an information network that describes literature as an information network" (DN 371). But does this indicate an increase of system complexity, a cultural version of renormalization, or an immanent mutation of the network? In order to describe discourse networks as differentiated and contrasting systems, "at least *two* delimiting events" are indispensable. For the two networks Kittler analyzes in *Discourse Networks 1800/1900*, "universal alphabetization circa 1800 and technological data storage circa 1900 constitute just such turning points, for which there is sufficient evidence within about fifteen years" (DN 370). However, methodological constraints determine that an event inaugurating another discourse network can only be identified retrospectively. Despite intriguing possibilities raised by the current telecommunications assemblage and computer chip architectures, Kittler must therefore remain silent about DN 2000.

Communications and/or Computation

When Foucault brought *Les mots et les choses* to a close with sybilline proclamations concerning the effacement of "man" and the dissolution of the modern episteme, readers at the time wondered where— that is, within what episteme—Foucault's writing was or should be situated. A similar ambiguity shadows Kittler's methodological relationship to the discourse network of which his work is (presumably) a part. His recent writing, however, makes even more pressing the question of the historical and theoretical status of the systems or communicational model which he derives from Claude E. Shannon's *The Mathematical Theory of Communication* (*the* foundational text for information theory), and, more generally, from Norbert Wiener, John von Neumann and contemporary systems theorist Niklas

Luhmann. Are these theoretical sources—all but the last published in the late 1940s and early 1950s—part of the discourse network of 1900, or do they constitute the second of "at least *two* limiting events"—one on each side, as it were—that enable it to be demarcated and contrasted with a succeeding network, even if the latter is not yet fully articulated? There is, moreover, an ambiguity in the communications model itself, inasmuch as the computer's capacity for automated calculation tends to subsume and displace communications—an effect Kittler himself highlights without comment (see the quotation above, p. 2).

Yet these are fruitful ambiguities. If, on the one hand, there are noticeable continuities between the "random generators" of psychophysics and neurophysiology and the theoretical import of information theory and cybernetics as developed by Shannon, Wiener, von Neumann and others (which, despite their opposition to behaviorism also tended to level the differences between natural and artificial machines) on the other hand it can be argued that the work of this group made possible a genuine "epistemological break," the full consequences of which we are only now beginning to witness. Indeed, Kittler himself provides the evidence in his recent writing. The most visible effects, of course, are those brought about by the computer and its associated technologies, and it is all to Kittler's theoretical credit that they occupy a key position in his recent analyses. Paradoxically, Kittler's understanding of the computer's effect on "mediality"—as both completing the triad of data storage and transmission through calculation and bringing about the end of medial differences through digitalization—at once establishes media studies on a more secure basis and sounds its death knell.

Nevertheless, much of what is theoretically exciting in systems theory today reacts against the atomized and mechanistic ethos of the discourse network of 1900. The development of chaos theory and complexity (the study of nonlinear dynamic systems), self-organization and emergence, connectionism and neural networks, strides in molecular biology and artificial life all problematize the computational model, and deviate from or contest basic modernist assumptions in ways that have led many to claim that a new paradigm may well be in the making.[8] One can only hope that Kittler, who is usually unassailable on technical details, will direct his attention to developments that may date (or further confirm) the terms he has laid out for recognizing our present "situation."

In the meantime, Kittler's work confronts us, extending and contesting the very best of twentieth-century theory on technology (by Benjamin, Heidegger, McLuhan, Baudrillard, Virilio, et al.), as well as recontextualizing and to a certain degree transforming the work of the French poststructuralists.[9] Indeed, what is perhaps most striking and useful in Kittler's work is how fundamental poststructuralist concepts and assumptions are deployed to revitalize and update media and literary theory, while implicitly raising the question of the degree to which technology was always the *impensé* or blindspot of poststructuralism itself. Moreover, while information theory has been applied to literature before—notably by Umberto Eco in *The Open Work* and Jurij Lotman in *The Artistic Structure of the Text*—no one (to my knowledge) has done so with the degree of resonant detail and historical specificity that one finds in Kittler's analyses. In sum, by making discourse analysis "high tech," by providing the means for connecting scientific discourse with literary and cultural discourse, and by bringing brute positivist history into catalytic contact with contemporary theory, Kittler's writing pushes beyond the most intractable and supposedly deconstructed antinomies of our time.

Nervensprache: The Discourse Network Circa 1900

Among these antinomies, the discourse of our modernity stands as the most central and widely encompassing. In relation to the usual accounts, a text like Daniel Paul Schreber's *Memoirs of My Nervous Illness* can only appear to be marginal and eccentric; for Kittler, however, it proves essential. Published in 1903 by a German high court judge, the book soon attracted Freud's attention.[10] His analysis, published in 1911 as "Psycho-Analytic Notes on an Autobiographical Account of a Case of Paranoia," made Schreber a paradigm case for the psychoanalytic study of paranoia. Significantly, Freud admitted that a perilously thin line separated Schreber's delusional account of his becoming-woman under the influence of God's rays from Freud's own theory: "these and many other details of Schreber's delusional structure," Freud writes, "sound almost like endo-psychic perceptions of the processes whose existence I have assumed in these pages as the basis of our explanation of paranoia."[11] Indeed, with rigorous and self-critical honesty, Freud left it to posterity to decide "whether there is more delusion in my theory than I should like to admit, or whether there is more truth in Schreber's delusion than other people are as yet prepared to believe." But why should knowledge and delirium exhibit such a precise symmetry of structure? Because, as Kittler shows, both depend on the existence of the discourse network of 1900, within which Schreber's *Memoirs* occupies an essential and privileged place.

"Discourse network" is one possible English translation of the German compound word *Aufschreibesystem*, which is Schreber's neologism for the "notation" or "writing-down-system" that transcribes and exhausts by means of a mysterious *Nervensprache* or "nerve-language" all of Schreber's thoughts as soon as they flash into his head. Here is how he describes the *Aufschreibesystem*:

> Books or other notes are kept in which for years have been written down all my thoughts, all my phrases, all my necessaries, all the articles in my possession or around me, all persons with whom I come into contact, etc. I cannot say with certainty who does the writing down. As I cannot imagine God's omnipotence lacks all intelligence, I presume that the writing down is done by creatures given human shape on distant celestial bodies . . . but lacking all intelligence; their hands are led automatically, as it were, by passing rays for the purpose of making them write down, so that later rays can again look at what has been written. (quoted in DN 298)

From the "writing down" that both produces and records Schreber's intricate and highly detailed paranoid delirium Kittler takes two things: first, the idea of an automatic and impersonal notation system that depends on no single individual and that articulates several discourses into a single discourse network; and secondly, the positioning of Schreber, both as body and text, in relation to a new and historically specific discourse network.

First the *Aufschreibesystem*. Kittler deploys the *term* to designate the archive of what is inscribed by a culture at a particular moment in time. The notion of the discourse network points to the fact that at any given cross-sectional moment in the life of a culture, only certain data (and no other) are selected, stored, processed, transmitted or calculated, all else being "noise" (in information theory "noise" is precisely what disrupts a communication channel). Whether implicitly or explicitly, an outside is thereby defined and a system of addresses and commands (or instructions) is established. In other words, on the basis of this particular selection of data not only perceptions, ideas, and concepts—all that is coded as meaningful in short—but also a system authorizing certain subjects as senders and others as receivers of discourse is instituted. However, by replacing causal and expressive models with a communicational one, Kittler in no way cuts off discourse from its material context. While a discourse network by definition has no center or origin, it serves precisely to link bodies to institutions. In fact, an insistent theme in Kittler's analysis of the discourse networks of 1800 and 1900 is the human price paid—the exclusions, the pathologies, the suicides—for these linkages.

Kittler's notion of the discourse network thus owes something to Foucault's theory of discourse, with its subsidary notions of "author function," discursive regularity, the archive, and diverse articulations of power/knowledge.[12] At the same time, it also reveals the latter's historical and technological limits. As Kittler himself points out, "Foucault's historical research does not progress much beyond 1850" (DN 369). As a consequence, Foucauldian discourse analysis has difficulty with the modern period, wherein new data-processing methods and technologies destroy "the alphabetic storage and transmission monopoly, that old-European basis of power" (DN 369). Whereas for Foucault the archive assumes the monologic dominance of written sentences, discourse then designating precisely how they would have to be organized in order not to be excluded from inscription, for Kittler "technologically possible manipulations determine what in fact can become a discourse" (DN 232). More succinctly: "all books [or libraries] are discourse networks, but not all discourse networks are books" (DN 298).

But if, as Kittler argues, "archaeologists of the present must also take into account data storage, transmission, and calculation in technological media" (DN 369), it is precisely because a new discourse network emerges around 1900 as a result of innovations in the technology of information. Specifically, the recently invented technical media of film, phonograph, and typewriter brought about a new division or differentiation of the human and cultural sensorium. With the invention of the phonograph and film, acoustical and optical data could now be stored "serially with superhuman precision" (DN 245); for the first time in human history, "writing ceased to be synonymous with the serial storage of data" (DN 229). Concomitantly, language could no longer be conceived as the expression of prelinguistic meanings, nor a conduit for the *inflatus* of spirit, as in the 1800 discourse network. Instead, it becomes one medium among others, its logic one of pure differentiality. As Ferdinand de Saussure theorized about the same time, language is a system of signs in which only differences matter: phonological or acoustic on one side (the signifier) and conceptual or imagistic on the other (the signifier). What joins the two realms of diacritical difference is simply the arbitrariness of the discrete linguistic sign.

Poetic "Alphabêtise"

What was it like to read a book—or more precisely, a work of imaginative literature—150 years ago, when language still retained its sovereignty, and cinema, phonographs, and typewriters had not yet separated the data flows of optics, acoustics, and writing and rendered them autonomous? Kittler answers this way:

> As long as the book had to take care of all serial data flows . . . words trembled with sensuality and memory. All the passion of reading consisted of hallucinating a meaning between letters and lines: the visible or audible world of romantic poetry. And all passion of writing was (according to E. T. A. Hoffmann) the poet's wish "to pronounce the inner being" of these hallucinations "in all its glowing colors, shadows, and lights" in order to "hit the favorable reader as if with an electric shock." (infra, 40)

This experience of reading can be attributed to alphabetization (or the oralization of language), and specifically to the new phonetic method of learning to read and write instituted in Germany by Heinrich Stephani (among others) around 1800.[13] Kittler demonstrates how the new method brings about a major discursive event, effecting both the way language is produced and received, and how it is linked with nondiscursive domains, the human body first of all. Basically, the phonetic method substitutes sounds for letters in a kind of dematerializing of the linguistic sign. As a result, one no longer decyphers, but seems to hear what is written as an inner voice. It is, moreover, a voice one has already heard, a variant of the voice that emanates from the mother's mouth in the hazy depths of childhood. Indeed, in a major shift of social roles the new method was administered by the mother, who does not simply teach language but transmits the living sounds of nature as the intelligible utterances of an inner voice, the prototype of all transcendental signifieds. For the male child, enshrouded in an eroticized, reverberating orality, nature becomes the organic continuum whose meaning only he (as poet) can express. But while poetry results from this maternal gestation, the mother herself remains woman under erasure, a stand-in for nature whose function is to insure that men can speak.

Expression as such thus requires several displacements and denials. They are, in part at least, enacted in Goethe's *Faust*, which Kittler reads (like Foucault reads the literary texts between epistemes in *Les mots et les choses*) as a telescoping from one discourse network to another. Specifically, the scholar-poet Faust tries unsuccessfully to slot himself (as individual man) into a no longer functional discourse network, the Republic of Letters.[14] What is lacking is the means to express a moment of originary self-constitution, which Faust discovers in an exercise of free translation. "In the beginning was the *Word*." But what, exactly, is the Word? Is it mind, force, act . . .? Out of a series of crossed out signifiers the transcendental signified itself emerges, but only as glimpsed in the displacements/translations of Faust's own search. Moreover, the same spirit that brings Faust to this realization also calls up Mephisto, and poetic license ends in a pact with the devil.

As Kittler brilliantly demonstrates, the other signatory in the pact with Mephisto is actually the state. Thus, while poetry, at once means and goal of understanding, presides over the new discourse network of 1800, it is watched over at "a modest distance" by an apparatus of power that operates not through understanding but control. It is a power, consequently, that remains inaccessible to the new methods of reading and understanding that it supports:

> The State remains closed off to every hermeneutic. Because understanding, despite its claim to universality, is one speech act among others, it cannot get behind the speech act that instituted it. Texts that are part of the hermeneutic net allow the power that governs them to

come to light only in a masked fashion. The translator Faust is watched
over by a devil in poodle's garb. (DN 21)

Thus shadowed by state surveillance, Poetry stands at the apotheosis of the discourse network of 1800—Hegel himself attests to it—
precisely because of its capacity to dematerialize and universalize.
This power is simply the poetic faculty or Imagination, the sense
that can replace all other senses: "It was not enough that in their own
domain the flow of sound rather than letters should dominate; poetic
words would liquidate, that is, liquefy, stones and colors, sounds and
building materials, all kinds of materialities and techniques of the
body, until the Imagination could replace all senses" (DN 114).
However, there is a price to be paid for this power. First, women are
excluded from the author position. Since a woman can only function
as a stand-in for nature, as the woman or mother who inspires
poetry, she cannot speak it herself (she cannot be both source and
medium.) And as Goethe himself also understood, the poet is not
always a poet, but must work as a functionary of the state, or as a
schoolteacher (which amounts to the same thing). Summarily, even
while the discourse network of 1800 provides a maximum number of
addressees (or readers), it also denies its own status as a discourse
network.

Electricity brings to an end the classical-romantic experience of
reading and writing. Among other effects, the synthetic, hallucinatory power of the word will be (re)produced in the twentieth century by other media: movies will replace the fantasia of the library;
the entertainment industry will flourish. Literature is left with two
options: it can join the other media, transposing its own textual
resources in a general degradation of effects; or it can reject them,
taking as its "infallible criterion" that it cannot be filmed, and
henceforth occupy the margins left to it by other media. The
French poet Stéphane Mallarmé immediately grasped the problem,
as well as the solution: the essence of literature derives from the fact
that it consists of rearrangements of twenty-six letters printed on a
white page.

Which brings us (back) to the typewriter. In a letter typewritten
to Peter Gast in 1882, Friedrich Nietzsche observes that "our writing instruments contribute to our thoughts." Kittler turns to the
first philosopher of media—or, as he calls Nietzsche, the "first

mechanized philosopher"[15]—in order to understand how the typewriter, through its capacity to implement "a logic of chaos and intervals" (DN 192), converges with the research of the new science of psychophysics.

Nietzsche's Typewriter

Nietzsche's writing machine, a Malling Hansen he purchased in 1880 for 450 reichmarks, remained serviceable for only several weeks. Long enough, apparently, to confirm his insight that writing was not—as it was for Goethe—the continuous translation from nature to culture, but a violent inscription or mnemotechnique: "Rather than presenting the subject with something to be deciphered, [writing] makes the subject what it is" (DN 196). Indeed, as Kittler goes on to show, Nietzsche's experiments with a new "telegraphic style" in which "the logic of the signifier has become a technique of sparseness and isolation, and minimum signs release maximum energy" (DN 190) already called for a new method of transcription, one that would accord with writing conceived not as the spiritualized expression of a subjective plenitude but as the transposition of signs over and against an empty ground. Or literally, as the striking of letters onto a white expanse.

How then could Nietzsche not be interested in the typewriter? In *Eperons*, a study of Nietzsche's many styles, Jacques Derrida reminds us that the notion of style itself derives from *stylus* or writing instrument, thus implying a concept of style as a labor of differential inscription that is both prior to, and hence irreducible to, meaning.[16] More attentive to the material articulation of the body in writing, Kittler demonstrates that the typewriter's unlinking of hand, eye, and letter decomposed the organic shroud that in the discourse network of 1800 enclosed the speaker in a reverberating orality which, emanating first from the Mother's mouth, ultimately signified Nature as an organic continuum that included Man. Thus, with the invention of the typewriter, "Woman" is liberated from the role as both idealization of and stand-in for Nature, and enters the work force as secretary/typist.

In the twentieth century, Alan Turing, whose "Universal Machine" will become the intellectual prototype of the digital computer, apologizes to friends for typing—rather than handwriting—

his letters with the remark that he has come to prefer discrete as opposed to continuous machines. Turing's preference for discrete machines reveals a significant difference, in contrast to Heidegger's remark (in his seminar on Parmenides) that the typewriter, which is "something between a tool and a machine," alters our relationship to being.[17] Whereas for Heidegger technology itself prevents any experience of its essence (as he famously insists in *Holzwege*),[18] for Turing it is precisely technology that allows one to avoid this (paradigmatic) confusion of writing with experience.

Yet it was Nietzsche who had already pointed the way out of the woods. According to his theory of language, we are twice removed from the continuities of nineteenth-century nature. Or rather, if there is a nature, it is physiological, the domain of nerve impulses. As Nietzsche points out in "Truth and Falsehood in an Extramoral Sense," the trajectory from this domain to articulate language entails two leaps, each one a metaphor: "First of all a nerve impulse is translated into an image. First metaphor. The image is again further formed into a sound! Second metaphor. And each time there is a complete leap, from one sphere into a completely different and new one" (quoted in DN 187).

Language, consequently, has nothing to do with truth or adequate expression; it only designates the relations of things to human beings by utilizing the most daring metaphors; it is literary in its foundations.

But the real significance of Nietzsche's theory, as Kittler underscores, is that it resolves language not into a common ground or origin but into two kinds of physiological data:

> Optical and acoustic responses to impulses, images and sounds, bring about the two aspects of language, as signified and signifier. Yet they remain as separated from one another as they are from the pure stochastic processes to which they respond. The break between the imaginal signified and the acoustic signifier cannot be bridged by continuous translation; only a metaphor of transposition can leap the gap. Separate sense media come together against the background of an omnipresent noise—as "completely different and new spheres." Instead of deriving media from a common source like the poetic imagination, Nietzsche divides optics and acoustics into a "world of sight" and a "world of sound." (DN 187)

By thus rendering the eye and ear autonomous, Nietzsche's theory of language anticipates in its very formulation the differentiation that new technological media—typewriter, phonograph, film—will soon bring about.

Pink Noise, or Psychophysics

Theodor Ziehen, Nietzsche's psychiatrist and a witness to the philosopher's collapse and transmogrification into a howling paralytic, was a renowned specialist on aphasia and the "flight of ideas." Yet scientific studies of the physiology of eye, ear and brain—privileged objects of scientific research circa 1880—could hardly have astounded the formerly mechanized but now debilitated philosopher. Basically, they simply extended his theory of language to include the operations of a typewriter: just as the latter's working parts are connected by rods and levers, so sensory and motor, acoustical and optic as well as language centers in the brain are linked by nerve paths that function autonomously, that is to say, independently of consciousness (see DN, 251). But, as Kittler insists, the new positivities of brain physiology and psychophysics can only have a disunifying effect on the discourse network of 1800:

> Because not every local center has direct nerve connections to every other, there is no unity of the transcendental signified capable of organically developing speaking and hearing, writing and reading out of one another. . . . Children circa 1900 learned to read without understanding and to write without thinking. The investigation of aphasia is always already its production. (DN 216)

Experiments in psychophysics, such as those carried out by Gertrude Stein at Harvard, measured the parameters of memory, sensory and motor response by excluding meaning as an independent variable. Psychophysics thus proved theoretically what was already becoming a basic operating assumption of the twentieth-century office, where every modern secretary was required to do what no nineteenth-century one ever dreamed of doing: to type and take dictation proficiently at a high speed with little attention to the meaning or even content of the work. Not surprisingly, psychophysics also laid the theoretical groundwork for a new conception of language based on this disintrication of sign and meaning (and here again Nietzsche proved prescient). For only on the basis of psychophysics, Kittler observes, does it make terminological sense for Saussure, in founding a new linguistics, to decompose the linguistic sign into the notion of a concept (signified) and an acoustic-sensory image (signifier), or for Freud . . . similarly to divide "thing representation" [*Sachvorstellung*] from "word representation" [*Wortvorstellung*]. (DN 216)

Psychophysics subverted not only the assumed referentiality of language but of sense experience itself, the "referential illusion" of which is unsparingly laid bàre in an exacting analysis of the brain, sense organs and nerve tissue. Early in the nineteenth century, in a paper entitled "Idea of a New Anatomy of the Brain," Sir Charles Bell observes that electrical stimulation of the nerves can produce such different responses as vision, hearing, and taste, without the proximity of any specific referent. Such is the context for this sample text from Hermann von Helmholtz's *On the Sensations of Tone*, published in 1863:

Nerves in the human body have been accurately compared to telegraph wires. Such a wire conducts one single kind of electric current and no other; it may be stronger, it may be weaker; it may move in either direction; it has no other qualitative differences. Nevertheless, according to the different kinds of apparatus with which we provide its terminations, we can send telegraphic dispatches, ring bells, explode mines, decompose water, move magnets, magnetize iron, develop light, and so on. *The same thing with our nerves.* The condition of excitement which can be produced in them, and is conducted by them, is . . . everywhere the same.[19]

More recently, Jonathan Crary has shown how the very absence of referentiality in the new theory of specific nerve energies illustrated by this passage becomes "the ground on which new instrumental techniques will construct for an observer a new 'real' world." Thus, Crary writes:

Far from the specialization of the senses, Helmholtz is explicit about the body's indifference to the sources of its experience and of its capacity for multiple connections with other agencies and machines. The perceiver here becomes a neutral conduit, one kind of relay among others allowing optimum conditions of circulation and exchangeability, whether it be of commodities, energy, or information.[20]

All of which goes to show how psychophysics does to the culturally integrated human sensorium what the new technological media do to language: it breaks up and redistributes constitutive elements according to a multiplicity of particularized functions. In nineteenth-century Europe, culture [*Bildung*] was "the great unity in which speaking, hearing, writing, and reading [Kittler oddly leaves out seeing] would achieve mutual transparency and relation to meaning" (DN 214). In these terms the very existence of psychophysics heralds a paradigm shift, since it singles out and tests "autonomic functions" with no ideal completion or endpoint: "There is no universal norm (inwardness, creative imagination, high idiom, Poetry) transcending the particular functions. Each has a standard only in relation to defined experimental subjects and conditions" (DN 214).

The experiments conducted by Hermann Ebbinghaus in the 1880s serve as example *par excellence* (just as Heinrich Stephani's new pedagogy did for the discourse network of 1800). Ebbinghaus quantifies human memory capacity by counting the number of times a sequence of nonsense syllables randomly generated must pass before "the subject" (first himself, then others) before said subject can be said to have memorized the sequence. Postulating no universal or statistical norm, such experiments draw attention to the white noise that precedes and surrounds every discourse. In fact, in its investigations and research programs, psychophysics renders massively visible the evidence of aphasia, alexia, agraphia, agnosia, and asymbolia; white noise becomes at once theme and method. As Kittler summarizes: "Psychophysics transmits white noise through a certain filter so that what comes across is, say, pink noise; whatever the eyes and ears of the receiver make of this is then the experimental result" (DN 218).

The Simulation of Madness
Yet what is "noise" on one information channel can be transposed and inscribed on another. Thus Judge Schreber, or rather the *Aufschreibesystem* whose writing instrument and surface of inscription he *is*, will record the new positivities of psychophysics, albeit transposed into delirious form. In a moment of extravagant lucidity, or perhaps just a lull between the sandstorms of hallucination, Schreber decided that the only way to fend off the rays transcribing his thoughts while transforming him into a voluptuous woman for God's enjoyment was to write down a detailed account of God's "new world order" and his special place within it, thereby "proving" his own sanity. To counter the bawdy nonsense of tormenting voices, Schreber

memorizes poetry and reads widely for new understanding ("reading a book or a newspaper always stimulates new thoughts" [quoted in DN 301]). But such strategies of resistance are of no avail, and Schreber simply ends up demonstrating that the "basic principles of the classical discourse network have thus deteriorated into being the defensive weapons of a mental patient" (DN 301).

Yet Schreber does not flinch from drawing the full consequences of his condition. Since, according to the best scientific sources of the day, the physical evidence of his ordeal could be confirmed directly only by inspecting his nerves, his body itself would be his most effective testament. While the *Memoirs* could explain what had happened to him, only by submitting his own nerve tissue to a postmortem dissection could he deliver empirical proof of his ordeal. Although differing in his premises, Dr. Paul Flechsig had proposed no less in his treatise *The Corporal Basis for Mental Disturbances*, published in 1882. And so Schreber argues, with infallible logic; but unnecessarily, as it turns out, for there were already important precursors. As Kittler laconically observes: "the corpse of Hölderlin, an insane or, in other words, not bureaucratically employed teacher, was among the first to enter the new order of things via the dissection table" (DN 295).

As both body and text, "Schreber's mania archives . . . the libido theory that psychoanalysis reached only through long detours of interpretation" (DN 292). Long detours, because Freud substitutes the Oedipus complex for an examination of Schreber's information channels. Systematically replacing the name of Dr. Flechsig— Schreber's alleged "soul murderer"—with the name of Schreber's own father, Freud ignores the fact that Flechsig was not only an experimental neurologist but as such the information "source" for the language of Schreber's nerves and delirium. Not simply an exemplary case for the evidence of libido theory, then, Schreber also provided the link between psychophysics and psychoanalysis.

And literature as well. As Foucault had already reminded us, instead of Lancelot, we have Judge Schreber.[21] For Kittler, however, Schreber's full participation in the discourse network of 1900 reposes on changes in the functional basis of literature. Circa 1900, the "ersatz sensuality of Poetry" (DN 245) is replaced, not by nature, but by the noise produced by the "random generators" of psychophysics, while newly invented technical media automatically store acoustical and optic data streams that formerly supplied poetry's aesthetic and affective charge:

> The gramophone empties out words by bypassing their imaginary aspect (signifieds) for their real aspects (the physiology of the voice). . . . Film techniques like projection and cutting, close-up and flashback technically implement psychic processes such as hallucination and association, recollection and attention, rather than, like plays or novels, stimulating these processes descriptively with words (DN 246).

In short, circa 1900 the production of verbal hallucination through the synthetic power of words gives way to the writing down of delirium, since "a delirium written down coincides with what sciences and media themselves were doing" (DN 305).

In the discourse network of 1900, doctors who experiment on themselves and writers interested in their own mental pathologies become interchangeable. Not surprisingly, literary delirium takes its content from the detritus of two new discourses: from psychophysics it takes the randomly generated white noise of neurological experiments, from psychoanalysis the exhaustion of nonsense in transpositions of desire. Drawing material from the new psychiatric archive, which provided "rough drafts of poetry and . . . methods for pure writing," modern literature finds a new definition for itself in the simulation of madness. Only aesthetic formalization insures the difference. To Kittler's stream of examples—Rilke, Kafka, Gottfried Benn, the dadaist and surrealist writers—others can be added: T. S. Eliot's *The Waste Land*, Yeats' "Crazy Jane" poems, Faulkner's *The Sound and the Fury*, Beckett's prose fiction.

Modern literature however is doubly articulated with the discourse network of 1900: on the one hand through its simulations of *anomie*, madness and neurosis, but on the other through its concern with "language channels" and the effects of modern technical media. What appears to be "abnormal" or idiosyncratic in Schreber's *Memoirs* is simply the glaring exposure of these articulations. Moreover, by suppressing or ignoring precisely this evidence—i.e., that of the discourse network as such—modern literary criticism remains bounded by formal and hermeneutic models. Novels like Andrey Bely's *Petersburg*, where what is called "the biology of shadows" and the "cerebral game" bring the city and the brain into topological contact, or Joseph McElroy's *Plus*, where a decorticated brain hardwired to a communications satellite emerges as the source of narrative consciousness, likewise can only appear as the more or less idiosyncratic preoccupations of authors, and never as textual evidence of a twentieth-century writing-down system.

Literature and War

War, as opposed to mere fighting, depends not only on a communications structure of command and control (C^3I, the Pentagon calls it), but on strategies of persuasion in the art of getting other people to die for you. As Kittler notes, Frederick the Great needed almost as many troops in the field to control and 'motivate' his own troops as he did to attack the Austrian enemy. With the development of technical media, the generals disappear from the battlefield (the nature and shape of which also change) and the soldier's perspective as well as the very possibilities of wartime "experience" are altered.

From Homer, Goethe and Kleist to Bram Stoker, Ernst Jünger and Thomas Pynchon, works of literature textualize the changes in military strategy and technology that make the soldier's experience possible (or not). But if certain modern literary texts map information networks and display the efficacy of modern technical media, it is simply because "information technology is always already strategy or war" (DN 371). Or, as Kittler also puts it: "The writing of novels is a continuation of espionage by other means" (infra, 60). *Dracula* and *Gravity's Rainbow* demonstrate why. In *Dracula*, the undead arrives in England by a self-guided packetboat only to be ultimately defeated by a lawyer's fiancée turned secretary who gathers, collates and redistributes apparently unrelated information from diaries, phonographs and typewriters, autopsies and newspaper reports— information which allows the men to define and track the enemy. The horrors revealed are not only those of vampirism but the means of its defeat: the machinery of bureaucracy, democracy and colonialization. ("Vampirism is a chain reaction, and therefore can only be fought with the techniques of mechanical reproduction." (infra, 71).)

Two world wars later, during (and because of) which the media of information storage and transmission are perfected, certain parallels repeat themselves. In *Gravity's Rainbow*, the self-guided V-2s targeted on London would make the "Lord of the Night" or death itself a statistical probability deniable only through the "Monte Carlo

Fallacy" were it not for the inexplicable oddity that the rocket strikes coincide point for point with an American soldier's sexual encounters. Beginning with this perfect (and unexplained) congruence between two instances of stochastic scattering, the novel operates as a device for historical data retrieval, most notably concerning the increasing entropy of the German national state and the transfer of new technology east and west in the postwar period. However, a literary text that proceeds according to Claude Shannon's formula (increasing entropy means increasing information) also demands that the reader adopt Salvador Dali's paranoid-critical method as a reading strategy. Whereas in Stoker's novel the characters deploy an information network and new technical media in order to vanquish a mysterious enemy from the East whose utterances constitute the very "discourse of the Other," in Pynchon's novel technology becomes the very stakes of war now that nationalism has been transcended by the military industrial complex and "information" has replaced "dope and women" as the only medium of exchange. Needless to add, self-guided missiles (or yesterday's "smart bombs") solve automatically the problem of getting other people to die for you.[22]

Machines at the Scene

In a well-known chapter in *Writing and Difference,* Jacques Derrida analyzes the scriptural metaphors in a series of texts wherein Freud attempts to account for the apparent fact that in the psychic apparatus, memory and conscious perception function by mutually exclusive means.[23] For Derrida, noting that in Freud's writing psychical content is always represented by an irreducibly "graphic" text, the stakes are clear: "What is a text, and what must the psyche be if it can be represented by a text? For if there is neither machine nor text without psychical origin, there is no domain of the psychic without text" (WD 199).

If psychic processes cannot be conceived apart from or exterior to a certain site of inscription (a "scene of writing"), then technological devices can no longer serve (or be understood) as mere metaphors. Accordingly, Derrida argues, Freud's last and most developed model of memory and perceptual consciousness, the "mystic wax writing pad," cannot be taken to be a metaphor for memory; instead, the writing apparatus "founds memory," and therefore makes metaphor possible. If there is an analogy between the child's writing device and the operations of the psychic apparatus, it is because the latter is already inhabited and made possible by a machine, a writing machine. This machine "—and consequently, representation—is death and finitude *within* the psyche"; it therefore demands the "historical production of a *supplementary* machine, *added to* the psychical organization in order to supplement its finitude" (WD 228, Derrida's emphases).[24] However, according to Derrida's "logic of supplementarity," the invention of a new machine or technology added to what was already functionally complete only reveals that the latter was already always a machine. The relation between the two apparatuses, or, in more general terms, between the temporality of the present and its representation, between life and death, is what Derrida calls writing [*écriture*]. As a consequence, and to the scandal of university literature departments in the 1970s, the "subject" of this writing disappears into a "system of relations": "The 'subject' of writing does not exist if we mean by that some sovereign solitude of the author. The subject of writing is a *system* of relations between strata: the Mystic Pad, the psyche, the society, the world" (WD 226).

Yet Derrida's use of the word "system" appears rather general, perhaps even too metaphorical. In a commentary on Jacques Lacan's "Seminar on the Ego," Kittler offers a more technologically precise description of Freud's psychic apparatus.[25] The most salient fact about Lacan's "Seminar on the Ego" is that it is elaborated in relation to cybernetics and information theory.[26] For Kittler, therefore, the differences between Freud's model (and psychoanalysis more generally) and Lacan's rewriting of it simply reflect the differences in the operating standards of information machines and technical media in their respective epochs. In constructing his model of the psychic apparatus, "Freud's materialism reasoned only as far as the information machines of his epoch—no more, no less" (infra, 134). According to the scientific imperatives to which Freud willingly bent himself, ineffable emanations of Spirit had to be replaced by systems of neurons which differ according to separable functions, in this case the recording (memory) and transmission of data (perceptual consciousness).

In Freud's time, however, storage functions could only be conceived of on the model of the *engram*, which includes not only the graphic inscriptions highlighted by Derrida but also the grooves on

Edison's newly invented phonograph. Significantly, for both his "case studies" and lectures, Freud relies on his own "phonographic memory," as he emphasizes on several occasions. Psychoanalysis ("the talking cure") is actually a form of "telephony" (in fact a telephone cable was laid in Freud's house—but not in the consulting room—in 1895), a communication circuit between patient and analyst in which the former's unconscious is transformed into sound or speech and then back into the unconscious. As Kittler puts it in *Discourse Networks*: ". . . because mouths and ears have become electro-acoustical transducers, the [analytic] session remains a simulated long distance call between two psychic apparatuses . . ." (DN 284). Freud, however, does not limit himself to the phonographic. In *The Interpretation of Dreams* the transmission medium was optical, a cameralike apparatus which converted latent dream thoughts into a system of conscious perception, the virtual images of which Lacan would understand as cinema. Summarily, then, in constructing his model of the psychic apparatus, Freud implemented all storage and transmission media available at the time: print, phonograph, telephone and film (even though the last term never appears in his writing).

Lacan grasped not only the importance of these technical media for Freudian theory (as suggested by the titles of his own works: *Ecrits*, the *Seminars*, *Television*, "Radiophonie," etc.), but also the extent to which the foundations of psychoanalysis rested on the end of the print monopoly and the historical separation of different media. Thus, for Kittler, Lacan's triple register of the imaginary, the real and the symbolic corresponds exactly to the separation of media, that is, to film, phonograph, and linguistic signifiers respectively. As Kittler takes pains to show, however, the Lacanian symbolic corresponds not simply to the system of signifiers inscribed mechanically by the typewriter (as Lacan himself puts it, the most complex machine is made of words), but to the entire domain of calculation. For this reason, the most important technological invention between Freud and Lacan was the computer, or more specifically, Alan Turing's Universal Machine of 1936. Lacan's rewriting of Freud is thus to be understood as an attempt to redefine the psychic apparatus according to fully contemporary conditions of mediality. Lacan simply implements in a functional model the most up-to-date media of information storage, transmission and computation.

Computer Chips, and What They Tell Us

For Kittler, today's computerized communications assemblage only brings to the foreground a whole set of questions raised by the invention of Turing's Universal machine.[27] These questions range from the mathematically specific (can the body of real numbers formerly known as nature be digitalized?) to the philosophically general (what is the possibility of constructing strong forms of artificial intelligence?). Behind them all lies the recurrent specter of a totally programmable world. Alan Turing first raised it in 1936; electronics and digitalization–and the communications assemblage often referred to as the Net—make it pertinent once again.

The theory of communication and control: it all seems to come down to the basic question of whether nature is a Turing machine or, as Jacques Lacan would have it, the real is what is impossible in relation to our machines and systems.[28] Yet it can hardly be a matter of a simple either/or formulation, above all not of the technological versus the human, however the latter may be (re)defined. Instead of seeking essences in the pursuit of what Heidegger called the question of technology, it is from the specific terms—the equations, blueprints, circuit diagrams—that technology itself provides that one must proceed, in order to see how and what is said (or not said), what mechanisms determine and set the limits of our bodies, our subjectivities, our discourse.

Two of Kittler's most recent essays (both in this volume) constitute an analysis of the political implications of the contemporary "scene of writing" as defined by computer word processing. In "There is No Software," Kittler points out that there are inherent limits to programmability and computing power due simply to the discrete nature of switching components. In contrast, "on the other, physical side" one defines "nonprogrammable systems, be they waves or beings," which show "polynomial growth rates in complexity." Sensing that this "nonprogrammable system" begins to sound too recognizably human, Kittler adds that

[O]ur equally familiar silicon hardware obeys many of the requisites for such highly connected, nonprogrammable systems. Between its million transistor cells, some million to the power of two interactions always already take place. There is electron diffusion; there is quantum-mechanical tunneling all over the chip. Technically, however, these interactions are still treated in terms of system limitations, physical side-

> effects, and so on. To minimize all the noise that it would be impossible
> to eliminate is the price we pay for structurally programmable machines.
> The inverse strategy of maximizing noise would not only find the way
> back from IBM to Shannon, it may well be the only way to enter that
> body of real numbers originally known as chaos. (infra, 135)

In order to provide a more easily functional, 'user-friendly' interface, computer technology must substitute its zeros and ones for real numbers, thereby reducing noise and warding off chaos, but also confusing hardware and software, matter and information. Kittler draws attention to the limits of this technology, and to the price we pay for the service it renders. In short, we become subjected to it: as subjects of Word Perfect or Microsoft Word, its commands become our commands, its limits, our limits, our "writing" a repression of our necessary interface with a new "machinic phylum."[29]

The central thrust of "There is no Software" is to lay bare the obfuscating layerings of language—from the "originary" writing on the silicon microchip to assembler code, BIOS, DOS and finally Word Perfect (with the obvious irony)—which blur not only the distinction between matter and information but the ultimately political difference between hardware and software. In a companion essay, "Protected Mode," Kittler shows how this difference is further embedded (and obscured) in the architecture of the Intel 80386 processor chip. Basically, the chip makes certain segments of the computer's operating system inaccessible and unusable by secretly encoding a "Protected Mode" different from the system's "Real Mode." By "protect[ing] the operating system from the users," Intel deliberately obscures the difference between the two modes and hides the inefficiency such doubling brings about; more seriously, this new architecture actually transfers the logic of separation from the military-industrial complex into that of the information technology itself. The same strategy of separation that blocks access to power also blocks full access to writing machines, thereby producing a certain kind of subject (i.e. the public, the governed). "Software" simply names (and obscures) the strategy of simulation that secretly governs today's writing subjects and the bureaucracies within which they operate.

Essays by Friedrich A. Kittler

PREFACE TO GRAMOPHONE, FILM, TYPEWRITER

Tape my head and mike my brain,
Stick that needle in my vein.

Pynchon

*M*edia determine our situation, which (nevertheless or for that reason) merits a description.

As everyone knows, situation reports were discussed—on a broad scale in the middle of the day and in detail during the evening—in front of sand tables and staff maps at meetings arranged by the German High Command during war and so-called peace. Until Dr. Gottfried Benn, M.D., author and medical staff chief, elevated the identification of situations to the task of literature and literary criticism as well. His justification (in a letter to a friend): "As you know, I sign as follows: On behalf of the Commander-in-Chief of the Armed Services: Dr. Benn."[1]

And indeed, in 1941—with full knowledge of official documents, technologies, enemy positions and deployment plans, and especially with offices in Berlin's Bendlerstraße, headquarters of the armed services' high command—it still might have been possible to take stock of the situation.[2]

Today's situation is more obscure. First of all, the pertinent documents are located in archives that will remain secret for as long as there is a gap between files and facts, between targeted goals and their execution. Secondly, even secret files lose their impact when the actual data streams, by-passing the printed word and authorship, circulate through computer networks in the form of unreadable rows of numbers. However, technologies that not only by-pass writing but suck in and carry off so-called humanity render their own description impossible. More and more data streams, originally from books, later on from phonograph recordings or films, disappear into the black holes or boxes that, as mere artificial intelligence, abandon us on their way to nameless high commands. In this situation, only hindsight remains, and that means stories. How that which can no longer be found in any book came about can just barely be recorded in books. Operating at their limits, even antiquated media become sensitive enough to register the signs and indices of a situation. Then, as at the sectional plane of the surface edge of two optical media, scanning lines and dots emerge: myths, scientific fictions, oracles . . .

This book is a story woven from such stories.* It collects, comments on and engages positions and texts, in which the newness of technical media has inscribed itself in outmoded book pages. Many of these papers are old, or already entirely forgotten. Yet it was precisely when the mechanical media were founded that their shock effect was so overwhelming. Therefore, literature recorded it more accurately than in today's fictitious media pluralism where everything is allowed to flow on, as long as it does not disrupt Silicon Valley's control circuits in their accession to world domination. A communications technology, on the other hand, whose monopoly is just ending, records precisely the following message: the aesthetic of shock. What reached the page of the surprised author between 1880 and 1920 by means of the gramophone, film and typewriter—the very first mechanical media—amounts to a spectral photograph of our present as future.[3] That is to say, with those early and seemingly harmless devices that could store and thereby separate as such, sounds, faces and documents, a mechanization of information began, which—in the hindsight of stories—already made today's self-recursive number stream possible.

It is obvious that such stories are no substitute for a history of technology. They remain without numbers, even if they were innumerable; and as such, they already miss the real on which all innovations are based. Conversely, rows of numbers, blueprints and circuit diagrams never again turn into the printed word, always and only into appliances and devices.[4] Heidegger's beautiful maxim that technology itself prevents any experience of its own essence, signifies no

---

* [Tr.—The book referred to is Friedrich Kittler, *Grammophon Film Typewriter* (Berlin: Brinkman & Bose, 1986.)]

more and no less.[5] To be sure, the confusion of writing with experience (which Heidegger learned in school) is not necessary. Instead of ontological questions, plain and simple knowledge is sufficient.

The technical and historical data on which authorial texts on the media are also based can be supplied. Only then do the old and the new, books and their mechanical successors, come across as the communication that they are. It remains an impossibility to understand media, in spite of the title of McLuhan's book *Understanding Media*, because—quite conversely—the communications technologies of the day exercise remote control over all understanding and evoke its illusion. Yet it seems entirely feasible to read historical figures of the unknown, i.e., bodies, out of the blueprints and circuit diagrams themselves, whether they command printing presses or electronic calculators. We can only ever know about people what the media are able to store and transmit. What counts, therefore, are not the messages or contents with which communications technologies literally equip so-called souls for the duration of a technological era, but (strictly after McLuhan) only their circuit arrangements, those diagrams of observability in general.

Whoever manages to hear the circuit diagram itself in the synthesizer sounds of the compact disc, or to see the circuit diagram in the laser storm of the discotheque, finds happiness itself. A happiness beyond the polar ice, Nietzsche would have said. At the moment of relentless subjugation to laws—which is our case—man's illusion as inventor of media vanishes. And the situation can be identified.

Already in 1945, in the partly charred, typewritten minutes that recorded the last situation reports of the army's high command, war was called the father of all things: it was supposed to have been responsible (borrowing loosely from Heraclitus) for most technical inventions.[6] And since 1973 at the latest, when Thomas Pynchon's *Gravity's Rainbow* was published, it has also been made evident that true wars are not waged over people or fatherlands, but rather between various media, communications technologies, and data streams.[7] Scanning lines and dots of a situation that forgets us . . .

September 1985
Translated by Stefanie Harris

GRAMOPHONE,
FILM,
TYPEWRITER

Optical fiber networks. Soon people will be connected to a communication channel which can be used for any kind of media—for the first time in history or for the end of history. When films, music, phone calls, and texts are able to reach the individual household via optical fiber cables, the previously separate media of television, radio, telephone, and mail will become a single medium, standardized according to transmission frequency and bit format. Above all, the optoelectronic channel will be immunized against disturbances that might randomize the beautiful patterns of bits behind the images and sounds. Immunized, that is, against the bomb. For it is well known that nuclear explosions may send a high intensive electromagnetic pulse through traditional copper cables and cripple the connected computer network.

The Pentagon is capable of truly far-sighted planning. Only the substitution of optical fibers for conducting cables can accommodate the enormous rates and volume of bits that are presupposed, produced, and celebrated by electronic warfare. Then all early warning systems, radars, missile bases, and army headquarters on the opposite coast, in Europe,[1] will finally be connected to computers, safe from an electromagnetic pulse and able to function when needed. And for the intervening period there is even the by-product of pleasure: people can switch to any medium for their entertainment. After all, optical fibers can transmit any imaginable message but the one that counts—the one about the bomb.

But even now, before the end, something is coming to an end. The general digitalization of information and channels erases the difference between individual media. Sound and image, voice and text have become mere effects on the surface, or, to put it better, the interface for the consumer. Sense and the senses become mere glitter. Their media-produced glamour will last throughout the transitional period as a waste product of strategic programs. In computers everything becomes number: imageless, soundless, and wordless quantity. And if the optical fiber network reduces all formerly separate data flows to one standardized digital series of numbers, any medium can be translated into another. With numbers nothing is impossible. Modulation, transformation, synchronization; delay, memory, transposition; scrambling, scanning, mapping—a total connection of all media on a digital base erases the notion of the medium itself. Instead of hooking up technologies to people, absolute knowledge can run as an endless loop.

But right now there are still media; there is still entertainment. One is informed—mainly, unfortunately, thanks to jumbo jets. In the jumbo jet, media are more densely connected than in most places. They remain separate, however, according to their technological standard, frequency, user allocation, and interface. The crew is connected to radar screens, diode displays, radio beacons, and nonpublic channels. The crew members have deserved their professional earphones. Their replacement by computers is only a question of time. But the passengers can benefit only from yesterday's technology and are entertained by a canned media mixture. With the exception of books, that ancient medium which needs so much light, all the entertainment techniques are represented. The passengers' ears are listlessly hooked up to one-way earphones, which are themselves hooked up to tape recorders and thereby to the record industry. Their eyes are glued to Hollywood movies, which in turn must be connected to the advertising budget of the airline industry—otherwise they would not so regularly begin with takeoffs and landings. Not to mention the technological medium of the food industry to which the mouths of the passengers are connected. A multi-media embryonic sack supplied through channels or navels that all serve the purpose of screening out the real background: noise, night, and the cold of an unlivable outside. Against that there is muzak, movies, and microwave cuisine.

The technological standard of today, and not only of the jumbo jet, can be described in terms of partially connected media systems. All can still be described in the terms McLuhan provided. According to him, the contents of one medium are always other media: film and radio constitute the content of television; record and tape the content of radio; silent movie and magnetic sound that of cinema; text, telephone, and telegram that of the semi-media monopoly of the postal service.[2] Since the beginning of this century, when Lieben in Germany and deForest in California developed the electronic tube, it has become possible, in principle, to amplify and transmit signals. The vast systems of connected media that have come to exist since the '30s can tap into writing, film, and phonography—the three storage media—and connect and emit their signals at will.

But between those systems of connected media there are incompatible data channels and differently formatted data. Electrotechnics and electronics are not quite the same. Within the spectrum of the general data flow, television and radio, cinema and the postal service function like individual windows for one's sense perception. In contrast to the perfected optoelectronic future, today infra-red radiation or radar echoes of approaching missiles are still sent over separate channels. Our systems of connected media can only distribute words, sounds, and images as they are sent and received by people. Above all, the systems do not compute data. They do not produce an output which, under computer control, would transform any algorithm into any interface effect, to the point at which people will no longer be able to make sense of their senses. Right now only the transmission quality of the storage media, which in the connected media systems represents the content, is being computed. A compromise between engineers and sales people regulates the degree to which the sound from a television set can be poor, the pictures in the cinema can be fuzzy, or a beloved voice on the telephone can be filtered. The dependent variable of this compromise is what we take for our sense perception.

A composite consisting of a face and a voice, which, as in the case of Kennedy, remains calm during a TV debate, even when faced by someone like Richard Nixon, is telegenic and wins presidential elections. Voices which would become traitors in an optical close-up, however, are called *funkisch* ("radiogenic") and rule over the VE301, the *Volksempfänger* of World War II. For, as a student of Heidegger, one of Germany's early commentators about radio, remarks, "Death is primarily a radio topic."[3]

But what we take for our sense perception has to be fabricated first. The domination and the connection of technical media presuppose a kind of coincidence, in Lacan's particular sense of the term: something had to stop not writing itself. Long before the electrification of the media, that is, even before their electronic end, there were modest, merely mechanical apparatuses. Those apparatuses could neither amplify nor transmit, but they could still store data for our sense perception: there was the silent movie for sights and Edison's phonograph for sounds (Note that Edison's apparatus—in contrast to Berliner's later gramophone disk—could also be used for the recording of sound.)

On December 6, 1877, Thomas Alva Edison, lord of the first research laboratory in the history of technology, presented the prototype of the phonograph. In the same town of Menlo Park, on February 20, 1892, the so-called kinetoscope was completed. Thus, three years later the Lumière brothers in France (or the Skladanowsky brothers in Germany) only had to provide a means of projection for this apparatus in order to turn Edison's kinetoscope into our cinema.

Since this epoch-making event storage systems have been developed that can record and reproduce the temporal flow of acoustic and optical data. Ear and eye have become autonomous. This has brought about a far more radical change than have lithography and photography, which in the first third of the nineteenth century merely propelled the work of art into the age of mechanical reproduction (according to Walter Benjamin's thesis). Media "define what constitutes reality"[4]; they are always already ahead of aesthetics.

What was new about the storage capability of the phonograph and cinematograph—and both names refer, not accidentally, to writing—was their ability to store time: as a mixture of audio frequencies in the acoustic realm, as a movement of single picture sequences in the optic realm. Time, however, is what determines the limits of all art. The quotidian data flow must be arrested before it can become image or sign. What is called style in art is only the switchboard of these scannings and selections. The same switchboard also controls those arts that administrate in writing a serial, that is, a temporally transposed data flow. In order to store the sound sequences of speech, literature has to arrest them in the system of twenty-six letters and thereby exclude noise sequences from the beginning. It is no coincidence that this system includes, as a subsystem, the seven tones, the diatonic system from *a* to *h* that forms the foundation of occidental music. In order to fix an acoustic chaos assaulting European ears as exotic music—according to the suggestion of the musicologist von Hornbostel—one first of all interpolates a phonograph, which can record the chaos in real time and reproduce it in slow motion. When the rhythms then become paralyzed and the "individual measures, even individual sounds resound," occidental alphabetism, with its staves, can proceed to an "exact notation."[5]

Texts and scores were Europe's only means to store time. Both are based on writing; the time of this writing is symbolic (in Lacan's terms). This time memorizes itself in terms of projections and retrievals—like a chain of chains. Nevertheless, whatever runs as time on a physical or (again in Lacan's terms) real level, blindly and unpredictably, could by no means be encoded. Therefore all data flows, if they were real streams of data, had to pass through the defile of the signifier. Alphabetic monopoly, grammatology.

If the film called history is wound back, it will become an endless loop. What soon will end in the monopoly of bits and fiber optics began with the monopoly of writing. History was that homogenous field which, as a subject in school curricula, included only cultures with written language. Mouths and graphisms dropped out into prehistory. Otherwise events and their stories could not have been connected.[6] The commands and judgments; the announcements and prescriptions that gave rise to mountains of corpses—military and juridical, religious and medical—all went through the same channel that held the monopoly on the descriptions of those mountains of corpses. This is why anything that ever happened ended up in libraries.

And Foucault, the last historian or the first archeologist, had only to look it up. The suspicion that all power comes from archives to which it returns could be brilliantly illustrated, at least within the legal, medical, and theological fields. This is the tautology of history or merely its calvary and tomb. For libraries, the archeologist's rich places of discovery, gathered and catalogued papers which differed greatly according to address, degree of secrecy, and writing technique: Foucault's archive as entropy of a post office.[7] Before it falls into libraries, even writing is a communication medium of which the archeologist only forgot the technology. That is why his analyses end immediately before that point in time when other media penetrated the library's stacks. For sound archives or towers of film rolls, discourse analysis becomes inappropriate.

Nevertheless, as long as there was history, it was indeed Foucault's "endless bleating of words."[8] More simply, but not less technically than the fiber optics of the future, writing functioned as the general medium. For that reason the term *medium* did not exist. For whatever else was going on dropped through the filter of letters or ideograms.

"Literature," Goethe wrote, "is the fragment of fragments; the least of what had happened and of what had been spoken was written down; of what had been written down, only the smallest fraction was preserved."[9]

Accordingly, today oral history confronts the writing monopoly of the historians; accordingly, a media theoretician like Walter J. Ong, who, particularly in his function as a Jesuit priest, must take a professional interest in the spirit of the Pentecostal mystery, celebrates a primal orality of tribal cultures, as opposed to the secondary orality of our media acoustics. But that kind of research was inconceivable as long as the opposite of "history" used to be simply (again in Goethe's terms) "legend."[10] Prehistory disappeared in its mythical name; Goethe's definition of literature did not even have to mention optical or acoustical data flows. And under pretechnical, though literary, conditions even legends, those spoken segments of what had happened, could last only when they had been fixed in writing. Since it has become possible, however, to record on tape the epics of those last Homeric bards, who until recently were wandering through Serbia and Croatia, oral mnemotechniques or cultures can be reconstructed in an altogether new way.[11] Then even Homer's rosy-fingered Eos is transformed from a goddess into a piece of chrome dioxide, which used to be stored in the memory of those rhapsodists and could be combined with other pieces into whole epics. Primal orality or oral history are technological shadows of the apparatuses which they can document, only, however, after the end of the writing monopoly.

Writing can store only writing, no more, no less. The holy books testify to this fact. The second book of Moses, chapter twenty, fixes a copy of what Jaweh originally had written with his own finger on two stone tablets: the law. Of the thunder and lightning, the dense cloud and very powerful trumpet that accompanied the writing-down on the holy mountain of Sinai, the Bible could store nothing but mere words.[12]

Even less is handed down of the nightmares and visitations that came to a nomad called Mohammed after his flight to the holy mountain of Hira. The Koran does not begin until, in place of the many demons, the one God rules. Archangel Gabriel descends from the seventh heaven with a roll of scripture and the command to decipher it. "Read," he says to Mohammed, "read in the name of your Lord, who has created all and made man out of his own coagulated blood. Read, in the name of your Lord, the glorious, who taught man the use of the quill and all he did not know before."[13]

But Mohammed answers that he, the nomad, does not know how to read, not even the divine message about the origin of writing and reading. The archangel has to repeat his command before this illiterate man can become the founder of a book religion. For soon, or all too soon, the illegible roll starts making sense and offers to Mohammed's magically alphabeticized eyes exactly that text that Gabriel already uttered twice as the oral command. It is the twenty-sixth sura that, according to all traditions, was at the beginning of Mohammed's enlightenment—a beginning which then has "to be learnt by heart by the believers, to be written down on primitive surfaces such as palm leaves, stones, wood, bones, and leatherpieces, and to be recited again and again by Mohammed and elect believers, especially during Ramadan."[14]

Thus, writing stores only the fact of its authorization. It celebrates the storing monopoly of the god who has invented it. And because this god rules over signs that are not meaningless only for readers, all books are books of the dead, like those from Egypt that stand at the beginning of literature.[15] The realm of the dead beyond the senses to which they lure us coincides with the book itself. When Zeno asked the delphic oracle what was the best way to live, the answer he was given was: " 'To mate with the dead.' Which he understood as the equivalent of to *read* the *ancients*."[16]

How the teaching of a god who taught the use of quills went from Moses and Mohammed to simpler and simpler people—this tedious history can be written by no one, since this would be history itself. Comparable to how, in electronic warfare, the memory capacities of the computers will soon coincide with the war itself, gigabyte upon gigabyte shall exede all the processing capacities of historians.

Suffice it to say that one day—in Germany, perhaps, this was already so at the time of Goethe—the homogenous medium of writing was additionally homogenized by the state apparatus. General compulsory school attendance pulled a hide of paper over everyone. No longer a "misuse of language" (according to Goethe) struggling with cramped muscles and individual letters, they learned a way of writing which went on even in darkness or intoxication. They learned a "silent and private way of reading" which, as a "sad surrogate of speech,"[17] could easily consume letters, bypassing the oral organs. Whatever they were emitting or receiving was writing. And since whatever exists depends on what can be posted, the bodies themselves were submitted to the regime of the symbolic. This is unthinkable today, but it was once a reality: no movie stored the movements that they produced or perceived, no phonograph the noises they uttered or heard. For whatever existed failed before time. Silhouettes or pastel drawings fixed the play of features, and the staves failed before the noise. But whenever a hand would take the quill a miracle occurred. Then that body that had not yet stopped not writing itself would curiously, unavoidably leave traces.

> I am ashamed to admit it. I am ashamed of my handwriting. It exposes my naked mind. In that handwriting I am more naked than when I get undressed. No leg, no breath, no dress, no sound. Neither a voice nor an image. Everything is emptied out. Instead the full man is shriveled, shrunk, and stunted into his scribbling. His lines are all that is left of him and his propagation. The unevenness between the upstroke and the blank paper, minimal and hardly to be felt by the fingertips of a blind man, forms the last proportion that comprises the fellow once again in his totality.[18]

The shame that overcomes the hero of Botho Strauss's *Widmung* whenever he sees his own handwriting exists only as an anachronism. The fact that the minimal unevenness between upstrokes and paper can store neither a voice nor an image of a body presupposes in its exclusion the invention of phonography and cinema. Before their invention, however, without any competition, handwriting could guarantee the perfect securing of traces. It wrote and wrote, in an energetic and ideally uninterrupted flow. For in this continuous flow of ink or letters the alphabetic individual had, as Hegel correctly observed, "its appearance and exteriority."[19]

And what applies to writing also applies to reading. Even if the alphabeticized individual of the "writer" finally had to fall out of the private exteriority of his handwriting into the anonymous exteriority of print in order to secure beyond distance and death "what is left of him and his propagation"—alphabeticized individuals called "readers" could nevertheless reverse those exteriorizations. "If one reads correctly," Novalis wrote, "the words in us will be unfolded into a visible world."[20] And his friend Schlegel added that "one believes one hears what one merely reads."[21] Perfect alphabetism was supposed to supplement precisely those optical and acoustical data flows which refused to stop not writing themselves under the monopoly of writing. In order to naturalize writing, writing had to be made painless, and reading had to become silent. Educated people who could skim letters were provided with sights and sounds.

Around 1800 the book became both film and record simultaneously—not, however, as a media technological reality, but only in the imaginary of readers' souls. General compulsory school attendance and new technologies of alphabetization helped to bring about this new reality. As a surrogate of unstorable data flows the book came to power and glory.[22]

In 1774 an editor named Goethe had the handwritten letters or *The Sorrows of Young Werther* printed. Even the "unknown masses" (as they are called in the *Dedication of Faust*) "should have the chance to hear a song," which, "like an old, almost forgotten legend," evoked "first love and friendship."[23] This exactly describes poetry's new road to success: voices or handwritings are unnoticeably turned into Gutenbergiana. For the same reason, we find Werther's last letter before his suicide still sealed, though not yet mailed off, giving his lover the promise of poetry itself: during their lifetime she would have to remain the wife of the unlovable Albert, but thereafter, "before the eyes of the infinite being," she would be united with her lover in an "eternal embrace."[24] And indeed, that addressee of the handwritten love letters which were given into print by a mere editor/author was to be rewarded with the same kind of immortality as the novel itself. The novel, and only the novel, will constitute that "beautiful world"[25] in which, also in 1809, the lovers in Goethe's *Elective Affinities* "will once reawaken united" according to the hopes of the novelist.[26] During their lifetime Eduard and Ottilie already had a marvellously similar handwriting. Therefore, their death had to take them into a paradise which, under the storage monopoly of writing, used to be called poetry.

And it might very well be that that paradise was more real than our media-manipulated senses can imagine. The suicides among *Werther's* readers might have perceived their hero, if they only read correctly, in a real, visible world. And the lovers among Goethe's female readers, like Bettina Brentano, might very well have died with the heroine of his *Elective Affinities* in order to be reborn through "Goethe's genius" "into a more beautiful youth."[27] Possibly the perfect readers of 1800 were a living answer to the question with which, in 1983, Chris Marker ends his film essay *Sans Soleil*:

> Lost at the end of the world, on my island Sal, in the company of my dogs strutting around. I remember January in Tokyo, or rather I remember the images that I filmed in January in Tokyo. They have put themselves in the place of my memory, they *are* my memory. I ask myself how people remember if they do not make movies, or photographs, or tapes, how mankind used to go about remembering.[28]

It is the same with language in which one has merely the choice of remembering the words and losing the meaning or, vice versa, of remembering the meaning and losing the words in doing so.[29] As soon as optical and acoustical data can be put into some kind of media storage, people no longer need their memory. Its "liberation" is its end.[30] As long as the book had to take care of all serial data flows, however, words trembled with sensuality and memory. All the passion of reading consisted of hallucinating a meaning between letters and lines: the visible or audible world of romantic poetry. And all passion of writing was (according to E. T. A. Hoffmann) the poet's wish "to pronounce the inner being" of these hallucinations "in all its glowing colors, shadows, and lights" in order to "hit the favorable reader as if with an electric shock."[31]

Electricity itself has brought this to an end. If memories and dreams, the dead and the specters have become technically reproducible, then the hallucinatory power of reading and writing has become obsolete. Our realm of the dead is no longer in books, where it was for such a long time. No longer is it the case that "only through writing will the dead remain in the memory of the living," as Diodor of Sicily once wrote.

The writer Balzac was already overcome by fear when faced with photography, as he confessed to Nadar, the great pioneer of photography. If the human body (according to Balzac) on the one hand consists of infinitely thin layers of "specters," and if on the other hand the human spirit cannot be made of nothing, then the daguerreotype must be a shady trick: it fixes, that is, steals those layers, one after the other, until finally nothing remains of those "specters" and of the human body itself.[32] Photo albums establish an infinitely more precise realm of the dead than Balzac's *Comédie humaine*, the competing literary enterprise. In contrast to the arts, the work of media is not limited to the grid of the symbolic. Media can reconstruct bodies beyond the systems of words, colors, or sound intervals. It is only media that can fulfill the "high standards" which we have applied to the "image" since the invention of photography. According to Rudolf Arnheim: "It [the image] is not only supposed to resemble the object, but it is also supposed to guarantee this resemblance by being the product of this object itself, i.e., by being mechanically produced by it—in the same way as the illuminated objects in reality mechanically imprint their image onto the photographic layer";[33] or, as the frequency curves of noises inscribe themselves onto the phonographic plate.

A reproduction authenticated by the object itself has physical precision. This kind of reproduction refers to the real of bodies which necessarily slips through all the symbolic grids. Media always already provide the appearances of specters. For, according to Lacan, in the real even the word *corpse* is already a euphemism.[34]

And the tapping specters of the spiritistic séances, with their messages from the realm of the dead, appeared quite promptly at the moment of the invention of the Morse alphabet in 1837. Promptly, photographic plates—even and especially with the camera shutter closed—provided images of ghosts or specters which, in their black-and-white fuzziness, only emphasized the moments of resemblance. Finally, one of the ten uses Edison predicted (in 1878, in the *North American Review*) for the recently invented phonograph was to preserve the "last words of the dying."

From those kinds of "family archives,"[35] with their special attention to the returning dead, it was only a small step to fictions which connect the living and the dead via telephone cables. This was something wished for by Leopold Bloom on the occasion of his visit to the Dublin cemetery.[36] It had already been turned into science fiction by Walther Rathenau in his double role as chairman of the board of AEG and as a writer. In his story *Resurrection Co.*, the cemetery administration of a town—Necropolis, Dakota, USA—reacts to the scandal of people being buried alive by founding a daughter company, the Dakota and Central Resurrection Telephone and Bell Co., with a capital stock of $750,000 and the sole purpose of ensuring that even the inhabitants of graves are connected to the public telephone network. Whereupon the dead take advantage of their opportunity and, long before McLuhan, proceed to prove that the content of each medium is another medium—which is, in this concrete case, a specific professional deformation.[37]

Paranormal voices on tape or radio, as they have been spiritistically researched since 1959 and preserved even in rock music since Laurie Anderson's 1982 release, *Big Science*, tend to tell their researchers only their preferred wavelengths.[38] This is quite comparable to the case of Judge Schreber, in which, in 1898, a paranormal "base or nerve language" of beautiful autonomy revealed its code and channels,[39] that is, when channel and message became one. "You just have to choose a talk show station of the middle, short, or long wave, or the so-called white noise, a noise in between two stations, or the 'Jürgenson wave,' which, depending on your location, is to be found between 1450 and 1600 kHz, between Vienna and Moscow."[40] You then connect a tape recorder to the radio and, when you replay the tape, you will hear ghost voices which do not originate from any known station, but which will, like any official newscaster, result in sheer advertising for the radio. For the location and the existence of such a "Jürgenson wave" has been pinpointed by "Friedrich Jürgenson, the nestor of vocal research."[41]

The realm of the dead has the same dimensions as the storage and emission capacities of its culture. *Media*, as you can read in Klaus Theweleit, are always already flight apparatuses *into the other world*. If grave stones stood as symbols at the beginning of culture,[42] our media technology can bring back all the gods. The old lamentations about temporality that always used to measure the distance between writing and sensuality have been suddenly silenced. In the media landscape immortals have come to exist again.

War on the Mind is the title of a book on psychological strategies of the Pentagon. In it we are told that the planning staff for electronic warfare, which is merely continuing the battle of the Atlantic,[43] has already made lists of those days that mean luck or mishap for other peoples. This allows the U.S. Air Force "to choose the time of a bomb attack in accordance with the predictions of some local god." Voices of those gods have been tape recorded in order to be able "to frighten primitive native guerillas and confine them to their villages" when played from a helicopter. And finally, the Pentagon has had developed special film projectors which can project those tribal gods on low-hanging clouds.[44] The technologically implemented beyond. . . .

There is no need to mention that the lists of those good and black days are not kept in the Pentagon in the form of manuscripts. Office technology keeps up with media technology. Cinema and phonograph, Edison's two great developments, which inaugurated our present, have their third term in the typewriter. The authors of books and their publishers, however, have become so accustomed to dealing with typescripts that cultural histories, which recently have regained so much popularity, generally tend to forget about the typewriter. Since 1865 (in Europe) or 1868 (in America) writing has no longer consisted of those ink or pencil traces of a body, whose optical or acoustical signals were irretrievably abandoned in order that the readers, at least, might flee into the surrogate sensuality of handwriting. In order to allow for a series of sounds and sights to be stored, the old European storage technique had first of all to be mechanized. Hans Magnus Johan Malling Hansen in Copenhagen and Christopher Latham Sholes in Milwaukee developed typewriters that could be mass-produced. Edison thought highly of the potential of this invention at the time when Sholes went to see him in Newark to show him his recently patented model and to invite the man who had invented invention itself to cooperate with him.[45]

But Edison turned the offer down—almost as if the phonograph and the kinetoscope had, already in 1868, been waiting for their inventor, thus limiting his time. Instead, the offer was accepted by an arms manufacturer that had been suffering from a loss in sales since 1865. Remington, and not Edison, took over the discourse machine-gun from Sholes.

Finally, it was not the marvelous One from whom the three media of our age would have sprung. At the beginning of our age there is quite the opposite situation: there is division or differentiation.[46] On the one hand there are two technical media which can, for the first time, fix unwritable data flows; on the other hand there is "something in between tool and machine," as Heidegger wrote so precisely about the typewriter.[47] On the one hand there is the entertainment industry with its new forms of sensuality; on the other hand there is a writing which already separates body and paper in the process of production, not just in the process of reproduction (as in the case of Gutenberg's movable type). The letters and their order are standardized from the beginning as type and keyboard, while media are placed in the noise of the real—as the fuzziness of the pictures in the cinema, as the hissing on tape.

In a standardized text, paper and body, writing and soul fall apart. Typewriters do not store an individual, their letters do not transmit a beyond which could be hallucinated by perfect alphabets as meaning. Everything which, since Edison's two innovations, can be taken over by the technical media disappears out of the type-scripts. The dream of a real, visible, or audible world arising from the words is over. The historical synchronicity of cinema, phonography, and typewriter separated the data flows of optics, acoustics, and writing and rendered them autonomous. The fact of this differentiation is not altered by the recent ability of electric or electronic media to bring them back together and combine them.

In 1860, five years before Malling Hansen's mechanical writing ball, this first typewriter that could be mass-produced, Keller's *Missbrauchte Liebesbriefe* announced the illusion of poetry: love had only the impossible alternative either to "speak with black ink" or "to let the red blood speak."[48] When typing, filming, and taking photographs become three equal options, however, writing loses those aspects of a surrogate sensuality. Around 1880 poetry becomes literature. It is no longer the red blood of a Keller or the inner forms of a Hoffmann that have to be transmitted by standardized letters; it is a new and beautiful tautology of technicians. According to Mallarmé's instant insight, literature does not mean anything but that it consists of twenty-six letters.[49]

Lacan's "methodological distinction" between the real, the imaginary, and the symbolic is the theory (or merely a historical effect) of this differentiation. The symbolic includes the signs of language in their materality and technicity; that is, they form, as letters and ciphers, a finite set which does not address the philosophical dream of an infinity of meaning. What counts are only differences (or in terms of the typewriter) the spaces between the elements of a system. For that reason the world of the symbolic, in Lacan, is already called "the world of the machine."[50]

The imaginary, however, is constituted as the mirror image of a body which appears to be more perfect as regards its motor control than the body of an infant.[51] The imaginary thereby implements precisely that optical illusion which was being explored at the birth of film. A body that is fragmented or (in the case of the film) cut apart is confronted by the illusory continuity of movements in the mirror or movie. It is not merely accidental that the euphoric reactions of infants at the sight of their double in the mirror were fixed by Lacan in a documentary film.

From the real, nothing more can be brought into the daylight than what Lacan had presupposed in its being given—nothing. It forms that residue or waste which can be caught neither in the mirror of the imaginary nor in the grids of the symbolic: physiological accident, stochastic disorder of bodies.

Methodological distinctions of modern psychoanalysis and technical distinctions of the modern media landscape coalesce very clearly. Each theory has its historical a priori. And structuralism as a theory only spells out what has been coming over the information channels since the beginning of this century.

Only the typewriter provides a writing which is a selection from the finite and ordered stock of its keyboard. The typewriter literally illustrates what Lacan shows in terms of the antiquated letter-box. In contrast to the flow of handwriting, here discrete elements separated by spaces are placed side by side. The symbolic has the status of block letters. Film was the first to store a moving double in which men, as opposed to all other primates, misrecognize their bodies. That is to say that the imaginary has the status of cinema. And the phonograph was the first to fix what is being produced by our larynx as noise before any semiotic order or semantic units. To obtain pleasure, Freud's patients need no longer want the good of the philosophers; they just have to babble.[52] The real—particularly in the talking cure of psychoanalysis—has the status of phonography.

The technical differentiation of optics, acoustics, and writing around 1880, as it exploded Gutenberg's storage monopoly, made the fabrication of so-called man possible. His essence runs through apparatuses. Machines conquer functions of the central nervous system, not merely the muscular system as they did previously. And it is only then—not yet with the steam engine and railroad—that we have a clean division between matter and information, between the real and the symbolic. In order to invent phonography and cinema, the ancient dreams of mankind do not suffice. The physiology of the eye, ear, and brain have to become objects of research. In order to optimize writing for machines, it must no longer be dreamt of as an expression of individuals or as a trace of bodies. The forms, differences, and frequencies of letters have to be reduced to formulas. So-called man becomes physiology on the one hand and information technology on the other.

When Hegel summed up the perfect alphabetism of his time, he called it spirit. The readability of all history and all discourse transformed man or the philosopher into god. The media revolution of 1880, however, laid the grounds for all theories and practices which could then avoid the confusion of information and spirit. In place of thinking we have Boolean algebra; instead of consciousness we have an unconscious which is transformed from "The Purloined Letter" (at latest with Lacan's reading) into a Markoff-chain.[53] The fact that the symbolic is called the world of the machine liquidates the megalomaniacal assumption of so-called man that he is distinguished by the "quality" of having a "consciousness" and that he is anything more than a computer. For both people and computers are subject to interpellation by the signifier, that is, both are programmed. Already in 1874, eight years before he decides to buy a typewriter, Nietzsche asks himself whether there are still men or simply thinking, writing, and computing machines.[54]

In 1950 Alan Turing, the practitioner among England's mathematicians, will answer Nietzsche's question. With formal elegance he shows that the question is not a real question. Turing's essay, "Computing Machinery and Intelligence," which appeared in the philosophical periodical *Mind*, of all journals, proposes an experiment, the so called Turing game:

A computer A and a man B communicate data via the interface connections of some sort of telewriter. The exchange of texts is monitored by a censor C that also receives merely written information. A and B pretend to be men. C has to decide which of the two does not simulate and which of the two is merely Nietzsche's thinking, writing, and computing machine. But because the machine, each time it gives itself away by making a mistake or rather by not making any, can improve its program through learning, the game remains open ended.[55] In the Turing game man and his simulation coalesce.

This is already the case because the censor C receives no manuscripts, but plotter outprints or typescripts. Certainly computers could also simulate human hands, with their routines and occasional mistakes, their so-called individuality, but Turing, as the inventor of the universal discrete machine, was a typist. He was not a particularly good typist—not much better than his tom cat, Timothy, who was allowed to jump on the key board of his typewriter in his chaotic secret service office[56]—but nevertheless, his typing was less catastrophic than his handwriting. Already the teachers of the honorable public school Sherborne could hardly forgive their pupil his chaotic lifestyle and messy handwriting. He got bad grades for brilliant exams in mathematics only because his "handwriting was worse than ever seen before."[57] This shows how faithfully schools cling to their old duty of fabricating quite literally in-dividuals by drilling them in a beautiful, continuous, and individual handwriting. But Turing, a master in subverting all kinds of discipline and self-cultivation, escaped. He made plans for the invention of an "incredibly primitive" typewriter.[58]

Those plans were not realized. But when on the meadows of Grantchester, the meadows of all English lyrics from the romantics to Pink Floyd, he came across the idea of the universal discrete machine, the student's dream was realized and transformed. The principle of Sholes's typewriter, patented in 1868, has survived until today. Only the man or stenotypist who was needed by Remington & Son for writing and reading has been rendered obsolete by Turing.

And this is so because a Turing machine is even more incredibly primitive than the Sherborn plan for a typewriter. All it has to deal with are a paper ribbon, which is at once its program and its data material, its input and its output. Turing has slimmed down the common typewriter page to this one-dimensional ribbon. But there are even further economizations: his machine no longer needs those many redundant letters, cyphers, and signs of a typewriter keyboard; all it needs is one sign and its absence, 1 and 0. The machine can read this binary information, or (in Turing's technical word) can *scan* it. It can move the paper ribbon a space to the right, or a space to the left, or not at all. It moves by jerks and therefore discretely, like typewriters, which have, in contrast to handwriting, block letters, back spacers, and space bars. (In a letter to Turing we find: "Pardon the use of the typewriter: I have come to prefer discrete machines to continuous ones."[59]) The mathematical model of 1936, however, is no longer a hermaphrodite between a machine and a mere tool; as a feedback system it beats all the Remingtons. For the sign on the paper ribbon, or respectively its absence, which is read, steers the next step, which is a kind of writing; it depends on the reading whether the machine keeps the sign or erases it or, vice versa, whether it keeps a space blank or puts a sign on it. And so on, and so on.

That is all. But no computer that will ever be built can do more. Even the most advanced Von-Neumann machine (with program storage and computing unit), though faster, is in principle no different from Turing's infinitely slow model. Furthermore, not every computer has to be a Von-Neumann machine, while all imaginable computers are only a state n of the universal discrete machine. In 1936 Turing proved it mathematically, two years before Konrad Zuse built the first programmable computer out of simple relays.[60] At that point the world of the symbolic really turned into the world of the machine.

The age of media—as opposed to the history that ends it— moves in jerks, like Turing's paper ribbon. From the Remington, via the Turing machine, to microelectronics; from mechanization, via automatization, to the implementation of a writing which is cypher and not sense—one century sufficed to transform the ancient storage monopoly of writing into the omnipotence of integrated circuits. Like Turing's correspondents, everything goes from the analogous machine to the discrete. The compact disc digitalizes the gramophone, the video camera the cinema. All data flows end in a state n of Turing's universal machine: numbers and figures become (in spite of romanticism) the key to all creatures.

*Translated by Dorothea Von Mücke
with the assistance of Philippe L. Similon*

DRACULA'S LEGACY

> *Something is going out; I can feel it pass me like a cold wind. I can hear, far off, confused sounds—as if of men talking in strange tongues, fierce-falling water, and the howling of wolves.*

*T*he master spoke.* He was still speaking. He had not yet stamped with his foot, which stops all speech with the power of a koan.[1] He had not yet knotted his silent topology of string. He was not yet dead.

The master was still speaking, yet only a moment more, and only to say that he was just speaking for a moment.

Needless to say, not to the countless people, women and men, who filled the lecture hall of Saint Anne.[2] They were not even listening; they only wanted to understand (as the master once revealed to the radio microphones of Belgium).[3]

Only tape heads are capable of inscribing into the real a speech that passes over understanding heads, and all of Lacan's seminars were spoken via microphone onto tape. Lowlier hands need then only play it back and listen, in order to be able to create a media link between tape recorder, headphones, and typewriter, reporting to the master what he has already said. His words, barely spoken, lay before him in typescript, punctually before the beginning of the next seminar.

Speech has become, as it were, immortal.[4]

One hundred years before the discoveries of Lacan, *Scientific American* announced Edison's phonograph under the headline:

---

* This article was written on the occasion of the death of Jacques Lacan. It was first published under the title "Draculas Vermächtnis" in the volume *Zeta 02/Mit Lacan*, ed. Dieter Hombach (Berlin: Rotation, 1982) 103–37 (translator's note).

"Speech Capable of Indefinite Repetition from Automatic Records."[5]

Endless repetition thanks to automatic recording—just one more reason to keep on speaking. To speak in particular about what writing is, and what it means psychoanalytically to be able to read one's own speech,[6] even what is merely spoken off-the-cuff. All friends of wisdom and deep thinking in Germany, who have pondered signifier and signified, could (if they only wanted to) hear how simple this distinction is. It exists only technically, "in the dimension of writing as such": "The signified has nothing to do with the ears, but only with reading, the reading of what one hears in the signifier. It is not the signified, rather the signifier which one hears."[7]

A law that is of course valid in precisely that place where it is proclaimed. For the master, because a small media link transcribes all of his speeches, is in the fortunate position of being able to continue these speeches on the basis of a lecture previously produced, while the participants in his seminar, because they only hear him speak, are exposed to the power of pure signifiers. It requires a special gift to be able to play back this chain of signifiers without a technical interface. What the master speaks off-the-cuff—and that means to and about women—is received only by women. Since the winter semester of 1916, when the University of Vienna heard certain *Introductory Lectures on Psychoanalysis*, with the equally unheard-of and overlooked salutation "Ladies and Gentlemen!" this type of feedback is no longer impossible. With their own ears women hear discourses concerning the secrets of their desires. Hearing that even they have a connection to the signifier called phallus (at least in its anatomically miniature form),[8] simply because they are no longer, as they had been for an entire century before fundamentally barred from all academic discourse.

Everything that the Herr professors have told the Herr students about mankind and nature, spirit and alma mater, becomes ridiculous as soon as women are allowed to sit in the lecture hall. To women the master reveals very different things. Namely, that their wishes and myths conjure up, rather than the universal mingling of spirit and nature, a Don Juan, who takes them one after the other.[9] It is therefore not surprising that precisely in place of this feminine myth, a feminine pair of lips acts as a tape recorder. According to Leporello, one thousand and three women—one after the other—allowed themselves to be seduced; but what this signifies for Lacan psychoanalytically and mathematically, "was noticed, needless to say, by only one person—my daughter."[10]

The language and subject matter of psychoanalysis, according to Lacan's nice play on words, always include an Anna, who, as the daughter of the master, brings his words back to him. There is no difference in this respect between Berggasse and the Chapel of Saint Anne. Even if this daughter (as Anna Freud did) defines her activity as "the restoration of the unity of the Ego."[11] In actuality she only makes certain that an intact Moebius loop known as text is produced from the ventriloquism of the master. Speech has become, as it were, immortal.

The discourse of psychoanalysis runs through two parallel-switched feedback loops, one feminine and one mechanical. On the one hand is the daughter, the only one who understands Don Juan's counting games, and on the other is the son-in-law, or daughter's husband *(Tochtermann)*, to express it more nicely (and in the dialect of Baden). Of course he is not called by name, but he lurks in all of the seminar meetings as a "someone," whose editorial "efforts" make it possible for the master "to stick his nose into the speeches he himself has given over the years."[12] It is well-known that Jacques-Alain Miller directs the media chain that transcribes and puts into text Lacan's seminars, one after the other.

A discourse, brought back by the daughter and turned into text by the daughter's husband, circumvents certain dangers. Words fail many speakers simply because, according to Lacan, stupidity—at least of the type that can be spoken—doesn't get one very far. Within the current discourse, it just spins in place. Which is why the master never returns without fear to things he once spoke simply off-the-cuff. And thanks only to this "someone," who transcribes every lecture with his machines, can he allow himself the feeling of occasionally passing the test. After the fact, these re-lectures indicate that what he said off-the-cuff was not so stupid after all.[13]

In this manner, two parallel-switched feedback loops—the word of the daughter and the transcription of the daughter's husband—create a discourse that never stops inscribing itself: Lacan's definition of necessity. His books, whether they are called *Seminar* or *Television* or *Radiophonie*, are all works of art in the age of technical reproduction. For the first time since man has thought, stupidity is allowed to go on indefinitely. Even if Freud's basic rule commands that one speak at random, and even if the "most direct" path "to the pleasure principle" (not including all of those chin-ups "to higher spheres, which form the basis of Aristotelian ethics")[14] leads through this gibberish *(Blabla)*,[15] there really is no other option. After all, tape recorders, television cameras, and radio microphones were invented for the very purpose of recording gibberish *(Blabla)*. Precisely because they "understand nothing," technical media take the place that, on other occasions, was reserved for Lacan's seminar participants. In both cases the master "thanks" completely thoughtless recorders that his teachings are not insanity, or, in other words, "not self-analysis."[16] And in case the seminar participants should still not be aware whose subjects, and that means whose subordinates, they are, the media link also records the following statement: "From now on you are, and to a far greater extent than you can imagine, subjects of gadgets or instruments—from microscopes to radio and television—which will become elements of your being. You cannot now understand the full significance of this; but it is nevertheless a part of the scientific discourse, insofar as discourse is something that determines a form of social cohesion."[17]

Psychoanalysis in the age of technical reproduction is an open provocation. Because there is no such thing as pre-discursive reality,[18] discourses can, by means of the tie called discourse, themselves create precisely this social tie. It is not a coincidence that the master liked to demonstrate the tying of knots that apparently cannot be untied. The social tie of the Lacan seminar consists of provocations that describe it as a social tie and nothing else. "I have," says someone to his listeners, "been saying for a long time, that feelings are always mutual. And I have said this that it might return to me again: 'Yes and then, and then, love, love, is it always mutual?'—'But-of-course, but-of-course.' "[19]

So the Chapel of Saint Anne serves as a giant echo chamber (and it is quite likely that chapels have always had this architectural significance). The word of love is sent forth, is received, is sent out again by the receiver, picked up again by the sender, etc., until the amplifier reaches the point that, in studies of alternating current, is called oscillation amplitude, and, in the contemporary discourse is called love. Because no one in the seminar attempts to protest, or, in other words, to produce inverse feedback,[20] these provocations fulfill their intention—love has become a resonant (oscillating) circuit.

It spins and oscillates, it oscillates and spins, dum da dum da, in waltz rhythm. Love, technically employed, is a shellac disc with the eternal title *Parlez-moi d'amour*. "Speaking of love, in the analytic discourse, basically one does nothing else. And how could it escape us that, as regards everything that the discovery of scientific discourse has made it possible to articulate, it has been one pure and simple waste of time. What analytic discourse brings to bear—which may after all be why it emerged at a certain point of scientific discourse— is that speaking of love is in itself a *jouissance*."[21]

In this respect, however, the psychoanalytic discourse is not in any way privileged. *Parlez-moi d'amour*, the recording of the seminar *Encore*, is also available elsewhere. How love functions and does not function, how it is made and not made, "is an important part of the analytic discourse; but one must emphasize, that it is not its privilege. It also expresses itself in what I have just called the contemporary discourse," the master explains, by way of technically implementing our fluid discourse with untranslatable word plays—as one more recording. This is what becomes of speech in the days of its reproducibility. If from now on we were to write instead of *disque-oucourant* or discourse-recording (with a pitiful German play on words) disc(ourse) [*Disku(r)s*], then Lacan's discourse on disc(ourse) runs more or less like this: "The contemporary disc(ourse), in other words the record, spins and spins, to be precise, it spins around nothing. This disc(ourse) appears precisely in the area from which all discourses are specified and into which all again disappear, where one discourse can speak exactly like any other."[22]

As we know, Lacan establishes four specific or officious discourses. There is a discourse of the master or lord, and one of the university, an hysteric and an analytic discourse. But since all four disappear again in the droning of the record, it does not bode well for their privileges and differences. "If there were no analytic discourse," the master reveals to his listeners, "You would all still and forever twitter like sparrows, singing the disc(ourse), droning out the record."[23] What he does not reveal to them is that this sort of provocation is more fittingly the business of masters than of analysts. (The latter are indeed paid to listen even to sparrows). But there are good reasons for his silence. People who cannot bear these provocations will simply stop listening to the drone of the record, and most certainly put a different one, called *Encore*, onto the turntable.

Encore, Da capo, Play it again . . .

"We are bringing the plague, and they don't even know it," said Freud to Jung, as their ship moved into New York harbor. "This was the being I was helping to transfer to London, where, perhaps, for centuries to come he might, amongst its teeming millions, satiate his lust for blood, and create a new and ever-widening circle of semi-demons" (52),[24] said Jonathan Harker when he realized that his best efforts as a lawyer were only going to aid a certain Count Dracula. When Lacan was translated to Germany, voices of this nature were not even heard. The currently popular record keeps on spinning, as if nothing had happened; this record, which has only recently been placed on the turntable, spins in ways that tell of all sorts of things, except, that is, of records and radios, television or excerpts from seminars. Academic discourses about Lacan (exactly as the master defined them) swallow the subject that holds them, into the abyss of its requirement to place an author named Lacan within a system of knowledge. Philosophical discourses about Lacan (exactly as the master defined them) remain variations of a male discourse of the master that still preserves the phantasms of Ego and world,[25] and in an emergency still send its court jesters[26] into battle. Only the analytic discourse on Lacan—if only because of its name *Wunderblock* (mystic writing-pad)[27]—is protected from the danger of forgetting mystic writing-pads, typewriters, systems, and discourses, as the very name *Wunderblock* brings these things into play.

1. Vienna, May 2, 1890, 7:46 A.M. The Orient Express, already an hour late (in keeping with its reputation), is at the station. For a moment the path of Jonathan Harker, a legal assistant from Exeter in England, crosses with that of a young doctor from Moravia, who has gone among the builders of civilization to bring them the plague. But since there is no poetic justice, the disaster runs its course. Unfortunately the Orient Express experiences no mechanical problems; Freud continues to write his functional *Aphasia (Auffassung der*

Aphasien), and Harker in his stenographic travel diary. This concise refutation of the localization of physiological speech centers in the brain *(hirnphysiologischer Sprachzentren-Lokalisierungen)*, as soon as it is hooked up to the collected slips of the tongue of hysterical girls— will inaugurate a psychoanalytic discourse. The hand-written diary, as soon as it is hooked up to phonographs and typewriters, autopsies and newspaper reports, will kill the Lord of the East and the Night, leaving him only the miserable immortality granted the hero of a novel. 1897, while the mystery of the interpretation of dreams is becoming clear to Doctor Freud, Bram Stoker's *Dracula* appears in print. And even if the guest of the Count did not visit Freud on his journey, at least poetic justice has spread the rumor that the novelist of the Count had been initiated into the new system of knowledge. Stoker is said to have heard reports in 1893, at the Society for Psychical Research, on Freud's "Observations on the Psychical Mechanism of Hysterical Phenomena" ("Vorläufige Mitteilung über den psychischen Mechanismus hysterischer Phänomene").[28] And indeed, sending people to Transylvania, to the "Land Beyond the Forest," even if they are merely office clerks and characters from novels, could not occur to anyone who had not heard that an Ego can develop where there once was an Id.

In order to replace the Id with an Ego, to replace violence with technology, it is necessary that one first fall into the clutches of this violence. The beginning of every romance reverses for a certain period of time the roles of hunter and hunted. On his journey to the Count, Jonathan Harker, the imperial tourist, is forced to abandon the Orient Express and be content with Balkan cuisine, provincial hotels, post carriages, and horses. In order to enter the "eye of the storm," which (as if to support the theories of a certain Vámbéry) mixes together various Eastern European myths and races,[29] the English office assistant must step beyond the point of no return. The conversation of his fellow travelers becomes incomprehensible, and since it is not possible to hear the signifieds themselves, only Harker's polyglot dictionary can inform him that signifiers like *vlkoslak* and *vrolok* all mean "vampire." English tourists are simply not polyglots; and the name Mahdi must therefore have sounded to the troops of General Gordon, when they advanced toward Khartum—the city of their destruction—as the word *vlkoslak* did to Harker.

But in the heart of darkness and the Carpathians, high on the Borgo Pass between Transylvania and Bukovina, a rescuer appears: Harker steps from the post carriage into the count's calèche, where the coachman speaks of the night through which they ride in fluent German. In this way Eastern Europe's former language of trade reconciles the extremes of the continent. And when the calèche finally escapes the horrible howling of the wolves and drives into the castle courtyard, the traveler greets the excellent English of the Count as if his reaching of this destination were already his return to the eastern edge of Austro-Hungary.

Negotiations with a foreign power, itself more concerned with England than with Transylvania—since the Count plans to purchase properties in Whitby, Purfleet, and Exeter, and to this end has horded British address lists and railway time tables, lists of lawyers and aristocrats—: this is how it goes in the first few nights of Harker's stay, and very much in keeping with the wishes of an empire whose primary secret is handling all foreign policy as if it were domestic policy. The legal assistant of a lawyer from Exeter is supposed to provide the Transylvanian territorial lord with advice and data, which are necessarily missing from his imported and out-of-date reference works.

But lords of the east are not merely customers of western data banks. Every tourist, having once reached the point of no return, comes to realize that the others have only learned English in order to be able to tell about the Other. Late at night, while Harker has dinner and his host is curiously fasting, the Count makes a habit of speaking about the land and the peoples who have owned it and spilled blood on it. He speaks of Saxons and Turks, Hungarians and Wallachs. He speaks of the Huns, in whom witches and devils once mated, and his own ancestors, who were descended from the union of these nomads and Wotan's werewolves and Berserkers. He tells of Draculas as crusaders against the Turks, Draculas as betrayers of the crusaders to the Turks—the race of the Count is the history of Transylvania, his blood a different sort of memory than reference works.

2. For there was the Count. In the period of transition, when Rome finally fell to the attack of nomadic hords, there was in Transylvania a Count Vlad Tsepes, who on coins also referred to

himself as Dracula or little dragon. When he was 13 the Turks took him as a hostage from his father, the ruling lord or voivode, into the near east. When Vlad was released in 1448 and took the throne of his father who, needless to say, had been murdered, these years of Turkish captivity provided him with a nick-name. Tsepes means "the impaler," and impaling was the slow form of execution he had learned in Asia. He was the defender of the Occident, on its most threatened border, but with the torture methods of the Orient, whole forests of stakes on which corpses rotted—enough reason for Hungary to make a prisoner of him when he was fleeing the Turks a second time in 1462, a prisoner this time in the camp of his Christian allies. The despot, who had impaled heathens and Saxons by the thousands, had 12 years in a Budapest prison to continue his experiments, this time on birds and mice. And when Vlad the Impaler finally regained his freedom and power, he met with a horrible fate himself. The military stratagem of disguising himself as a Turk brought him death in battle, at the hands of his own troops.[30]

Dracula, until his dying breath, a double counterfeit between east and west, was never the vampire Dracula. The blood of Huns and Berserkers that flowed in his veins, desired blood, but within the economy of waste rather than of need. No folklore of Transylvania equates him with those Un-Dead who can only eke out an existence on the blood of strangers. The despot impaled his opposers and servants, while he sat in the midst of the dying, giving a feast in pure excess. The Un-Dead is impaled by others, in order that he too might become a Christian corpse.

The first impetus for making the territorial lord into a vampire was provided by a Hungarian orientalist, whose own name is found just before "Vampyr" in old reference works. And this is no coincidence. It is as if Arminius Vámbéry, vain as he was, had wanted to occupy the lexical place of the terrible one. He changed "Bamberger," the surname of his Jewish grandfather, into "Vámbéry," playing a game of signifiers with vampire.

And Arminius Vámbéry (1832–1913), the adventurer and professor from Budapest, actually was a sort of vampire. Like Vlad Tsepes before him, but without the fatal consequences, like Lawrence of Arabia after him, but without the ingratitude of the men behind the scenes, he traveled the Orient in oriental disguise, gathering information that found open ears upon his later travels to London. It was not the linguistic footnotes, which his polyglot mind also brought along, which aroused the interest of the practical Britons; what he had discovered about peoples and despots, dealings and politics in the east, however, was paid for only moments after arrival—while he was still in the Dover-London express train—by a Mr. Smith, whose name and ready cash apparently remained a lifelong mystery to Vámbéry.

But even autobiographies cannot be so naive. Vámbéry, with his inside information and oriental connections—no contemporary gossip doubted this—became a useful spy for the Empire, welcome at Whitehall and Downing Street. After dinner, when the women had been excused, he preached his geo-political credo to the Prime Minister, that the East should be freed from the medievally backward emperors of Austro-Hungary and Russia, and be allowed to flourish as a part of the Empire. This should not be accomplished merely by a concentration of troops, but after the model of the czarist secret service, in the manner of the enemy himself. At this point Lord Palmerston ordered certain measures to be taken in Kandahar or Teheran and, since the women were gone, asked the orient expert openly about harem secrets. Vámbéry's question "Who shall be lord and master in Asia?" also included the sex lives of lords and masters, who, like Stoker's count, have three playmates, and incestuous ones at that.[31]

The traitor shared different, although not very different, interests with Abraham ("Bram") Stoker, with whom he met on several occasions in London's Lyceum Club. There was the cholera epidemic of 1832, which, along with a few Prussian state philosophers, had done away with Vámbéry's father,[32] and had also brought Stoker's family into the greatest danger. There was the Romanian folk tale of another epidemic, one that was transmitted through almost imperceptible bites on the neck, and finally the suddenly once again very apropo history of Vlad Tsepes, the two-faced crusader against the Orient. Stoker simply needed to combine the historical and the legendary, the prince and the vampire, in order to start work on a novel. Arminius Vámbéry had made the vampire Dracula possible.

3. The writing of novels is a continuation of espionage with other means. This is why the names of scoundrels and informants are kept more or less obscure. Vámbéry's numerous writings avoid the all too similar word vampire;[33] Stoker's novel, which makes the word proverbial, avoids, on the other hand, the surname Vámbéry, mentioning as a confederate simply a certain "Arminius of Buda-Pesth University" (240). But it takes more than this to dispel the shadow of espionage, even from a so-called fantastical novel. Vámbéry received a medal from Queen Victoria for "active," in other words, covert "participation in the defense of British interests in the Orient."[34] Jonathan Harker, Stoker's representative, deserved the same honorable title.

Small wonder then, that Harker, even before his meeting with the Count, suffers from acute paranoia. An English spy, sent to the front on the information of an English spy, would have to see within foreign eyes what has been the object of his desire all along: the evil eye. For this reason, it is not of much help that concerned inn keepers' wives in Bistritz want to protect him from the Malocchio by giving him crucifixes. The spy prefers to rely on modern defensive techniques of espionage: Like Vámbéry, who wrote his secret travel notes in Hungarian and sewed them into his dervish robes, Harker writes all of his travel journal in stenography. The eye of the Count, however red it may glow through the night, cannot read shorthand. Imaginary terrors pale before this technology of symbols, developed by the most economical of centuries. All that the Count can do is complain of the meaninglessness of these symbols, and burn every letter of Harker's that is not legible to him as a host. Because of this cryptic writing, the broken piece, whose Greek name is symbol, itself falls to pieces. But imperial tourism was never anything different, nor were its consequences.

Half spy, half prisoner, Harker creeps through the dusty hallways of a castle in which there are no mirrors and no coins that could still be legally circulated. Small wonder that his British ego gradually loses its foundation. "Here I am," muses the stenographer at a small oak table, "where in old times possibly some fair lady sat to pen, with much thought and many blushes, her ill-spelt love-letter, and writing in my diary in shorthand all that has happened since I closed it last. It is nineteenth century up-to-date with a vengeance. And yet, unless my senses deceive me, the old centuries had, and have, powers of their own which mere 'modernity' cannot kill" (36–37).[35] The old Count will neither allow himself to be bought, nor to be made into an image. He remains the Other, whom no mirror can reflect, a paranoic hallucination with desires that Harker does not even dare mention in his secret diary. Minutely, like Dr. Seward later in the novel, he notes how many times per evening the Count refills his glass, trying to separate insanity from reality. But even with this counting there remain plenty of shocks. Simply the fact that the keeping of his journal—like the discourse of Hamlet's father, or the stories of the Arabian Nights, or the material for *The Interpretation of Dreams*—always ends with the crowing of the cock, deeply disturbs him, although this diary is the only thing keeping him from an imminent insanity. But when the last mirror Harker possesses under the dictates of the Other, reflects only darkness . . .

A darkness as if ready-made to create nightmares for the spy. When he pleads with the Count to let him depart for home early, it materializes itself as wolves, which, as is well-known, always travel in packs,[36] and can therefore actually block the castle entrance. When he takes advantage of a suspicious absence of the Count, in order to spy behind castle doors that have been violently broken open, the darkness forms itself—as soon as one moon beam falls on it—into dancing motes of dust, from which dancing female shapes appear before Harker's spellbound eyes. And although he is happily engaged to be married, he imagines that he has seen these three women before, who come to him either threateningly or seductively. The nightmares have thus become transparent coverings for desires that would cause him to lose either his blood or his sperm.[37] But in the middle of this daydream the Count appears and calls the three women back, much as he had called back the blood thirsty wolves in the last minute. It is strange, however, that these orders (even if in a strange accent) are uttered in the best commando English. Women and wolves of the Balkans obey signifiers that make sense, not to them, but to Harker's ears. Only half-conscious, the eavesdropper understands every word with which the Count betrays his more than incestuous desires to the three women.

A count who forgets not to speak English when he is not even speaking to his guest, a count who dislikes garlic as otherwise only

Anglo-Saxons dislike it, a count who refers scornfully to the "employer" of his guest as "lord and master," a count whose words are simultaneously commands, and whose desires (as aspiring lawyers really ought to notice) presuppose an *ius primae noctis*—Harker finds in Dracula his Lord Signifier. This is how it goes when someone reaches the heart of darkness. Conrad's novella, Copolla's film, Stoker's novel—they all lead to that point where the power of the Other or Stranger would become decipherable as their own colonialism, if it were not so unbearable to read the writing on the flesh.

One day at noon Harker stands before the corpse of the Count. But just when he wants to drive a stake through the Un-Dead, an all powerful eye catches and restrains him.

"The signifier commands above all else."[38]

Men want nothing to do with the Lord Discourse and his lordly definition. Harker saves the only thing he has, his diary, which has been spared from the Count as if by a miracle, and flees. In the middle of June a nameless patient stumbles into a hospital in Budapest. He has seen the Count dead, and heard him give commands—in order that this single and double truth become unspeakable, a brain fever overcomes the spy, with the result that they are inscribed instead on his brain. A few decades before, a Hungarian adventurer arrived in Teheran in a similar condition, after he had seen his certain death in the eye of the Emir of Buchara. Vámbéry as a skeleton, Harker with brain fever, this is the way spies return home. And while caring nuns do everything to remove the prints left on his brain, Harker's boss dies in far off Exeter. Without knowing it, he has carried out the business of a dead man with another dead man. Without realizing, because of the directions of a will and testament, he takes the place of his boss.[39] Careers of men.

4. While the unconscious Harker is taking over for his dead boss, and an all-powerful dead man—because this boss sold him four houses in England—is sailing out from the Black Sea, a very new career is beginning. Dracula's project, which (in the opinion of a critic who is, not coincidentally, Anglo-Saxon) anticipated Operation Sea Lion,[40] is shattered by women of a sort never before seen in the history of Western discourse formation. "Western Democracy" (whatever that may be) would fall helplessly into the hands of a

discourse of the master, if there were not young women in Exeter who could ultimately destroy this discourse with the technology of democracy. For it is not the Count who controls the modern media with which he would corrupt the Empire (as the interpretive counterfeit of the above-mentioned Anglo-Saxon would suggest), but, on the contrary, Harker's fiancee, a certain assistant school mistress by the name of Mina Murray, who, with the weapons of a new age, undermines the very possibility of a discourse of the master. By profession Mina Murray is an assistant school mistress, but, not satisfied with this preliminary movement toward women's emancipation, she practices her typing and stenography arduously, in order to do one day "what the lady journalists do" (55).

Everyone knows how marriages come about: He plans and woos, he manipulates and commands.[41] Harker would have been satisfied with the simple title of office assistant, had his wife not found it intolerable. Harker is automatically called to his position by the death and final testament of his boss; Miss Murray has no choice but to want her (and his) career.

Everyone also knows what journalists do: they defer, re-work, and augment speeches and texts, in whatever form they appear. While her groom is writing down a terrifying discourse of the master, in order to stave off madness, Mina is herself busy creating mountains of paper. For this purpose, a form of handwriting, like the one she can see in Jonathan's shorthand letters from Transylvania, would simply be a hindrance; whatever democracy may be, it is supported by the mechanical processing of anonymous discourses (if only because there is no social record apart from discourses). Without the armies of women steno-typists (as women have been called for the last 90 years, who, like Mina, are proficient in both stenography and typing), Houses of Commons and *Bundestage* would fall apart.

In 1871, the machine gun factory Remington brought the first mass-produced typewriter onto the market. Oddly enough, however, financial success was years in coming. All of the Jonathan Harkers—secretaries with the task of setting down discourses of the master in shorthand, transferring these discourses into fair copy, and, if necessary, somehow making office copies—scorned the new discourse machine gun. Perhaps they were simply too proud of their handwriting, a continuous, literally individualized bond, which they had developed only after long years of schooling, and which held them together as individuals and guarded them from insanity. It is, at any rate, not due to any technological backwardness of the Remington company that Harker does not bring a travel typewriter with him to Transylvania; when his future wife makes the same trip five months later these machines have, much to her joy, already been on the market for some time.

Things went much more smoothly: two weeks of intensive typewriter instruction made seven years of schooling obsolete. Women, simply because they were less oriented toward handwriting and individuality, were able to take over this gap in the market by storm, a gap their competitors, mostly male secretaries of the 19th century, overlooked purely out of arrogance. Remington's production departments and advertising agencies only needed to discover women in the noteworthy year of 1881, in order to make typewriters into a mass commodity.

Bruce Bliven has amusingly proven that the typewriter, and only the typewriter, is responsible for a bureaucratic revolution. Men may have continued, from behind their desks, to believe in the omnipotence of their own thought, but the real power over keys and impressions on paper, over the flow of news and over agendas, fell to the women who sat in the front office. And if the great word emancipation has any historical meaning, it is only in the area of word processing, which continues to employ more women world-wide than any other field.[42] Lacan's secretary Gloria was only one among millions . . .

. . . and Mina Murray, afterwards Harker, was in 1890 already at the pinnacle of present and future. She disdainfully left the erotic dreams of the free choice of partner to the so-called "new woman" (91); her own dreams circled around the much more practical desire of a position as secretary for her new husband. "If I can stenograph well enough I can take down what he wants to say in this way and write it out for him on the typewriter" (55), Mina writes (still by hand) to her girlfriend Lucy Westenra. In much the same way, the revolution of European bureaucracy and democracy creeps up silently. Harker's lord and master has the good fortune to be able to say that he, like the Count, is dead when this coup takes place. The female secretary replaces the male secretary, while the boss is replaced by a husband who, not without cause, has been incapacitated by brain fever. When Mina goes to Budapest, summoned by nuns with a written plea for help, an emergency wedding is performed with the sick (not to mention "impotent") man, followed by a *translatio studii sive imperii.* Jonathan Harker, in order not to fall again into madness, forbids himself any re-examination of his Transylvanian diary, and turns it over to the safe hands and eyes of his trusted typist. He does not even want to wonder if his depiction of events was recorded "asleep or awake, sane or mad" (107). Since there are no signs of reality within the unconscious, his output becomes, as it does on the couch, a mass of data to be interpreted by others. Trusted typists, however, are made for the neutralizing of discourses. Mina does not need to hord a copy of Bradshaw, the English train schedule, like the Count, nor does she need to consult one like Sherlock Holmes (who is otherwise a walking data bank);[43] she has Bradshaw memorized.

5. While Harker is languishing in a hospital in Budapest, the schedule of the aspiring journalist prescribes a trip to Whitby, where—far better than the slavish dictates of a lawyer husband—the first interviews and investigations call. The object of research is Mina's friend Lucy, with whom she shares a room, and with whom she has increasingly unpleasant experiences night after night, especially ever since a ship with the name of Demeter has come into the harbor at Whitby, a ship that, apart from dead sailors, brought only a terrifying animal to shore. Of course the amateur reporter can not yet guess that England is now one count richer; but nevertheless, newspaper reprints of the Demeter's log book, eye-witness accounts of harbor workers, and above all, descriptions of Lucy's strange illness, find their way into her diary. Even amateur journalists follow the motto: "All the news that's fit to print."

At first Lucy Westenra only shows the symptoms of a sleepwalker. Mina, however, smarter than many of her female interpreters, does not believe in an autochthonic "tendency toward somnambulism";[44] it becomes very clear from interviews with Lucy's mother that the hysteria of her daughter is related to her father's death. As Freud so rightly remarked in the same year in which the vampire novel appeared, when it comes to hysterical women "blame [is to be] laid on perverse acts by the father."[45] Proof is not hard to find: immediately after the arrival of a perverse count, Lucy's sleep-walking turns into a nightmare. Mina sees the somnabulist giving in, night after night, to the seduction of a shadow who disappears immediately, but leaves two small wounds in her neck, always in the same place. The sick woman feels nothing of this inscription into the real; she is left merely with dream memories, at first of something black and tall, with red eyes, and later of a feeling of sinking into deep, green water, hearing the singing it is said drowning people hear. In support of the truth of the signifier Demeter, there is then, even in hysterical women, a pleasure that goes beyond the long and black phallus.[46]

But since what counts in an hysteric discourse is only what other discourses write down about it, Lucy's oceanic feeling disappears from the files. What is verifiable to the relevant discourse, that is—to the scientific discourse, is only an abnormally high loss of blood and two bite wounds on the neck, always in the same place—like the strikes of a precisely aligned typewriter. Both are discovered by Dr. Seward, a young and successful psychiatrist who had courted Lucy in vain, and who now, instead of a lover, finds a patient, whom he hardly dares to examine, in the bed of his dreams. Where the Lord of the East goes courting, other men have no chance, not even men of knowledge. Dr. Seward is so baffled by Lucy's anemia that, since his rejection, he flees to his hideout of scientific work, to his new data technology, and to $C_2HCL_3H_2O$.

It is not Lucy's neurosis, but the psychosis of a male asylum inhabitant which absorbs Dr. Seward, whenever he awakes from his chloral sleep. He speaks the entire and exhaustive case study of a certain Renfield into the wax cylinder of a phonograph—by 1890 in mass production for precisely three years.[47] For the psychotic discourse, in contrast to Dr. Seward's object of love, at least has all the advantages of logic. That Renfield feeds flies, with which he feeds spiders, with which he feeds sparrows in order to feed a kitten, "a nice little, sleek, playful kitten" (71), with which he will finally feed himself, that Renfield thus works on a logical zoophagous chain according to the motto "blood is life," is easier to write or speak into a phonograph than the oceanic feeling of singing ears. Certainly this zoophagous mania presents a unique puzzle, why it is that Renfield's body has organs like a mouth and stomach, which is why it specifies the psychotic discourse as not needing the aid of any other discourse;[48] and yet, even the psychiatrist is not so sure what he should do with his mouth, when Lucy prefers a Lord by the name of Godalming to all medical proclamations of love. It appears the Name of the Father is still so powerful that nothing is left for the scorned mouth of the psychiatrist but the technical reproduction of deliria. Whatever Renfield hallucinates, Seward speaks into his phonograph. Speech has become, as it were, immortal.

The objective and exhaustive recording of his lunacy does not help the patient much, and has in fact—according to Seward's own admission—traces of cruelty, but "why not advance science in its most difficult and vital aspect—the knowledge of the brain? Had I even the secret of one such mind—did I hold the key to the fancy of even one lunatic—I might advance my own branch of science to a pitch compared with which Burdon-Sanderson's physiology or Ferrier's brain-knowledge would be as nothing" (72). Big words, although they only proclaim the most basic project of the psychiatry of 1890. Whether in Harker or in Renfield, since Broca's studies of aphasia, insanity must be localized in the brain. For this reason Dr. Seward does not even consider an idea that would save him both time and words: to send Renfield's delirious speeches, without the interface of his own doctor voice, directly into Edison's apparatus. But after Flourens and Flechsig, Ferrier and Fritsch had laid bare the individual brain nerve connections with their scalpels, and had stimulated animals with acids, poisons, and currents; insanity lost every verbal quality. It exists only as neuro-physiology[49] in "molecules and connections of the brain," which remind "us," according to the testimony of an art physiologist, "not coincidentally of a process similar to Edison's phonograph."[50]

Dr. Seward's brain is specifically useful for sending a sick brain into the brain of a phonograph. An "unconscious cerebration," suspected by Renfield's unconscious, but not allowed to reach the psychiatrist's Ego, should at least be made accessible on the cylinder.

"The scientific discourse is an ideology of the suppression of the subject, a fact well-known to the master of the progressive university." Placed before the psychoanlytic reading of the Cogito, which only allows one either not to live or not to think,[51] Dr. Seward chooses the phonograph on the one hand and love on the other. His patient Renfield receives the former, his patient Lucy Westenra the latter. Of course, both are going to die.

In contrast to the psychotic zoophagous, who in his asylum plays the role Vlad Tsepes played in prison, Lucy can say whatever she wants: Dr. Seward still sees nothing more than a sick body, because he still sees her as a lover. He does not investigate her fear of sleep and dreams, of wolves and bats, until her incurable condition forces him to call in a specialist from Holland. Van Helsing, although even he is working on a neuro-physiological theory concerned with "the continued evolution of brain mass," is at least old enough to believe what his patient tells him. He even takes those aspects of her symptoms seriously that appear fantastical or impossible according to normal medical standards, simply because Van Helsing dares to "follow the mind of the great Charcot" (191). In the over-filled lecture hall of the Salpêtrière this magician had proven quite forcefully that through hypnosis one can, if not heal, at least produce and interpret unexplainable ailments.

Van Helsing allies himself with Charcot. Even if he only sees Lucy as hysterical because he has "actual attacks of hysteria" himself, he, at any rate, switches from a scientific to an analytic discourse. Like Freud in his article on aphasia, he denies the brain localization impulse of his psychiatrist friend. Like the earlier Freud (before revoking his seduction hypothesis) the old doctor assumes, himself a sort of father, that Lucy is being seduced every night by a sinister father. (Both of them are far beyond the scruples of Charcot or Breuer, who dared to proclaim the psychical mechanism of hysteria, but not its sexual etiology). Like Freud, who, involved in the recording of hysteric discourses, brags of his "absolutely phonographically-reliable" ears,[52] Van Helsing also discovers sexual seduction through symptoms of conversion, secret notes, and remarks Lucy makes—much as if a phonograph (Dr. Seward uses his only for the study of psychoses, and Lucy herself simply leaves hers lying around) were applied to the hysteric discourse. Edison and Freud, Sherlock Holmes and Van Helsing—they all institute, according to Ginzburg's apt expression, a new paradigm of science: the gathering of clues.

This guarantees above all that certain clues, never before present, suddenly appear. Productive, like his great model Charcot, who could bring his female patients all the way to the point of hysteria, Van Helsing calls up amazing symptoms. After his methodical interference the patient divides into two personalities, just like those known to the history of medicine since Dr. Azam and his Félida. During the day Lucy becomes nicer and lovelier, in other words, more and more like her friend Mina. The patient now also has a discourse-technological toy, her phonograph—although it is used only by Dr. Seward, and she too makes a few diary entries, although only in "imitation" (111) of her journalist friend. At night, however, a very different personality comes to power who, as in the case of Félida, has nothing but disdain for virginal morality or even the happiness of secretaries. Lucy Westenra's second personality simply embodies the medical diagnosis.

After Van Helsing has resorted to sensational forms of therapy such as hanging garlic wreaths around the collar of Lucy's nightgown and attaching crucifixes to her bedroom window,[53] nothing remains for the second personality but vampirism, in other words: resistance, in a technically Freudian sense. Sometimes it is the blundering of her mother, but more often the angry movements of the sleeping patient herself which move the apotropaic garlic out of the way (of the count). It is well-known that not only patients, but also their families, often panic when threatened with healing.

The unconscious then, in keeping with its definition, develops artful strategies. Apparently Lucy, if she only sleeps deeply enough, does not really want to sleep with her lordly fiance, but prefers to sink and sink into red eyes and green waters. Accordingly, her daytime personality appears less frequently and always more sickly, and her night-time personality ever stronger and more often. And while the former only imagines with the vaguest disgust what forbidden lust the night brings, the latter is fully conscious of both day and night. She otherwise would not tear up the writing-pad (fortunately already read by Dr. Van Helsing) on which Lucy's day time personality has kept a record of her fear of sleeping. Every aspect of the two conditions, the asymmetry of awareness of the condition, as well as the postponement of passing through the null phase, operates exactly as it did with Azam's Félida.[54]

With the result that in the end, the second personality becomes the only personality. The moment of her death transforms Lucy into an Un-Dead and a bride of the Count. Already by September 10, however, the two doctors discover, because—following Van Helsing's plan—they make a note of even the smallest and least meaningful clues, that Lucy's gums are oddly receding. On September 19 they discover that her teeth are becoming increasingly long and sharp. "Ladies and Gentlemen!" Freud would comment, "Woman also has in her genitalia a small member that is similar to man's."[55]

Vampire teeth are the small member with which Lucy, at the moment of her death, goes after her prey. With a lustful voice never heard from her before, and with eyes both hard and sad, the woman who has been seduced by the Count attempts the first seduction of her own. Lucy Westenra tempts her fiancé with fatal kisses, and by so doing provides proof of the equivalence of vampires and "new women," who are defined by the fact that they do not wait when it comes to desire, but articulate it themselves. In light of this scandal, there is no alternative for Van Helsing and his assistants but to kill the Un-Dead a second time, following all rules of ritual. A few weeks later, Lord Godalming has the privilege of boring through the blood thirsty corpse of his former and traitorous fiancée with a stake that requires no commentary.

This also proves that in the case of bodies once possessed of language, it no longer matters whether they are dead or alive.[56] The main thing is that Dracula's wanton bride—even if it is by means of necrophilia—is brought back to the droning record of discourse.

6. According to the discourse-technological conditions of 1890 women have two options: typewriter or vampirism. Mina Harker and Lucy Westenra represent a systematic alternative which is only reinforced by Lucy's two personalities. As the novel ends, Mina holds a child in the lap that for 300 pages held a typewriter. Lucy, while she was alive, killed her mother, and after her own death, or apparent death, sucked the blood out of children. The two options are thus no longer simply mother or hysteria, as the dispositive sexuality had established them in classical-romantic times. Since our culture has begun to allow women into the sacred halls of word processing, far worse things are possible.

"Machines everywhere, wherever you cast your eye! A replacement for countless tasks that man before had to perform with his own industrious hand, and what a replacement of time and energy. It was only natural that, after the engineer had removed the symbol of feminine industry from the delicate hand of woman, a colleague of his would come up with the idea of replacing the quill pen, the symbol of masculine productivity, with a machine."[57] In other words: machines remove from the two sexes the symbols that distinguish them. In earlier times, needles created woven material in the hands of women, and quills in the hands of authors created another form of weaving called text. Women who gladly became the paper for these scriptorial quills were called mothers. Women who preferred to speak themselves were called overly sensitive or hysterical. But after the symbol of male productivity was replaced by a machine, and this machine was taken over by women, the production of texts had to forfeit its wonderful heterosexuality.

There are women who, under the influence of a despotic signifier, begin to write and record their desires. The two bites always in the same place, as Lucy Westenra received them from Dracula's teeth or typewriter hammers, are passed on by her to other necks. And so, "new women" prove, even beyond their death, that desires (as the concluding sentences of the *Interpretation of Dreams* proclaim) are indestructable.

There are other women who, because of the dictates of a career, stop leaving writing up to men or authors. Neutral apparata make an end of the erotic myth of quill and paper, Spirit and the Nature Mother. Mina Harker's typewriter does not copy the bites of a despotic signifier, but copies indifferent paper instead: hand writing and printed matter, declarations of love and land registry entries. Stenotypists no longer have a hand free for needles and cradles, the symbols of woman or mother.

And this is a good thing. Even under the conditions of mechanical discourse processing, a balance of terror is maintained. Let the femmes fatales lust after the radical Other; for every Lucy Westenra there is a Mina Harker. To hunt undead women and their despotic seducers, a man and his diligent hands are not enough. (Harker's stake failed him when he should have killed the Un-Dead in his castle dungeon.) Vampirism is a chain reaction, and can therefore only be fought with the techniques of mechanical text reproduction. Van Helsing therefore sends for Mina Harker as soon as the secrets of Lucy's transformation and Dracula's infiltration are brought to light. From this moment, the counterattack of a democratic empire is in motion.

No counterattack takes place without both a strategic discussion of the situation and the gathering of information. The situation: an enemy has infiltrated England who has already won over one accomplice and, through her blood-thirsty alliances, will make more accomplices. (The desire of vampirism is spread, like every epidemic, by means of contagious infection.) The information: the enemy has smuggled in 50 coffins filled with Transyvanian dirt, and has placed them in secret locations. This assures him, on the one hand, of a logistic base within a foreign country, but, on the other hand, makes him vulnerable. (Vampires, like all territorial rulers, can only sleep in the soil of their homeland.)

In a situation of this nature, every counterattack presupposes the necessity of: firstly, concentrating all information; secondly, democratizing it; and thirdly, storing it absolutely safely. Fourthly and lastly, it would be desirable to have assistants and agents in the camp of the enemy, because this is obviously no confrontation on the open battlefield, but rather (as Vámbéry viewed it) a war between two secret services.

Mina Harker becomes the girl for all four points. Only from the moment in which Van Helsing contacts her does the counterattack of the empire promise success. The head doctor and his men have only fragmentary information about an hysterical blood sucker and her shadowy seducer; Mina Harker can assemble facts from her own diary concerning Lucy's original vampire experience, and from the travel diary which her husband no longer dares to read, facts concerning the history and plans of the Count himself. Only the collation of all of this information makes an assessment of the situation possible. "In this matter," Mina Harker correctly remarks, "dates are everything" (224). The steno-typist therefore goes to work in a fully professional manner. All diaries, in longhand and shorthand, all useful newspaper articles, all private correspondences and land registry entries that are related to the Count and his bride, go onto her Remington. When they leave it, they are in perfect chronologi-

cal order as a group of signs made up of 26 uniform letters. A collation of data that guarantees general legibility as well as minimal
access time.

And since economy of access time is the thing that brings a counterattack against a supernatural Bliztkrieg even within the realm of
possibility, Dr. Seward's phonographic records must also be transcribed. These cylinders contain, on the one hand, irreplaceable
information about the late Lucy, when she still deserved Seward's
love, as well as about Renfield, who meanwhile has come to see the
Count as his long awaited lord and master. But on the other hand,
phonographic cylinders pay for their technical advantage of being
much quicker to record on than paper, with the disadvantage of having an extremely slow access time. Dr. Seward assures Mina "honest
Indian" that "although I have kept the diary for months past, it never
once struck me how I was going to find any particular part of it in
case I wanted to look it up" (221).

This is when Mina Harker comes to the rescue. She, who has
never before seen a phonograph, learns in record time, like countless secretaries after her, to work with her ear on the phonograph
and her hands on the keyboard. However shy Seward may be about
having the sighs of his rejected love publicized acoustically and
mechanically, it simply must be done. According to the conditions
of 1890, all that matters is the technological ordering of all previous
discourse. "True," as only machines can be, and "in its very tones,"
Mina hears, as she transcribes the cylinders, Seward's "heart beat"
(222–23). In this way the typewriter, as only it can, drives all of the
remaining hysteria out of the scientific discourse. When it comes to
liquidating the very conditions that make discourses of the master
possible, men and women can have no more secrets from each
other. Stoker's Dracula is no vampire novel, but rather the written
account of our bureaucratization. Anyone is free to call this a horror
novel as well.

Jonathan Harker's diary was written by his own hand, because it
had to defend his faithfulness to his fiancée, even against women
whose beauty makes English assistant school mistresses look like nothing more than English assistant school mistresses. Dr. Seward's diary
was spoken with his own voice, because it was meant to save his final
heartbeats from a scientific standstill as an insane-asylum director.

Reservations of this sort are exterminated by the media chain of phonograph, amplifier, and typewriter. This chain liquidates, as in Villiers' *L'Eve future*, love itself.

The role of love is usurped by the office. All characters in the novel, except for the vampires, receive copies of the first 250 pages of the novel. The broken English of Van Helsing, the American English of the millionaire, and the hyper-correct English of Dracula, are all fixated with phonographic reliability. And since the typewriter was invented to bridge the gap between documents and the printed book,[58] the gap between the heroes and the readers of the novel also disappears. Accordingly, Mina does not simply produce a typescript, but always, using a "manifold," "three copies" (224).

And this is a good idea. However late-medieval the attitude of Transylvanian counts may be, even they can sense the colonialism of mechanical discourse processing. While still in his castle the Count burned all of Harker's letters, whose secret writing was "an outrage upon friendship and hospitality!" (43). After the murderous intention of his hunters has become clear even to his "child-brain" (320), he acts more systematically. The Count no longer merely burns secret documents, but also the apparata that go with them. So he succeeds, in a night raid on Dr. Seward's insane-asylum, in discovering a copy of Mina's report and in casting it, together with the phonograph, into the flames of eternal judgement. It is thus not without significance that Edison's recording cylinders, before Emil Berliner invented the modern record disc, were made of wax. When the Count throws the collected psychiatry case-histories into the fire, "the wax helped the flames" (285).

But since the invention of the typewriter, fire and sword are obsolete. What the distressed counterattack does not reckon with is Mina Harker's clever forethought. "Thank God," Dr. Seward can cry out, confusing God with the secretary, "Thank God there is the other copy in the safe" (285). Secretaries do not merely collate and distribute information, each evening they bring the neutralizing and annihilating signifiers together into safety. The destruction of the Count begins with paper money and typewriter paper, as they survive indestructibly. Bribed transport workers and bribed lawyers reveal to his hunters all remaining unknown addresses that guarantee the home-sick vampire six feet of

Transylvanian earth in a foreign country. So they succeed (according to the technical term used in the novel) in "sterilizing" Dracula's 50 coffins, one after the other.

7. The cholera epidemic of 1832 made it to Ireland, the birth place of Abraham Stoker. Cholera, which, less than 20 years before the horrible Count, moved from India via Persia and Turkey in the direction of Europe—came to a halt at the Balkans. A certain medical doctor named Adrien Proust, known today only as the financial supporter of his novelist son, traveled under commission of the French government to the capital cities of Stambul and Teheran in order to organize a *"cordon sanitaire"* on the borders of the Occident. Adrien Proust's wonderful neologism is reflected in the words and deeds of Stoker's vampire hunters. Once again the advancing infectuous hordes are first sterilized, and then, after the Count has been robbed of his logistic base and forced to retreat, the Transylvanian nest of the disease is sterilized as well.

Hygenic measures of geo-political importance make it understandable that Van Helsing and his brave disciples—Lord Godalming, Dr. Seward, Johathan Harker, and a Texan millionaire with a Winchester rifle—decide to spare Mina Harker the details. They meet, plan, and act, while the only woman who is still alive is meant to return to her role as housewife. Since Lucy Westenra's terrible metamorphosis, the end awaiting women who do not live as wives and future mothers is no longer a secret. But however well-intentioned the professional, or in other words masculine, vampire hunters may be, according to the conditions of 1890, their sexual hygiene is a fatal mistake.

When a Hanoverian administrative director from the *Goethezeit*, in harmony with all other thinkers and poets of the time, called "the barring of women from all council meetings of corporations" "extremely prudent,"[59] he was speaking an historical truth. Of course not the whole truth, as Truth is herself a woman and therefore not meant to speak. But in the discourse of the university, as the personel union of thinkers and employees of the state discussed authorship and motherhood, the barring of real women was the social tie, the Alma Mater itself. Only after the power of professors has gone to engineers, and the power of teachers to medical doctors, does the greatest wisdom become foolishness. A Mina Harker without type-writer and psychoanalyst is threatened by the same fate that destroyed her dead girlfriend.

While the corporation of all the novel's men is sterilizing tons and tons of Transylvanian earth, the Count ambushes the woman of all their hearts in an elegant counter-maneuver. It once again becomes clear that women of 1890 have only the choice of perforating paper with their typing, or being themselves perforated on the neck by gruesomely long eye-teeth.

All the work of the vampire hunters would thus have been in vain, if unexpected help had not come to them in their hour of greatest darkness. Mina's banishment from all tactical discussions distorts even her husband's discernment of the clear symptoms of illness. Only Renfield, the lunatic, realizes who is visiting Mina each night. And although he, much like more famous collaborators after him, had recognized in the Count his lord and master, the chastity of British women still means much more to him than lust and life. Renfield converts, from this moment on, to a hero of the resistance, simply because "even for lunatics English reason is strong enough to oppose eastern-European thirst for blood."[60]

Of course Renfield pays for this with a painful death, as the Count bashes his brains in; but in the circles of secret agents, even dead men are respected sources. The vampire hunters have finally fulfilled point four of their data flow program, and have a traitor at their disposal.

Because hemorrhaging in Renfield's brain is affecting "the whole motor area" (276), and therefore unfortunately affecting Broca's motor speech centers at the "back side of the lower, left curve of the forehead",[61] doctor Van Helsing dares to perform an emergency operation and trephine Renfield's skull. In this way the theoretician of a progressive cerebralization still gets to demonstrate his skill. Of course not to save the lunatic, but rather to maintain his powers of speech in his dying moments. Thanks to his brain, which has been broken open, suddenly the truth speaks from Renfield, the lunatic, quite possibly the whole truth. Even "those experiments, which nature carries out in the illnesses of the nervous system—for us," the neurophysiologists,[62] have their value, even when the role of nature is played by Dracula. One should not expect brains that have been broken open to formulate according to the rules of transcendental apperception, in other words, to have the power of speech. Their discourse, on the contrary, operates like a phonograph in a repeat mode where it is also not possible to correct poorly recorded passages or to return the needle to the precisely desired position. Yet, these access problems at least guarantee that the speech machine Renfield tells the whole truth—namely, that Mina Harker is in the process of becoming a female vampire.

After this horrible discovery there is, for the doctors, no more hesitation, and no more Hypocratic oath. Renfield is allowed to bleed to death on the operating table, as the men rush up one floor to the bed of the women of all of their hearts, just in time to catch a glimpse of a black shadow teaching her to suck blood from his own breast . . .

A scene that has set the typewriters of specialists on cross-sexual sadism, especially those forms focused on the mother's breast, into motion. But it too is nothing more than a flow of information. After the count has connected a living woman to his blood stream, there exists one more source of information for the hunters. The stenotypist has become an hysterical woman who, much to Dracula's future misfortune, has just as much hypnotic rapport with him, as he has with her. The hunters simply need to tap into her neurotic source, just as they have already tapped into Renfield's psychotic source. But what in terminally ill and bleeding patients can only be accomplished neurophysiologically by trepanation of the brain, can be accomplished through hypnosis, in female patients who can still be healed. Once again Van Helsing swings from the scientific to the analytic discourse, from Broca to his great model Charcot.

The Count, with the last of his 50 coffins—which he needs so badly during the daylight hours—has barely been able to flee over the ocean. A ship with the telling name "Czarina Catherine" carries him back to the homeland from which he once came forth in another great mother, hoping to bring the Empire the plague. Now he runs, beaten back but not destroyed, on seas that unfortunately are not yet controlled by observation airplanes, radar stations, and radio eavesdropping services. The "Czarina Catherine" cannot even put telescopes to use, since the Count, besides wolves, rats, and bats, can also control the fog.

Occidental sanitarians have no choice but to take the Orient Express again. Following nothing but suspicions, Van Helsing and his men move into the Land Beyond the Forest. But Mina, who was before barred from full participation, is with them. In order to gain technical information about the routes and landing harbors of a camouflaged enemy, the barring of women must become a new inclusion of women in the realm of knowledge. It is decided that "Mina should be in full confidence" (290). If it is possible for the Count to seduce women with hypnotism, then it is also possible for another hypnotist to use this method against him. Every day Mina is placed in a trance by Van Helsing, while the Count is sailing upon the unknown seas and rivers of the East, and a young Viennese doctor is performing his first experiments with hypnosis.

" 'Where are you?' The answer came in a neutral way:—'I do not know. Sleep has no place it can call its own.'

'Where are you now?' The answer came dreamily, but with intention; it were as though she were interpreting something. I have heard her use the same tone when reading her shorthand notes.

'I do not know. It is all strange to me!'

'What do you see?'

'I can see nothing; it is all dark.'

'What do you hear?' I could detect the strain in the Professor's patient voice.

'The lapping of water. It is gurgling by, and little waves leap. I can hear them on the outside.'[63]

'Then you are on a ship?'

'Oh, yes!'

'What else do you hear?'

'The sound of men stamping overhead as they run about. There is the creaking of a chain, and the loud tinkle as the check of the capstan falls into the rachet.'

'What are you doing?'

'I am still—oh, so still. It is like death!' " (312–13).

Hypnosis is a transposition to another place, the place of "the Other." As a subject of an experiment in trances and death, Mina Harker makes the euphemism with which the vampire hunters refer to the enemy literally true. Only within the hysteric discourse is there an unconscious.[64] For this reason, Mina Harker speaks, not from

Friedrich Kittler

where she is, but from where the Count is; as if she too were in the darkness of a coffin, the coffin in the darkness of a ship's hold, the ship's hold beneath the surface of a Black Sea. There is no articulation within the Heart of Darkness, however. Neither names, like that of a despotic Czarina, nor the longitude degrees related to the imperial center of Greenwich, pass the lips of a medium—nothing but optical and acoustical data, yet with the hypersensitivity that is the current criterion of hypnotism.[65]

Oceanic feelings, yet no longer within Lucy Westenra's lonely dreams, but within the frame of experimentation. The unconscious as a discourse on "the Other" has technological status. Dracula's feminine mouthpiece speaks in the same tone as she does when repeating shorthand notes. Only machines are capable of storing the real of and beyond all speech—white noise, which surrounds the Count in his Yellow Submarine. Regardless of whether Vlad the Impaler once ruled with gruesomely precise commands, his shadow Dracula—as he alone survives under technological conditions—has become nothing more than the stochastic noise of the information channels. It is not without reason that vampires arise before Harker's eyes from motes of dust in the moonlight, in other words, as Brownian molecular movements. It is not without reason that Van Helsing calls "every bit of dust playing in the wind a horrid monster in embryo."

Discourses of the master have played in the key of the symbolic; the scientific discourse knows only the key of the real. "Every record, as we know, works through incidental noise."[66]

It follows that Mina Harker, this double agent between two hypnotists, when she receives and transmits noises from the hold of a faraway ship, is merely a sensor or radio transmitter. Wireless data transmission functions even before Marconi's discovery electrified all of the world's battle ships. Hypnosis, as the analytic discourse can call it forth, achieves physiologically what engineers will later implement technically. And of course it has the same practical function. Mina Harker, the telepathic radio transmitter in the coffin of an un-British despot, is as good an asset to the Secret Service as the BBC would be 30 years later. Britain's state radio (not to mention the UFA and the transmitter Nauen) will be founded by discharged Air Force and Naval Intelligence officers who, at the end of the

First World War, foresaw the second one more clearly than some prime ministers.[67]

"More a voice than a person, a voice that could only come out of the radio, a voice that does not ex-ist, as it says nothing"[68]—even it has an effect. For days, there is nothing but noise, of the ocean or of the news channels, until finally anchor chains rattle, people holler in foreign languages, the water flows more rapidly as if over stones, and at night the wolves howl—Van Helsing only needs to write down Mina's radio signals one after the other, and have her mechanically transcribe them herself, in order to create a small mystic writing-pad. What was formerly transcribed in the unconscious, is now permanently accessible in typescript. Mina Harker herself reads and writes what she received in the place of the Other. Double inscription—in hysteria and typewriter—is the historical trick that can only be accomplished with the inclusion of women in the sphere of knowledge. With the files of her own trance speeches and a map of Transylvania in front of her, the steno-typist begins to gather clues, the move that is decisive for the outcome of the campaign. Even the sounds of hypnotic and hypnotizing waters can be located on the map: from the harbor at Galatz, via the Sereth and the Bistritza, to the Borgo Pass . . .

After this brilliant deduction by the feminine secret agent, the actual Search and Destroy (as it was called in Vietnam) is only child's play. Three Englishmen, one Dutchman, and one American—who of course acts as the arms supplier—can hold a whole troop of gypsies in check with their Winchester rifles, while the unhappiest and sickest of them breaks open Dracula's coffin. It is Jonathan Harker, and he is also allowed to perform the final action with his Kukri knife. Seconds before sunset, before the Count regains his nocturnal omnipotence, Harker cuts open his throat.

One last time he sees the Evil Eye, as "the eyes saw the sinking sun, and the look of hate in them turned to triumph" (376).

8. I dedicate this prose to Lucinda Donelly and Barbara Kotacka, two American students who, I am told, pointed out to a truly weak-minded Dracula interpreter, that the killing of the Count is not effective according to the novel's own standards. As this interpreter explained, the two students pointed out to her that "at the final moment a look of triumph comes into Dracula's face, and that his

heart is stabbed with a hunting knife, but not with the prescribed stake." If therefore, "the men do not repeat the complicated rituals when killing Dracula, which were apparently so necessary when killing women," it necessarily follows "that Dracula is still lurking somewhere."

Even if seminar leaders do "not believe"[69] in logic, there are other women whose desire remains the desire of the Other. Precisely because the discourse of the novel has killed him, "the Other, which we can only identify with feminine desire," experiences a "resurrection"[70] in other discourses. Even Salome did not believe that the object of her desire could be dead. She sang of a desire that Mina Harker, although, and because, she had received fatal kisses, suffocated with the clatter of her typewriter.

> Ah! I have kissed thy mouth, Jokanaan.
> I have kissed thy mouth.
> There was a bitter taste on thy lips.
> Was it the taste of blood . . .?
> But perchance it is the taste of love . . .
> They say that love hath a bitter taste . . .
> But what of that? What of that?
> I have kissed thy mouth, Jokanaan.

But Salomes and Lucys are rare. What they attempted to do, all those brave people in the epoch of Van Helsing and Stoker, Charcot and Freud, was as quickly as possible, and that means as scientifically as possible, to trace the origins of that other desire back to dirty stories.[71] It is no wonder then, that Abraham Stoker kills the Count twice: once with the Kukri knife of his fictional counterpart, and again with the very fictionalization of an historical despot. The "tenacious immortality" of power[72] disappears in the "Note" at the end of the novel; what remains is "hardly one authentic document; nothing but a mass of type-writing" (378). In other words, Stoker's novel itself, which is identical with Mina Harker's archive.

It is also no wonder that Freud took back his hypothesis of seduction in the same year in which the novel was published. If this other desire—which hypnotized and later analyzed women kept whispering into his nearly phonographic ears—leads, according to theory, to nothing more than dirty stories, it was clear that "in every case the father must be accused of being perverse." Yet since "it was

hardly credible that perverted acts against children were so general,"
Freud decides: "I no longer believe in my *neurotica*."[73] He too then
fictionalizes an "Other," whose existence is clearly affirmed by court
doctors and sexual hygienists, also in eastern Austro-Hungary, and
precisely at the time Freud was recanting. Their statistical material
concerning alchoholics and perverts who seduce their own daughters
was so great that the Danube monarchy was forced to re-examine the
nature of parental rights, while a young doctor from the same eastern
country was just inventing his new concept of the family romance . . .

Stoker and his novel, Freud and the novel he ascribed to his
patients—the liquidation of the discourse of the master is achieved by
means of other discourses. Literarily murdered, sexual-hygienically
disempowered, psychoanalytically phantomized—the Other no
longer has a place of refuge. With help from the criminal psycholo-
gists Lombroso and Nordau, the sharp-witted Mina reduces the discourse of the master concerning Berserkers, Shaman and Boyars (to
which Harker is at first subjected) to simple psychopathology. She
turns a despot into an underdeveloped mortal. Van Helsing can only
applaud this and, very much in the spirit of his Austrian colleague,
establish systematic enmity between Dracula's "child-brain" and an
Occident which has the "power of combination," "sources of science," and the democratic freedom "to act and think" (238).

A colonial madness, whose path is strewn with corpses. "Despite
all projections, it is the 'Good Guys' of the novel who are responsible
for all actually described killing."[74] "Kill that woman!", the passion-
ate order with which Herod ends the opera Salome, could have been
spoken by Van Helsing about Lucy Westenra. With the result that
desire has no place of refuge among colonialists.

"With our *jouissance* going off the track, only the Other is able to
mark its position, but only insofar as we are separated from this Other.
Whence certain fantasies—unheard of before this melting pot.

Leaving this Other to his own mode of *jouissance*, that would only
be possible by not imposing our own on him, by not thinking of him
as underdeveloped."[75]

Dracula's underdeveloped child's brain only fills about 16% of
the novel's pages.[76] The rest are an apotheosis of freedom, combination and science. But since the Other alone constitutes our desire,
Dracula interpretations are forgetfulness itself. Psychiatry and

psychoanalysis, phonograph and typewriter, are neglected by an immense collection of secondary material that strives again for the colonizing of Transylvania. The suppression of the subject in the scientific discourse is thus quantifiable: 84%.

In order to make this forgetfulness complete, one only needs to hook up the machines that have supported this discourse since 1880 to the one machine (although it too had already been invented) that Stoker's novel—in contrast to phonograph and typewriter, telegraph and telephone—does *not* mention. The phantomizing of Dracula has been accomplished through motion pictures. Stoker the novelist long ago lost his ephemeral fame, in order to make ever new and imaginary resurrections of his title character possible. Perhaps, following the insight of the two students, Dracula has become immortal on the screen because the scientific discourse, out of pure technical efficiency, overlooks symbolic necessity. But perhaps it is also, following the insight of the first film theorist, due to the fact that motion pictures technologically implement every discovery of experimental psychology (concerned with attention and memory, consciousness and imagination).[77]

At any rate, the Dracula films, from Murnau via Polanski to Werner Herzog, are experimental-psychological channelers of attention which use all of their power—fangs and phallic castle ruins, wolves and half naked skin—to draw attention away from the hum of the projector. What never comes onto the screen, are Mina Harker's typewriter and Dr. Seward's phonograph. This is how closely connected they are with the film projector.

Under the conditions of technology, literature disappears (like metaphysics for Heidegger) into the un-death of its endless ending.

Only on one occasion did Stoker's novel find its way back to its own textuality: in the Second World War the US Army, on its crusade, distributed free copies to the GIs.[78]

"And perhaps that is what incites the anger of certain linguists against Lacan, no less than the enthusiasm of his followers: the vigor and the seriousness with which Lacan traces the signifier back to its source, to its veritable origin, the despotic age, and erects an infernal machine that welds desire to the Law."[79] At least the late despot left behind a legacy "which you cannot now comprehend in its full significance."

That you are from now on subject to gadgets and instruments of mechanical discourse processing.

I turn off the hum of the office machine, lift my eyes and see in the fog over the bay, the Golden Gate Bridge, our hyper-realistic future.

Berkeley, March 22, 1982
Translated by William Stephen Davis

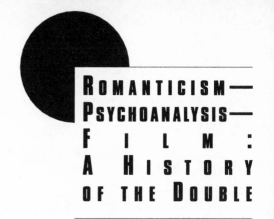

*O*n a winter night in 1828, one of the minor Romantic poets met the ghost of poetry itself. Aldelbert von Chamisso, a Berlin drinking-buddy of Hoffmann and Contessa, Hitzig and Fouquè, had once again been drinking with his Serapion brothers. As usual, the "uninhibited revelry"[1] lasted until midnight. Afterwards, as Chamisso himself describes his condition, the "tired boozer" snuck home through the city streets, pursued by the echo of his lonely footsteps.

But the familiarity of home is not always—and, according to Freud, never—the opposite of the uncanny.[2] Having arrived before his own windows, Chamisso sees—or in his delirium, thinks he sees—a light in his study. He "freezes" in terror, hesitates a long time at the door, and—only after a resolute decision to put an end to the alcoholic daze—turns the lock. Only to see what the echo has already made audible: that he has a Double.

The Double is the ghost of poetry. While the Romantic poets were still gathered together "clinking glasses" in order to elicit professionally, so to speak, the inspiration that prompted poems like Chamisso's *Erscheinung* [*Apparition*], another apparition had already long ago occupied the seat at the professional's desk. That is why the light in the study is not a hallucination of the Romantic poet, but a working condition of his Double. That is also why Chamisso's question, "Who are you, spook?", does not elicit a response, but rather the justified counter-question, "Who disturbs me so late at this ghostly hour?" Tired boozers must indeed appear like ghosts at the witching hour to a Double who has been at his desk all evening reading or writing, or at any rate engaged in authorial pursuits.

Roles are exchanged and—Lacan's theorem of the mirror stage and sibling transitivism could have predicted it—a duel becomes likely. As it comes to words, or more precisely, tercets, Poet and Double cross swords and things progress as though the two enemy brothers were not named Chamisso and Chamisso, but Sosia and Mercury. Their battle is waged over the "squaring of a circle" that could "drive anyone insane," that is to say, over the impossibility of proving oneself Chamisso. The two duelists must remain within the realm of the verbal or the poetic simply because in 1828, passport photos, fingerprint files, anthropometric figures and data banks do not yet exist. Because proof of identity is impossible, each agrees to present a definition of himself and then wait for the effect. Both proclaim their particular manner of being,* first Chamisso and then his Double.

What occurs to Chamisso is pure fiction and a mere cliché, astonishing only in that it comes from one who reeks of alcohol: "I am he who aspires solely to the beautiful, the good and the true." What occurs to his Double is novel and to the point, especially since he is sitting at the poet's desk: "I am a cowardly, lying wretch."

Insolence at the limits of poetry, barely possible in tercets and for that reason of devastating impact. Chamisso just manages to murmur that his Double, Chamisso, is the real Chamisso, before standing outside again in the Berlin night, found out and tearful. This time, however, for good—the tercets and the poem *Erscheinung* have come to an end.

The story does not continue until 1914, eighty-six years later; no longer, however, in tercets, but in scientific prose. Otto Rank, Freud's literary historical case worker or aide-de-camp, uncovers Chamisso's experience of his Double and those of countless others. As a result, alcoholic episodes from the era of Romanticism become the indispensable scientific data of the present century. Rank furnishes the proof of identity that Chamisso could not. First conclusion of the new science of psychoanalysis: authors who are plagued by "neurological and mental illnesses" are also haunted by their Doubles.[3] Second conclusion: what contemporary readers of

*[Tr.—The author employs the tem *Sosein*, meaning literally 'to be-like-that,' as opposed to the conventional *Dasein*.]

Chamisso had to call unbelievable or fantastic, at least as long as they did not take the story as moral metaphor, is literally true. Freud's theory of narcissism—whether it concerns live patients or dead authors—can adduce the psychic mechanism that "creates," as with Chamisso's Double, a "projection of inner turmoil." This duel between the beautiful, the true and the good on the one hand and the cowardly, lying wretch on the other is a reality in the unconscious. It measures, "as Freud has demonstrated, . . . the distance between the ego-ideal and the attained reality."[4] Thus, half a century after his death, Chamisso gets confirmation in writing as to who he was. The Double is "the phantom of our own ego," and not merely the double-vision of drunks or poetic-moralistic metaphor.

Whereby, I (leaving Kittler aside) cite Rank, who cites E.T.A. Hoffmann,[5] who cites a certain Clara. And that means: certain basic assumptions remain unquestioned in the psychoanalytic verification of the fantastic, precisely because it transfers poetry into science. First of all, Hoffmann's basic assumptions, or those of the literary era that produced the fantasm of the Double; secondly, Clara's basic assumptions, or those of the philosophy that provided for the empirical-transcendental doubling of man. Goethe and Fichte, Jean Paul and Hoffmann—Rank's historical memory extends back exactly one century. The question he never asks, however, is why the figure of the Double populates the literary record since then and only since then. Even if all psychoanalyses, which is to say dissections, of Romantic fantasies are correctly resolved, there is a remainder. Namely, the simple textual evidence that Doubles turn up at writing desks.[6]

Proof of this can be furnished quickly because one no longer needs to thumb through all the books. A re-reading of Rank's *Doppelgänger* suffices. All these ghosts of the writing desk are recorded; however, Rank never unmasks them.

Guy de Maupassant sat "one afternoon in 1889 . . . at the desk in his study. His servant had strict orders never to enter while his master was working. Suddenly, it seemed to Maupassant as if someone had opened the door. Turning around he sees, to his extreme astonishment, *his own self entering*, who sits down opposite him and rests his head on his hand. Everything Maupassant writes is dictated to him. When the author finished his work and arose, the hallucination disappeared."[7]

Thus what in 1828 occurred only under the influence of alcohol, became autobiographical reality in 1889. Naturalism and psychoanalysis are synchronous. It is as though Maupassant plays his own psychiatrist in order to gain insight into the genesis of *Lui* and *Horla*, his own stories that deal with the Double. He reports of a hallucinated dictator at the desk, who subsequently passes into the archives of contemporary psychiatry and through them to Rank. The sciences of the soul are satisfied. The question that no one asks, however, is why the Double turns up at the writing desk, of all places.

Yet the answer lies with Goethe himself. In *Wilhelm Meisters Lehrjahren* [*Wilhelm Meister's Apprenticeship*], a baroness places the hero, as is well-known, in the study of a count and dresses him in the count's dressing gown, in order to come up with an amatory surprise for the count's wife. Whenever the budding poet and citizen took on stage roles or recited verses of love, he only played to the countess, who, for her part, "could not take her eyes off him."[8] The trick of the Double is to ignite a love that is as secret as it is literary. Adorned with all the attributes of his rival, Meister sits in the count's study, where the light of a very modern Argand lamp, anno 1793, falls on him and on the "book" in his hands. Erudition can be staged this perfectly. It is not the countess and poet lover for whom the living picture was arranged who enters, however, but rather the count himself—only to sustain the shock of his life. And because the countess would rather leave him to his religious delusions than admit to her failed rendez-vous, the count never learns that his Double is only an artful arrangement and not a sign from God. The consequence for the count is a misrecognition that haunts psychoanalysts to this day. In order to see one's Double as the "phantom of our own ego," the cunning strategies by which others produced it must be thoroughly masked. Whether these others are schemers like the baroness or poets like Goethe makes no difference. Both invest their heros with the attributes of his paternal rival—the baroness at the castle of the one, the poet on the page of the other—because in order for the count to believe in the Double before him, the Double must for its part once again be believed by Goethe's readers. There is no guarantee of the optical identity of two male images except for the words that make that assertion. And indeed these assertions are all the more easily made by words, the emptier they are. The entire novel, very wisely, does not contain a single physical description of its hero. Wilhelm Meister remains as empty as a mere sketch.

"There are no individuals. All individuals are also *genera*," decreed Goethe,[9] who after all is the very individual German scholars credit with the literary invention of the individual. But as the title of Manfred Frank's book already discloses, the individual of 1800 was merely a generic individual and that means no individual at all.* The reason is clear given the technological conditions of the time. Meister and his count, Goethe and his readers—they could all believe in the phenomenon of the Double simply because words do not define singularities. Not even the word 'Double' itself. And other storage media besides words did not exist in the days of classical Romanticism.

The poor depressed count must already have suspected something of the sort, otherwise he would not have sent for Meister again that same evening in order to reconstruct his shock. Once again the budding poet receives a book in his hand—this time, however, not to play a count converted to the reading of Goethe, but simply to read aloud. Naturally, Meister trembles for fear that he may have been unmasked, but precisely this trembling in his voice is "thank goodness, appropriate to the content of the story" and is occasion for the count to "praise the expressiveness with which Wilhelm had been reading."[10] It can hardly be more clearly stated that the Double of classical Romanticism essentially emerges from books. Whoever, like Meister, employs reading and recitation as a means to identification, wins the love of a countess and the praise of a count.

That words do not define singularities, all legends about poets to the contrary, is not their weakness but rather their cunning. In their emptiness, identification clicks in as the mechanism of the text's readability in the new era. That goes for the story Meister recites, but also for the one his readers are reading. As Daniel Jenisch, author of the first *Meister* interpretation in 1797, already revealed, the episode of the Double simply serves to program readers in identificatory reading. According to the Berlin minister, one of "the most striking characteristics of *Meisters Lehrjahren*," or, better said, "that which

*[Tr.—Manfred Frank, *Das individuelle Allgemein: Textstrukturierung und -interpretation nach Schleiermacher* (Frankfurt a.M.: 1977).]

makes this novel typically Goethe's," was the literary history-making innovation of introducing a hero like you and me. Meister stands neither above nor below his readers; he has absolutely no "special characteristics" that could separate us from him. Because individuals were not recorded around 1800, he has only the "general character-istics of human nature."[11] In other words, it is Meister's characteris-tic to have no characteristics at all, and to be merely the Double of his readers. The logical result, then, is that all Germans are obligated to read Goethe. The novel provides no less than *"the story of us all.* In this Wilhelm Meister we see our own selves, as did the count in the costumed nightmare on the sofa; we are not frozen in panic, how-ever, but pleased and amazed by the magical force of the enchanted mirror the poet holds up to us."[12]

Enchanted mirrors from other lands and times revealed god-desses or demons. In classical Germany, they reflect the sheepish faces of citizens who confuse their lives with their reading. What the *Lehrjahre* teaches (with Friedrich Schlegel[13]) can only be called life for people who have always already been taken in by words. As long as only the *Laterna magica* competed with poetry's enchanted mirror, this trick was not at all difficult. As Novalis said: "If one reads cor-rectly, then a real, visible world unfolds itself in us internally accord-ing to the words."[14] The printed word was skipped and the book forgotten, until somewhere between the lines a hallucination appeared—the pure signified of the printed sign. In other words, Doubles in the era of classical Romanticism originated in the class-room where we learn to read correctly.

Musset's *Nuit de décembre* ["The December Night"], the long poem much loved by Rank—every other stanza or every other year of which the poet is again confronted by his Double—begins with a stanza that Rank suppressed.

> Du temps que j'étais écolier,
> Je restais un soir à veiller
> Dans notre salle solitaire.
> Devant ma table vint s'asseoir
> Un pauvre enfant vêtu de noir,
> Que me ressemblait comme un frère.[15]

That poor child in black—neither narcissim nor ego produced it; neither death nor immortality is its message. Things are much simpler than psychoanalysis imagines. The child in black is poor only because he has fallen victim to the general literacy campaign that seized Central Europe in 1800. Ever since then, new child-oriented methods for the teaching of reading sweeten and sensualize the alphabet; ever since then, people no longer experience words as violent and foreign bodies but can also believe that the printed words refer to them. Lacan called it 'alphabêtise.' And Baudelaire, as though to decode the ghosts of Chamisso and Musset, began his volume of poetry with the address: "Hypocrite lecteur,—mon semblable,—mon frère!" ["Hypocrite reader, —my double—my brother!"].

That is plain language indeed, and poetry's final reckoning. None of Baudelaire's successors in 'l'art pour l'art' will ever again muster the mendacity of writing for mendacious readers. Books no longer behave as though words were harmless vehicles supplying our inner being with optical hallucinations, and especially not with the delusion that there is an inner being or a self. Along with the true, the beautiful and the good, this Double vanishes as well.

The form that emerges from the depths of the mirror today is very different. It has nothing to do with literacy and poetry. In 1900, Ernst Mach described how he recently saw a stranger boarding the bus and thought, "What a shabby-looking school-master that man is!" That is to say, in practice, even the famed physicist and perception theorist required a few split seconds in order to recognize the stranger as his own mirror image. And Freud, who repeats the story of Mach's uncanny encounter, is immediately able to present his own parallel case. He "was sitting alone in [the] *wagon-lit* compartment when a more than usually violent jolt of the train swung back the door of the adjoining washing-cabinet, and an elderly gentleman in a dressing gown" enters, whom Freud "thoroughly disliked."[16] One's own mirror image in the looking-glass on the bathroom door is especially suited to prove the ambiguity of the familiar/uncanny [*heimlich*/ *unheimlich*], and furthermore to remind the father of psychoanalysis of his own bodily functions.

There are reasons, however, why these mirror images haunt buses and express trains, of all places. If the Double named the self, that poetic-philosophical phantasm, originated in the general literacy campaign of Central Europe, then the shabby figures that appear before Mach and Freud are the products of Central Europe's general mechanization. Of this, *Die Analyse der Empfindugen* [*The Analysis of Sensations*] remains silent; *The Uncanny* remains silent. And yet the mobile mirrors, the passing panoramas and the innumerable Doubles named commuters only came into existence with the train and the spark-ignition engine. The very same Mallarmé who put an end to reading and readability advised automotive engineers to move the car's engine to the back, so that happy passengers could enjoy unhindered the "magical" spectacle of passing perspectives through "bow-windows" with their own eyes. "Vision of a commuter with taste," as Mallarmé called his "invention"—the automobile as camera ride.[17]

Foremost, however, the vision of an author who devised protective strategies to seal off systematically his own medium, the printed word, from hallucinatory effects and Doubles. Mallarmé answered a survey on the illustrated book with a categorical 'no,' appending the counter-question: "Why don't you go right to the cinematographers, for their sequence of images will replace, to great advantage, both image and text of many a book?"[18] This, too, is plain language. Since 1895, a separation exists between an image-less cult of the printed word, i.e., e[lite]-literature, on one side, and purely technical media that, like the train or film, mechanize images, on the other. Literature no longer even attempts to compete with the miracles of the entertainment industry. It hands its enchanted mirror over to machines.

This, and only this, explains the horror on the part of the Professors Mach and Freud when even before their own eyes the antiquated medium of print must yield to the film of would-be reality, if only for a few split seconds. Silent films implement with technological positivity what psychoanalysis can only conceive of: an unconscious that has no words and is not recognized by His Majesty the Ego.

It is precisely the stupidity of film that makes it a favorable substitute of many books, particularly those of the Romantic era. It can store bodies that, as we all know, are just as stupid. When King Peter of the kingdom Popo ordered a search for his fugitive son in the last Romantic comedy, the grand-ducal Hessian police were not to be envied. They had only the "warrant, the personal description, the certificate" of a man: "walks on two feet, has two arms, in addition a mouth, a nose, two eyes, two ears. Special characteristics: is an extremely dangerous individual."[19] That is as far and only as far as poetry went when bodies were to be stored—up to the individualized generalities of Meister-like sketches. Film, on the other hand, as well as criminology and psychoanalysis, belongs to those modern technologies for the gathering of traces that, in Ginzburg's view,[20] optimize the control of bodies.

There is proof of this in all the stupid or crazy, idiotic or hysterical bodies that early silent films deploy. Every one of them is the shadow of the body of the one filmed, or in short, his Double. With only a swing of the camera King Peter would already have been in possession of the unmistakable, unfalsifiable certificate of his Leonce, charging through life as a Romantic actor. Whoever believes that he is referred to by the printed word is simply misled. And whoever is filmed is thereby already transported, even if only through mobile mirrors like Freud. On film, all plots appear more stupid; on sound recordings, which suppress the larynx-ear bone conduction, voices have no soul; on identification photos, one sees only the faces of criminals—not because the media lie, but because they fragment the narcissism of one's own conception of the body.

Media are an historic escalation of violence, which forces those affected into total mobilization. The first theoretician of the uncanny seems to have foreseen this even more than his critic Freud. Already in 1906, Ernst Jentsch compared the panic one senses before automatons or Doubles with the collapse of "a defensive position," that is, with a "lack of cover in the various stages" of a "war" that, according to Jentsch's prophesy, "would never end."[21]

UFA, Germany's feature film company, was created in 1917, as we all know, under the auspices of the General Staff's Office for Image and Film [BUFA] and at the instigation of the First Quartermaster-General, Infantry General Erich Ludendorff.[22] Small wonder that media wars never end. In Vietnam, elite troops like the U.S. Marine Infantry were only prepared to attack and risk death on the condition that NBC, CBS or ABC had a camera team on location.[23] The very fact that a body was torn apart by Vietcong grenades made its Double immortal in the evening news. *Apocalypse Now* or total mobilization . . .

Lacan's fragmented body is a positivity—to the understandable regret of *Lebensphilosophie*[24]—ever since film cameras first shot their 24 pictures per second by chopping up the body before the viewfinder with the blades of the shutter and a maltese cross. The fragmented body appears in the place of those whole persons that classical Romantic poetry celebrated or produced. It is not as though the great hysterical curve, that physiological mode of total mobilization, was produced merely by Charcot's staff and hand that, as we know, he obligingly passed over the abdomens and ovaries of his female patients.[25] The great psychiatrist was more modern than that, and said so. His Salpêtrière could secure the traces of hysteria for the first time in the history of medicine because new machines and their operators had converted a run-down Parisian insane asylum into a laboratory.[26] Charcot's engineer Albert Londe, inventor of the Rolleiflex, had already in 1883 built a camera with nine or twelve lenses that took successive snap shots on the command of a metronome—in other words, film *avant la lettre*. Object of this fragmentation: the female hysterics of the Salpêtrière; observer of this fragmentation: the young Sigmund Freud.[27] How beautiful and grand must the hysterical curve have turned out when cameras were able to store or produce it . . .

A total mobilization prepared the way for psychoanalysis, but Freud does not even take notice of this—the word 'Kino' [cinema, movies] does not appear in his writings. The application of Freud to film was left to his literary historical aide-de-camp. This is precisely the point of departure for Rank's study of the Double, which appeared immediately after the premiere of the first German auteur's film. Rank did not hesitate to pick a "random and banal subject"—Hanns-Heinz Ewers' silent film, *The Student of Prague*—in order to "uncover deeply buried and significant psychic material." He even speculated "that cinematography, which in numerous ways reminds us of the dream-work, can also express certain psychological facts and relationships—that the writer often is unable to describe with verbal clarity—in such clear and conspicuous imagery that it facilitates our understanding of them." Rank's precise quill transcribed into print all of the "shadowy, fleeting, but impressive scenes" of the student in a 60-minute duel with his mirror image and Double (because in 1914, video tapes, that is, the possibility of optical rereadings, had not yet been invented). All this merely to scrutinize a banal mass media for an unconscious symbolic—as though Freud's manifest dream content and the entertainment industry were on one and the same level. On the other hand, the latent dream-thoughts and/or film shape discourse and nothing but discourse (especially because the screenplay writer Ewers commendably followed literary "patterns"[28]). Of all things, a silent film is what brings Rank to the Romantic poetry of the Double, and from this poetry to mythology or psychoanalysis. There is nothing, then, to the promise to engage the dream-work and cinematography, Freud and Londe. The psychic apparatus obstructs any understanding of the technical. And even at the end of his historic methodological regression, when he cites the Fiji-Islander who called his first glance in a European mirror a glance into the spirit world,[29] it does not occur to Rank that occult media have always necessarily presupposed mechanical ones.

The psychoanalysis of film undoes filming again. Ignoring technological thresholds, it verifies a poetry that the film has just superceded. Freud's primal scene—his year at the Salpêtrière—is successfully repressed.

For that reason, it is also only partly true when Todorov concludes the following:

> Psychoanalysis has replaced (and thereby made useless) the literature of the fantastic. [. . .] The themes of fantastic literature have become, literally, the very themes of the psychological investigations of the last fifty years. [. . .] Here we need merely mention that the double was even in Freud's time the theme of a classic study (Otto Rank's *Der Doppelgänger*).[30]

Todorov is correct if he lets the Romantic Double come to an end around 1900. Yet, it is not credible to assume that theory alone can deliver such blows. The empirical-transcendental doublet Man, substratum of the Romantic fantastic, is only imploded by the two-pronged attack of science and industry, of psychoanalysis and film. Psychoanalysis clinically verified and cinema technically implemented all of the shadows and mirrorings of the subject. Ever since then, what remains of a literature that wants to be Literature is simply *écriture*—a writing without author. And no one can read Doubles, that is, a means to identification, into the printed word.

As we know, however, ghosts do not die; thus a new medium of the fantastic has emerged quite apart from literature. The cinema and its screenplay writers occupy the positions vacated by the Romantics. After all, as the first theoretician of film recognized: in film, "every dream becomes real."[31] What poetry promised but could only grant in the imaginary realm of the reading experience appears on the screen in reality. For this transfer into a real, visible world, Novalis' unconditional requirement of correct reading has become superfluous. In order to catch sight of Doubles, people need no longer be either educated or drunk. Even illiterates, or especially they, see the student of Prague, his lover and his mistress—all of Rank's "shadowy, fleeting scenes," which as such are already Doubles—as celluloid ghosts of the actors' bodies.

It only takes the arrival of a genius like Méliès and the documentary methods of Londes or the Lumières brothers with a full bag of tricks for film doubles to the first degree to be joined by film doubles to the second degree. With mirrors and multiple lighting, it is a simple matter to show two occurrences of the actor playing the student. No sooner is he practicing his fencing in front of the mirror, than his mirror image steps from its frame. Whether the "uniqueness of cinematography," as Rank states, "visibly portrays psychological images" is beside the point.[32] On the other hand, it is clear that the filming itself films. Cinematic Doubles demonstrate what happens to people who get caught in the way of mechanical media's firing line. Their mechanized likeness roams the data banks that store bodies.

Even the program notes to *The Student of Prague* pronounced "the double figure of the hero a possibility of expression that only the cinema, in contrast to the theatrical stage, is capable of showing to such perfection."[33] In the theater, the single student and his double, like Sosius and Mercury ever since Plautus, would have degenerated into two actors, and in the novel's pages, into empty rhetoric. On the other hand, early film was determined by the Doppelgänger effect— "the film problem of all film problems," as Willy Haas formulated it.[34] Ewers' *Student*, Lindau's *Anderer* [*Other*], Hauptmann's *Phantom*, Wegener's *Golem*, Wiene's *Caligari*, to say nothing of innumerable versions of *Jekyll and Hyde*—all are variations on the film trick of all film tricks, as it more simply and precisely had to be called.

The reason is obvious: tricks—whether in film, in love or in war—are strategies of power. It is only in the cliché of the Germanists that Expressionist films criticize the Wilhelminian bourgeoisie; in actuality, they indoctrinate with a new imperative: How to do things without words.*

Lindau's film *The Other* portrays a public prosecutor whose personality is split into public prosecutor and criminal, hunter and hunted, as a result of a neurological malfunction of his brain. From all the arguments of psychiatry and with all the weapons of criminology, an anachronistic government official has it drilled into him that his legal self (and not only legal self) was done for, from the moment that even silent traces of the body could be secured. The film is about powers to which he himself belongs.[35]

Therefore, it is only logical that the magic power of Rabbi Löw in Wegener's *Golem* blends into a film-within-the-film that he plays for Emperor Rudolf. (Kaiser Wilhelm, the renowned media freak of 1914, surely could have appreciated this.) In accordance with Wegener's imperative for mechanical media, "the true poet of the film must be the camera. The potential of an ever-changing point of view for the spectator, the countless tricks through mirrors and so on, briefly, the technology of the film must determine the choice of its content."[36] The fact that Rabbi Löw can build a mechanized automaton named Golem (or Wegener) hardly allegorizes (as the film historians believe) "the risk of a dictatorship—temporarily instituted by and under the control of the ruling classes— turning against its own instigators."[37] Leaving 'the greatest movie-maker of all time' (Syberberg) completely aside, Golems constitute a danger: stupid Doubles of a humanity that has no longer existed ever since media were also able to substitute for central nervous systems.

When a film begins in a projection room that has been darkened like an air-raid shelter (its prototype in the history of art can only have been Wagner's Festspielhaus[38]), the substitution of central nervous systems shifts to the public itself. Whether part of the ruling classes like Rudolf, Wilhelm or von Papen, or part of the classes being ruled like all the rest—everyone's retina is on the screen. "The

*[Tr.—Phrase appears in English in the original.]

spectator," wrote Edgar Morin, "reacts to the film screen as if to an external retina that is in telecommunication with his brain."[39]

Film is total power, even or especially when it displays that power once again (as in the case of Rabbi Löw and his magic tricks). As long as these same doublings remained literary—similar to the book-within-a-book of the *Lehrjahre*—they could be interpreted as reflection, or as an invitation to would-be criticism. Mechanical media and strategies of shock, on the other hand, are triumphant precisely because of their self-exhibition. That is to say, how could a simulacrum of the central nervous system—and that, after all, was at one time phrased 'of the Spirit'—be subject to further analysis?

A few authors in this century have understood that. A chain of the fantastic extends from Meyrink's *Golem* to Pynchon's *Gravity's Rainbow;* and it has nothing to do with Hoffmann or Chamisso and everything to do with film. Literature of the central nervous system is in direct competition with other media; and for that reason possibly always already intended for filming. To presentify* rather than narrate, simulate rather than verify—these are the maxims. Meyrink's *Golem*, which was published in 1915, begins with an unnamed speaker and a barely physiological presence. The speaker no longer "possesses" any "organ" that would enable him to pose the question "who am 'I' now." Therefore, a pure neurological data stream, which at the same time is always already retinal film, replaces reflexive speculation.

Bit 1: "The moonlight falls on the foot of my bed like a large, flat stone." This large, flat stone from the novel's opening sentence immediately forfeits its comparative function in order to be transformed from the metaphor of literature into the real of neurophysiology. Bit 2: "And the image of the stone, which looked like a hunk of fat, grows to monstrous proportions in my brain." This monstrous close-up—in accordance with the logic of camera movements—immediately fills the entire optical nervous system of the half-sleeping man. Bit 3: "I stride through a dried-out river bed and pick up smooth pebbles." This space, still the foot of the bed and already, simultaneously, the river bed, thus blends directly from close-up to

---

*[Tr.—The German verb is *Präsentifizieren*, which translates Jacques Lacan's *présentifier*.]

flashback. Bit 4: "All the stones that ever played a role in my life suddenly appear all around me."[40]

And so on and so on in the introductory chapter, until mere film tricks have turned a patch of moonlight in the life of A into the old-town ghetto of Prague in the life of B. The "cinematographic illusion of consciousness"—which is discussed in Bergson's contemporaneous theory[41]—causes the break between biographies and epochs to mend into the perfect continuum of a retinal film: through the hole in his non-existent identity, the nameless 'I' of the story frame topples into his Double, whose name is Pernath and who has lived the framed story a whole generation ago. That this Prague ghetto is also a film is proven by the doubling of the Double motif. Just as the nameless 'I' crashed into Pernath, so too does Pernath himself crash into a Golem who is quite explicitly and photographically called Pernath's "negative."[42] The ill-reputed mysticism of the novel is therefore only the precision of mechanical media. With Meyrink, literature for the first time presentifies the brain's physiological counterparts to film sequences. It is not the soul that is real, but the celluloid.

The dream-work and cinematography are much closer to one another than Otto Rank ever dreamed in 1914. No psychoanalytic theory of the Double can conceive of Meyrink's endless series of Doubles or even Schreber's "hastily sketched men."[43] Of all the sciences of the epoch, only one is responsible—and it is, of course, precisely that science whose groundwork first made film possible. Without the experimental psychology of people like Helmholtz and Wundt, there would be no Edison and no brothers Lumières; without the physiological measurements of the retina and optical nervous system, no film public. Therefore, the first competent theory of film came from the head of the Harvard Psychological Laboratory. In 1916 Münsterberg conceives what in 1915 Meyrink had described. This was simply because the great experimental psychologist—in word and deed—had founded a new science: psychotechnology.[44]

Film theory (to say nothing of the assembly line and combat training) first became possible with psychotechnology, this coupling of physiological and technical experiments, of psychological and ergonomic data. For the first time in the history of the art world, Münsterberg easily proved that film is capable of implementing the neurological data flow itself. Whereas the traditional arts treat orders of the symbolic or orders of things, film emits to its viewers their own process of perception—and this with a precision available only to experiment, which is to say, that it cannot be accessed either by consciousness or language. Münsterberg assigns every single camera technique to an unconscious, psychical mechanism: the close-up to selective attention, the flashback to involuntary memory, the film trick to day-dreaming, and so forth.[45]

But mathematical equations can be solved just as well from the right side as from the left. Thus, the designation psychotechnology already reveals that experimental psychological theories of film are also mechanical media theories of the soul. Just as in the *Golem*, involuntary memory becomes flashback, selective attention becomes close-up, and so forth. Unconscious mechanisms which previously could be found only in human experiments, abandon us in order to populate the film studios as Doubles of dead souls. One Golem as tripod or musculature, one as celluloid or retina, one as flashback or memory . . .

And having left Freiburg im Breisgau for Harvard, Münsterberg also takes the deciding step—he visits the New York film studios whose theory he wrote. That is the conclusive difference between Münsterberg and Rank, between the knowledge of an engineer and the viewpoint of a consumer.

Trends have resulted in Freud—self-authorized as prophet—enjoying the glory of all other discourses. Today, Hugo Münsterberg appears only in Freud biographies under the mistaken name Werner and as one of many in attendance at the psychoanalytic America-tour of 1908.[46] The truth about media technology has been this thoroughly repressed, ever since Münsterberg took one final step. His self-annointment in 1916 as strategist of the first world war brought with it scientific excommunication.[47] Without removing traces, traces cannot be gathered; without repression of the founding fathers, film companies cannot be founded by general staffs. In our current century which implements all theories, there are no longer any. That is the uncanniness of its reality.

Translated by Stefanie Harris

MEDIA AND DRUGS IN PYNCHON'S SECOND WORLD WAR

For David Welbery

*I*n the fall of 1983, the German Press Agency released the following bulletin:

> CSU [Christian Socialist Union] leader and Bavarian Prime Minister Strauss has publicly disclosed that according to "fairly reliable sources," the German Democratic Republic has been at work for some years reconstructing underground installations dating from the Third Reich, in which atomic rockets will be stored. Strauss stated at an international conference hosted by the Hanns-Seidel Foundation that the majority of these "natural defenses" are located beneath a solid layer of rock, 300 to 400 meters below the earth's surface, so as to ensure adequate security of the atomic weapons.[1]

What the German Press Agency neglected to state was that these "natural defenses," specifically those in Nordhausen in the Harz region, had already been employed as sites for the stockpiling and mass production of rockets. Whereby the SS20s in their rock bunkers or the Pershing missiles on our national highways[2] only signify the trajectory, or the rainbow, of an eccentric homecoming.

1. War

Gravity's Rainbow, the arc of gravity, describes the flight trajectory of the V-2 rockets that were launched from sites in Holland or Northern Germany and flew over the German-Allied front towards metropolitan targets like London and Antwerp during the last six months of the war—September 8, 1944, through March 27, 1945.[3] *Gravity's Rainbow* is also Thomas Pynchon's attempt to read the signs of the time as a novel. Despite any post-war fantasies,[4] these signs were written by the last world war, the "mother"[5] of the technologies that have effected us, as well as the notion of Postmodernity that "threatens the idea of cause and effect itself" (56).

The V-2, the first liquid-fuel rocket in the history of war, developed from an engineer's toy to a production-stage super-weapon through the work of Wernher von Braun and the Military Research Institute of Peenemünde; and in Pynchon's inexhaustible fiction, it even anticipates at the end of the war—according to Braun's blueprints—the manned spaceflight of our time. The rocket occupies, therefore, the focal point of a novel that reads our signs. At the far end of the horizon of the novel or the theater of war, the parallel development of American weapons technology turns up in Hiroshima and Nagasaki (480, 505, 539). One need only replace the conventional explosives of the V-2—resulting from the ignition of a metric ton of Amatol (96, 312) before impact (a suggestion made by Hitler himself[6])—with Uranium or Plutonium as the rocket payload in order to be current with the state of affairs in 1985. At the same time that a confidential military document of the German high command dated October 15, 1942, proposed "atomic decay and chain reactions" as a possible means for "rocket propulsion,"[7] Fermi and von Neumann were already working on a suitable payload, which (as improvements have since shown) was really too good for their own Enola Gays (588) and bombers.

Accordingly, Pynchon's subject matter is German-American friendship as technology transfer. The technology that began on the beach of Peenemünde and proceeded to production-stage in the bunkers of Nordhausen (built by IG Farben and taken over by the Reich)[8]—where, by the way, the first jet fighters were also manufactured (304)—finds its continuation in Huntsville (558-9) and Baikonur (705-6). The sum result of the push of innovations set off by World War II—from audio tape (522), color film and VHF to radar (388-9), UHF (325-6) and computers (259-60)—is a post-war period whose only secret is the marketing of super-weapons and whose future is already foreseeable.

To be sure, people still believed in dying for their homeland during World War II. But Pynchon, a former Boeing-engineer, makes it clear through precise details that "the enterprise [of] systematic death" (76) "serves as spectacle, as diversion from the real movements of the War" (105). That is to say, "the real crises were crises of allocation and priority, not among firms—it was only staged to look that way—but among the different Technologies, Plastics, Electronics, Aircraft," and so on (521).

If the war was literally a mere theater of war and its sea of corpses only simulacra, behind the screen of which various technologies fought for their or our future, then indeed everything works as it does in media, which, from drama to computers, only transport information. Competitions and priority controversies amongst technologies are always already struggles for information about those technologies. As one of the novel's characters from industrial espionage circles summarizes with despair: "life was simple before the first war," when "dope and women" were still of interest. Since 1939, however, "the world's gone insane, with information come to be the only real medium of exchange," to the point where even industrial espionage is poised at the verge of abandoning agents or people in favor of "Information machines" (258ff.).[9]

Under conditions of absolute semiotechnology, the only question remaining is which media are implementing these conditions. And if, as Pynchon formulates it, "[t]he more you dwell in the past and in the future, the thicker your bandwidth, the more solid your persona" (509), then media analysts would be well-advised to remember the military history of their own subjects. What appears as narrative and, accordingly, entertainment in media possibly only screens semiotechnical efficiencies. Media such as literature or film or phonograph records—and this is precisely why *Gravity's Rainbow* pursues their systematic combination—are all at war.

2. Literature
In that mythical past, when dope or women were still of interest, war may well have been a soldier's song, oral and narrative. But ever since general war duty was mandated, such that "no one can be missing from the field," there is no one—according to Goethe's profound insight—to listen to the stories any more: everyone is affected.[10] The liberation wars—which from 1806 to 1815 freed the people of Central Europe to become underlings of the nation-states, meaning peoples' militias—therefore required a new medium as well. Literature was the document and the order. The new, that is, absolute enemy[11] had first to be named, and then its destruction ordered—precisely this task was performed by dramas such as

Kleist's *Hermannsschlacht*, which operated from the propaganda war's elevated command position ['Feldherrnhügel'].

It is well known, however, that the playwright's good fortune did not last long. As the general's privileged hilltop position disappeared in the material battles of the First World War, literature was forced to descend to the perspective of the poor grunt at the front (as is demonstrated in Fussell's brilliant analysis of English texts).[12] An absolute enmity that would be taken over by machines no longer requires narration, motivation or planning. Confronted with incomprehensible orders and invisible enemies, literature was left only with—according to Jünger's astute title—the *Battle as inner experience [Kampf als inneres Erlebnis]*. And that was simply film. A technical substitute for the book appeared at the print medium's limit where all words are deformed by explosions.[13] When Lieutenant Jünger rejected the expressionistic study of his experience and encountered reality behind the morning fog and barbed wire, the enemy was a filmic hallucination of his Double.[14] Reason enough, as Remarque also proves, for the novelization of the grunt's perspective to develop into its filming.

If, however, the enterprise of systematic death and the simulation of ally-enemy relationships serve only to mask competing technologies—which for their part are based neither on experience nor narration but rather on blueprints, statistics and secret commands—then the perspective of the poor grunt at the front is rendered obsolete. Thus, from the outset, *Gravity's Rainbow* employs other narrative techniques in gathering the traces of the second and technological World War.

Instead of one war with its inner experience, there is a stochastic scattering of characters and scenes, of fronts and discourses, of Allied and German positions. Only the chance coincidence of two chance positionings creates the perspective of one hero and one plot. The Poisson distribution of the V-2 strikes in London coincides point for point with the private statistics that an American lieutenant named Slothrop maintains of his chance erotic encounters. And just as the super-sonic rockets that, through their speed, create ambiguity between cause and effect, between audible threat and visual explosion (23),[15] Slothrop's erections act as an index (in the double sense of Peirce and all prophets), already designating the next strike position.

The V-2s follow the erections, in the same way that the sound of flight follows the impact. In other words, even Slothrop's love-making or "fantasy has the structure of bombs."[16] This is reason enough for the Allied command to use the lieutenant as a test subject in the technical sense. He is smuggled into the collapsing Reich in order to find the traces of any final, extraordinary and mythical rockets that his German double orders into space and/or to death.

Slothrop escapes the "operational paranoia" (25) of the intelligence agent only to the extent to which it seizes him at the personal level. The medium of this transfer is print. The lieutenant is descended from puritanical paper manufacturers, that is, people who took America's "diminishing" forests and "converted acres at a clip into paper—toilet paper, banknote stock, newsprint—a medium or ground for shit, money and the Word" (28). This symbolic, in the Lacanian sense, catches up with him as he studies the captured V-2 documents. Reading and paranoia merge. All traces that Slothrop learns to decode in the European stronghold point to the fact that the military-industrial complex was always superior to battle fronts, meaning that it conditioned not only the innovations of German rocket engineers, but also the sexual reflexes of American GIs. In his personal file, which has indeed always controlled would-be experiences or anamneses, Slothrop reads that already as a child—on the historically correct track between IG Farben and Rockefeller's Standard Oil[17]—he was the behavioral test subject of the same Professor Jamf who would make manned space flight possible through his synthetic polymers. Subsequently, as always, it comes to light that the detective coincides with his double in the cockpit of the V-2. Even the coincidence of two iconic patterns, that is, the historically precise mapping of missile impact zones and the erotic-romantic London city map, is the opposite of chance. A thorough study of the files always reveals the conspiracy behind apparent coincidences.

Despite any assumptions made on the part of the reader (whose naiveté is addressed here), the premises of this sinister conclusion are not immanent to fiction. Rather, it is a process of the historical precision of that which the text itself calls "data retrieval" (582). Slothrop's paranoia within the novel corresponds precisely to a paranoiac-critical methodology that the novelist could have learned from Dali. Although there is a chronological inversion of the novelist's and the hero's confrontation with the 'files,' this alone does not render the work a fiction. *Gravity's Rainbow* is highly esteemed as a textual example of 'postmodernity'; however, the literary experts remain silent on the scope and exactitude of the research it incorporates. And yet the text, as is only the case in historical novels like *Salammbô* or *Antonius*,[18] is essentially assembled from documentary sources, many of which—circuit diagrams, differential equations, corporate contracts, and organizational plans—are textualized for the first time. (A fact easily overlooked by literary experts.)

Gravity's Rainbow is data retrieval from a world war whose classified files are made accessible to this degree only when their strategic goals become reality and no longer require what is called secrecy. Already for that reason, paranoia is knowledge itself—or, like all psychoses according to Freud or Morris, only a confusion of words and things,[19] of designatum and denotatum.[20] When the symbolic of signs, numbers and letters determine so-called reality, then gathering the traces becomes the paranoid's primary duty.

As a result, the paranoiac-critical methodology of the novel is transferred to its readers. These consumers of a narrative become hackers of a system, insofar as Slothrop, true to his puritan ancestry (207), by no means decodes every war secret that the novel has encoded. It is inconceivable that he could decipher that the fictitious U.S. Major Marvy, responsible for the transfer of the V-2 technology to the United States, is only a cryptogram of the historically accurate name of Staver.[21] Or that he could ascertain that Pointsman, the chief behaviorist of the British intelligence agency in the novel, is only so-named in order to merge into the multi-national conspiracy with his double bearing the same name—Weichensteller was an engineer at Peenemünde whose "responsibility," interestingly enough, was "the re-entry" (453) of the V-2s into British air space.

In *Gravity's Rainbow*, fictitious names and narrative structures mask a level of information that is connected, moreover, with other no less paranoid novels (cf. 587–8), and that for practical reasons can not be more satisfactorily revealed. In this way the novel is made up to date. In the emerging predominance of technologies over knowledge and aesthetics, only information counts. Indeed, certain roots of semiotics itself are concurrent with the very behavioristic semiotechnologies that Pynchon analyzes as war strategies.

Two problems remain, however, for the analysis and recombination of data that is no less scattered than cryptic: the closure and the self-application of the system. Slothrop "dances on a ground of terror, contradiction, absurdity" for good reason because his data retrieval of 1945 takes place some time precedent to the actual opening of the relevant secret archives. First of all, it would not have been difficult for the military-industrial complex to have "bought programmers by the truckload to come in and make sure all the information fed out was harmless" (582)—as harmless, for example, as a narrative novel. Secondly, Tyrone Slothrop's paranoid insight leads to his assumption that his desire is a desire of the self (216-7), when in reality—to borrow from Lacan—it has always been a desire of the other, or the director of the experiment. Exceeding his historical predecessors Watson and Baby Albert, Jamf conceives of the "elegant" idea— elegant in the sense of its "binary" nature—not to condition Baby Tyrone to an unquantifiable state such as fear, but rather to institute the uniform and unambiguous event of the erection as conditional reflex (84ff.). Slothrop dreams of a "very old dictionary of technical German" wherein "JAMF," the proper name of the director of the experiment, is translated as the English index "'I'" (287; cf. 623).

The "I," then, in other (but still Pynchon's) words, is only "a branch office in each of our brains, his corporate emblem is a white albatross, each local rep has a cover known as the Ego, and their mission in this world is Bad Shit" (712-3; cf. 285-6). End of citation, which could just as well have come from Foucault, and which is the end of all paranoia, insofar as there is no one left to make up the identity of an involuntary private detective who finally cracks the alibi, which is to say the "somewhere-else," of his own Ego. Under conditions of total remote-control, the narrativity of fictional heroes vanishes. In an endless series of clothes changes and metamorphoses, Lieutenant Slothrop loses his uniform, proper name and literacy; he dissolves into digressions, comic strips, myths and, finally, an album cover (742). In this and only this fashion, he escapes the trap that the print medium, itself a component of the military-industrial complex, presents to readers as such. If paranoia is said to exist in the anxiety provoked by the reading of a single, coherent and narratable plot (703), then "there is still also anti-paranoia, where nothing is connected to anything" (434).

And if the genre of the novel has been historically defined as a medium in which the bifurcation points of Markoff chains decrease in proportion to the path already covered by the hero until a structure or a solution is finally established, then one could state that the anti-paranoia of *Gravity's Rainbow* results in the opposite effect, which is an increase of information, and concurrently (according to Shannon) of entropy. In its progressive, that is, increasing mixture of characters, organizations and fronts, the novel systematically recalls the second principle of thermodynamics. This law, which states that a system always progresses towards increased entropy, directs time's arrow, and consequently—according to an attentive example presented by Eddington—can be used to ascertain whether films run forwards or backwards in physical time.[22]

3. Film

Gravity's Rainbow is film in this technical and temporal sense. Not because the novel could be filmed, as was done with Remarque, or because it hallucinates invisible enemies, as in Jünger, but rather because it offers up for inspection the progressive disintegration of the negentropy of the military-industrial complex. In contrast to the classical novel's use of the past tense, the constant and simultaneous presence of all episodes as such tends towards a state of forgettability that allows no room for the linear chains of cause and effect. "Each hit is independent of all the others. Bombs are not dogs. No link. No memory. No conditioning." In other words, the question as to "which places would be safest" is moot, and as a result of the experience, a "whole *generation* have turned out like this," whose Postwar is "nothing but 'events,' newly created one moment to the next" (56).

Only the "Monte Carlo Fallacy" (56) assumes that a rocket impact, a film still, or a novelistic event with the variable n is determined by the series 1 to $n-1$, as if it had a memory. Indeed, the rocket strikes on London are a signal to the chief behavioralist in the text that "reality is not reversible." It could only end if "rockets dismantle, the entire film runs backward: faired skin back to sheet steel back to pigs to white incandescence to ore, to Earth" (139). But as—of all people—Walter Rathenau, the inventor of the German war economy and, concurrently, Soviet five-year plans, explained in his capacity as conjured spirit, "all talk of cause and effect is secular history, and secular history is a diversionary tactic" (167) or even a "conspiracy" (164). It is well known that world history wreaked havoc in the print medium; on the other hand, technical media (besides the diversionary tactic of their status as entertainment) allow for the variation of precisely those parameters of which they alone are in total control. In other words, physical time as well. Just as the rocket strike mixes up the sequence of impact and sound, the numerous fictitious films within *Gravity's Rainbow* employ the trick that in the dialect of the electronics experts carries the name Time Axis Manipulation.

The final work of Gerhardt von Göll, who in the novel is representative of Papst, Lang and Lubitsch, his historical counterparts (112), is titled "New Dope," and it demonstrates "24 hours a day" how the drug leaves you "incapable of ever telling anybody what it's like, or worse, where to get any." "It is the dope that finds *you* apparently. Part of a reverse world whose agents run around with guns that are like vacuum cleaners operating in the direction of life—pull the trigger and bullets are sucked back out of the recently dead into the barrel, and the Great Irreversible is actually reversed as the corpse comes back to life to the accompaniment of a backwards gunshot" (745). Only that such film tricks are not restricted to imaginary hallucinations and visits to the cinema. The novel describes the wreckage from a British bombardment of a V-2 launch position in similar terms—"[t]he vehicles are back to the hollow design envelopes of their earliest specs" (560). The novel thus indicates the most sinister of its paranoid recognitions: Germany's industrial installations were constructed—according to the theory of the value of ruins developed by their architect, Albert Speer[23]—with the conscious intent to destroy the Royal Air Force, and they could fulfill this, their post-war assignment in the multinational conspiracy, only as "ruins," only after having been bombed (520–1).

Von Göll's first production, a forged documentary film following the guidelines of the Allied's Operation Black Wing,[24] achieves similar time reversals, if not quite as strategically. Masquerading as Hereros, Britons in stage make-up play the parts of one of Major-General Kammler's motorized rocket batteries. The completed film is artificially antiqued and damaged, that is, every tone is enhanced through which technical media are defined by their background (cf. 94). As a pseudo-document from a bogus V-2 installation, the film then serves to ignite German rumors over Blacks in the SS-Armed Forces (113 ff.). "'It is my mission,' [von Göll] announces . . . , with the profound humility that only a German movie director can summon, 'to sow in the Zone seeds of reality'" (388; cf. 275). And indeed, Lang's *Frau im Mond (Woman on the Moon)* of 1929 sowed the seeds for the countdown (753) and the future V-2.[25]

But as if this ambiguity between cause and effect, between programming and documentation, were not enough, the spiral continues. In von Göll's case, it subsequently comes to light that the Hereros of the SS-Armed Forces were not the effect, but rather the magical cause of their own propagandistic simulation. Because they already exist, von Göll's forgery would have to run in reverse, as all countdowns do. And so again the riddle surfaces as to the positions that programming and narrativity hold vis à vis each other in media.

Virilio's book, *Guerre et cinéma [War and Cinema]*, attempts to prove that world wars and film technology are not only concurrent phenomena, but are in strict solidarity. The command of a war that is militarily, technologically and propagandistically composed of velocity and information does not function without the concentration, the expansion and the reversal of time—that is, Time Axis Manipulation. Precisely that which would be impossible in the print medium or in literature—despite Ilse Aichinger's short story *Spiegelgeschichte [Story in a Mirror]*—has been an integral characteristic of film from the beginning, a beginning which can be found (among other places) in the six-shooter.[26] To be sure, literature was also able to manipulate that time which misrepresents the formative path or battle as inner experience. But in order to work with physical time itself, in which formative paths or mortal battles actually exist, technical media are mandatory. Rocket technology requires film technology and vice-versa. That the V-2 was ever able to find its mark precisely in London, despite all incredulousness on the part of the newly organized technical department of the British intelligence agency,[27] is in large part due to a brilliant innovation: the quantitative parameter of the rocket was neither its course, as was the case with ground troops, nor its velocity, as had most recently been employed with tanks, but rather acceleration, which is the only bit of information accessible to the rocket itself. Velocity is then calculated through simple integration of this figure, and trajectory through double integration (301ff.). A pendulum and two resistance-capacitance (RC) couplings in series—the construction of Virilio's Dromology was this simple. So simple, in fact, that it was easily overlooked (by the British experts, for example).

According to Pynchon, "there has been this strange connection between the German mind and the rapid flashing of successive stills to counterfeit movement, for at least two centuries—since Leibniz, in the process of inventing calculus, used the same approach to break up the trajectories of cannonballs through the air" (407; cf. 567). The technical medium that implements movement as infinitesimal calculus, however, is called film. Since the time of Marey's photographic rifle,[28] cinematic illusions of continuously moving pictures have been simple integrations similar to the velocity of the V-2, and their variables dependent on time axis manipulation, which is the only thing that counts in the optimization of weapons of destruction. As in the case of film's forerunners of 1885, the high-speed Askania cameras used in 1941 were not developed to serve the imagination of the movie-goer, but rather to permit the slow motion studies of the V-2 flight paths (407)—which in no way precludes these techniques, however, from "extend[ing] past images on film, to human lives" (407).

One of the many stories contributing to the entropy of *Gravity's Rainbow* questions narratability itself in terms of technology. It recounts the story of an engineer at Peenemünde on whom the trick of time axis manipulation is played. The simulacrum in this film or life is his 12-year old daughter, who, incidentally, is conceived thanks to the semiotechnology of film. Specifically, thanks to one of von Göll's late-expressionistic rape scenes, which was edited in the public version just before climax, but carried through to the bitter end in the studio and in the private archives of Joseph Goebbels. Besides the film-diva herself, this rape scene impregnated countless wives or girlfriends of returning film-goers. Under high-tech conditions, children are reduced to doubles of their filmscreen doubles: cannon fodder in the case of boys, pin-ups in the case of girls.

Thirteen years later. The film-generated cannon fodder entered the Blitzkrieg and pin-ups were needed. The rocket engineer—being the Pynchon character that he is—had naturally long since forgotten his daughter and her appearance. From 1939 onwards, however, she visits him during every summer holiday of the war, as a bonus reward from the Peenemünde military base. And only after the Pin-Up-Daughter herself deceives him does it become clear that year after year she was only assembled as a double without an original. Since 1939, the KZ Dora in Nordhausen—also the locale for V-2 mass production—simply granted a leave of absence to its female inmates, first a 12-year old, then a 13-year old, and so on until the end of the war. In Pynchon's words: "The only continuity has been her name, and Zwölfkinder, and Pökler's love—love something like the persistence of vision, for They have used it to create for him the moving image of a daughter, flashing him only these summertime frames of her, leaving it to him to build the illusion of a single child" (422). Film-goers are the victims, then, of a semiotechnology that deludes them into seeing a coherent and causal life story where there are only snapshots and flash bulbs. The feature film began, at least in Germany, with doubles who themselves directed and propagated the film version,[29] and found its peak, for Pynchon as well as for Virilio,[30] with the countless Japanese, who represented the bombs "as a fine vapor-deposit of fat-cracklings wrinkled into the fused rubble" of their city Hiroshima (588).

The exposure time? 67 nanoseconds or, literally, Blitzkrieg.

A war that coincides with its own depiction, however, becomes unrepresentable. *Gravity's Rainbow* assembles all of the obstacles to the portrayal of the technological wars in the character of Slothrop's German antipodes. Here the GI who sets out on the trail of the V-2 because of initial coincidences and marching orders; there a commander who controls not only the production and launching of these super-weapons, but also, through realistic film tricks, the sexuality of his engineers. A depiction of the Peenemünde commander would only be a revival of the war-film clichés of the evil German. The fact that Pynchon is able to circumvent this, and instead stage the enigmatic relationship between fact and fiction, has indeed led to the silence of his interpreters on this point. But it is the greatest aspect of the novel.

Historically, it is well-known that the Peenemünde military base was under the command of General Dornberger of the Army Ordnance Office. (In 1932, this same Dornberger, then a Captain and Aide to Professor Becker, had already discovered the young

Wernher von Braun.) The organizational map from Kummersdorf to Peenemünde remained stable until the methodically proliferating entropy of the Hitler state (427) created an SS-state within the state. For that reason, in 1944, after the Army Ordnance Office had done its technical duty and the Armed Forces were devolving into agony, the command over Peenemünde, Nordhausen and an army corps allocated 'by special decree'[31] (the only one in German military history) was given to Chief Squad Leader Dr. Kammler of the Chief Economic Administration Office of the SS.[32] Hans Kammler, born in 1901, shared with Thomas Pynchon, born in 1937, the distinctive feature of having destroyed all of his photographs.[33] He traverses the novel in a similarly unrepresentable fashion.

Pynchon's fictitious rocket commander erases his own identity because he is not a true figure, but only the result of a double exposure. As of 1932, the rocket commander is named "Major Weissmann," and with that name, designated an officer of the armed forces. He is (as was Dornberger) "a brand-new military type, part salesman, part scientist" (401). Even in his discussions with subordinate engineers over scientific interests, which for their part serve only to camouflage the pressure of the economics of war (416ff.), Pynchon's Weissmann pursues his own source: the involuntary exposure of Dornberger's memory book.[34] True to form, the name Dornberger does not appear in the novel in its exact construct, as if fact and fiction were two sides of the same sheet of paper.

In Peenemünde, this same Weissmann later acquires, without explanation, the SS-rank of "Generaldirektor" (418), and in 1944, eventually trades his name for the "SS code name" "Blicero," a transcription of death itself (322). As Blicero, Weissmann takes advantage of all the formalities due the German major general: he becomes a roaring animal, chasing the last rocket batteries over the bombed-out highways of the Reich. Dornberger, Braun and their stand-in ghostwriters report nothing else of Kammler and his belief that only he could have decided the war.[35] It is as if all entropies of the Hitler state had become flesh.

The coming together of Dornberger and Kammler, Weissmann and Blicero, of the armed forces and the SS, order and entropy, is the eccentric center of the novel, the space of its unrepresentability. Whether Blicero is dead or not remains a mystery (cf. 667), as was also the case with the real Kammler for many years after the war.[36] His deeds or deliria exist only as stories of stories from witnesses who for their part were under the influence of the drug Oneirine (463-4, 669-70ff.), another synthesized product of the fictitious Professor Laszlo Jamf (348), of course. "The property of time-modulation peculiar to Oneirine was one of the first to be discovered by investigators" (389; cf. 702-3). This is why it is possible for Blicero, the double exposure of 1932 and 1944, to be Dornberger and Kammler. This is why somewhere in the ruins of the Reich, his insanity can launch a manned spaceflight that would not exist for another 20 years. And finally, this is why Pynchon's Second World War is able to end with the intercontinental weapons of the next war, insofar as Blicero's manned V-2, shot down in Niedersachsen in 1945, lands on the last page of the novel in Hollywood, 1973, the year the novel is published. Its base delay-action fuse targets precisely the movie theater in which Pynchon and his readers are sitting. "For us, old fans who've always been at the movies," there finally begins "a film we have not learned to see," but have dreamed of since the days of Muybridge and Marey: the convergence of film and war (760ff.).

Oneirine is additionally distinguished, however, by other, less sensational, properties. In contrast to the structuralism of *cannabis indica* (cf. 347), the hallucinations prompted by Oneirine "show a definite narrative continuity, as clearly as, say, the average *Reader's Digest* article." They are, in other words, "so ordinary, so conventional" and so American (703). With these words, Pynchon makes his contribution to the topic of narrativity in media. It is furthermore his explanation why every medium, including the novel itself, is a drug and vice-versa.

According to Stresemann, people are praying "not only for their daily bread . . . but also for their daily illusion" (452). And corporations like the real IG Farben or Jamf's fictitious Psychochemie AG (250) do everything possible in the search for a positive, that is, a psychopharmaceutical, solution to "the basic problem" of "getting other people to die for you" after the disintegration of the illusions first espoused in theology and then in the philosophy of history (701). In 1904, when "the American Food and Drug people took the cocaine out of Coca-Cola," we are given the gift of "an alcoholic and death-oriented generation of Yanks ideally equipped to fight WWII" (452).

Thus all that remained—in the words of the Oneirine-user von Göll—was to hope for the eventual convergence of film and war. Even though Slothrop, according to whom "this ain't the fuckin' *movies*," may still rightfully continue to fear that people will shoot even though "they weren't supposed to," von Göll knows better. According to the film director, we are "not yet" in the film. "Maybe not quite yet. You'd better enjoy it while you can. Someday, when the film is fast enough, the equipment pocket-size and burdenless and selling at people's prices, the lights and booms no longer necessary, *then* . . . then . . ." (527).

In 1973, however, *Gravity's Rainbow* already organized a television quiz show, called "A Moment of Fun With Takeshi and Ichizo, the Komical Kamikazes," for its readers (805). And whoever guesses, like "Marine Captain Esberg of Pasadena," that this entire spectacle is "a film," only "another World War II situation comedy," wins the grand prize, a free flight (one way only) to the actual film set. There, in the midst of "torrential tropical downpours," he can "mak[e] the acquaintance of the Kamikaze *Zero*," control it, fly in it and—crash (691).

The narrative continuity of the feature film's Oneirine-hallucinations thus takes over the novel, which for its part makes them its theme. Plots and dialogues transpire as if they were written under the influence of the drug (cf. 704ff.), with the result that *Gravity's Rainbow* itself is a type of *Reader's Digest* article: ordinary, conventional and American. "There ought to be a punch line to it, but there isn't" (738). The enigmatic question of whether and how the technologies of the world war have programmed our so-called post-war period remains unsolved. The novel is but a novel, and its hero Slothrop, a "feeb." His allotment is "mediocrity," not Weissmann-Blicero's manned space rocket that he chased in vain.

And mediocrity, as is bitterly and explicitly revealed, "not only in his life but also, heh, heh, in his chronicler's too" (738).

4. Records

If the symbolic is stored in the text and the imaginary in the feature film, then the medium of stupidity is the countless number of songs found in the novel. Record grooves capture the vibrations of real bodies whose stupidity, as is well known, knows no boundaries. The effects ravaged on the body by wars and drugs and media find their continuation, for that reason, as music. "Tape my head and mike my brain, stick that needle in my vein," commences a song in *Gravity's Rainbow* (61-2). The novel comes to a repeated standstill because fictitious rumbas, beguines, foxtrots, blues improvisations, and so on, accompanied by exact performance specifications and distanced from all war-like games, deform the plots or conspiracies into a ritournelle, an endless recurrence of stanza and chorus. At the end of the text, while high over California a new world war is beginning, a song of consolation is sung for a "crippl'd Zone," whose referent is not only post-war Germany. Thus concluding song and novel: "Now everybody—"

Translated by Stefanie Harris

M E D I A
W A R S :
T R E N C H E S ,
L I G H T N I N G ,
S T A R S

*W*ar, as opposed to sheer fighting, has been for a long time an affair of persuasion. It came into being only when people succeeded in making others die for them. Before their probably fatal orders were obeyed, commanders had first to create subjects, both in the philosophical and political sense. Instructions, therefore, presupposed injunctions and these addressed an art of rhetoric. Following Nietzsche's analysis, this rhetoric proceeded as a "robbery" or "raid" directed against the listeners' self-conservation. How to think as a subject and how to die as a citizen—these were Socrates' teachings, and in a famous speech, Pericles, Socrates' political and military commander, taught exactly the same message.

This is why traditional warfare could simply not do without the physical presence of chiefs or seconds-in-command. In some famous battles, Frederick the Great needed almost as many troops to motivate and to control his own soldiers as were left to attack the Austrian enemy. Technical warfare, however, may have changed this whole configuration, balanced as it was between motivational techniques and strategies. In 1909, Count Alfred Schlieffen, chief of the Reich's General Staff, gave one of his articles the title "War in the Present Times." There he foresaw that one day commanders would become totally invisible to their troops, hidden in a bunker or technical lab. The traditional rhetoric of presence and persuasion would be replaced by technologies of telecommunication and control. Consequently,

"Media Wars: Trenches, Lightning, Stars," was originally presented as a conference paper at "Wars of Persuasion: Gramsci, Intellectuals and Mass Culture," 25 April 1987, University of Massachusetts at Amherst.

Schlieffen counted an exhaustive list of technical media among the musts of modern military command.

Five years later, as Paul Virilio has demonstrated, World War I put into operation all available storage media combined with early prototypes of transmission media. In turn these transmission media, technically perfected and serialized, supported World War II, but only to provoke, by further escalation since 1943, the development of computing media. Universal discrete machines settle the old question—how to make people die for others. If Star Wars took place or, rather, took place away, it would be fought by self-guided weapons, that is, by subjects who no longer need any persuasion. At about the same time that young Antonio Gramsci saw "the masses as [his] richest and most reliable source of information," Walter Benjamin proposed the opposite intellectual strategy: an ever grow-ing distrust in masses, democracy, freedom, etc., balanced only by his "unshaken trust in I.G. Farben and the peaceful perfection of air forces." Thus self-guided missiles wouldn't have come as a surprise to him.

To follow Benjamin is to gather military information. The binary architecture of our computers and missiles may well have per-fected what's at stake in every command. Therefore even if informa-tion about modern information systems has been classified by very explicit orders, let's try to tell a story of strategic command.

In the beginning, of course, was the word. The word was with God and it worked for six days at a binarization of day and night, heaven and earth, land and sea, sun and moon, as well as of good and evil. In those days before the day, the iterated sequences of digital encoding could not create anything that hadn't preceded them under the infamous name of *tohu-wa-bohu*. Consequently God's word was—in Lacanian terms—"nothing else than the creation—of noth-ing, indeed, of what?—of nothing but signifiers." Thanks to their very contingency, however, the first war of persuasion established what engineers would call an appropriate signal-to-noise-ratio. Digitalization separated God's ordered order from ancient chaos.

The World War II mathematician John von Neumann encoun-tered a very analogous problem. His *General and Logical Theory of Automata* had to admit that "our actual knowledge in technology as well as in physiology hardly indicates any existence of binary machines in a strict sense." As you know, nature and brain have remained close to ancient chaos. This empirical deficit, however, doesn't exclude by any means the existence of binary machines in strategy. From the Bible's first lines on, the language of chief commands continues to proceed by way of Yes's and No's, by commands and interdictions. In order to prevent the smallest misunderstanding which the ever-present noise-sources of physical channels could introduce, this language goes so far as to super-encode its own codes, to binarize its binarizations. For instance, every telegram issued by the German General Staff from Schlieffen's time on, made an explicit distinction between *westlich* and *ostwärts*. In German, this wording sounds as strange as if you had made up a binary opposition not between west and east, but between west and orient. Nonetheless, it solved on the elementary level of linguistics Schlieffen's foremost problem: a General Staff confronted with war on two fronts had to establish binary distinctions exactly as precise as God's distinction between Good and Evil. Therefore, when General Alfred Jodl, the last Chief of the Wehrmacht Operations Staff, tried to replace Schlieffen's artificial German with the current distinction between *westlich* and *östlich*, the consequences surpassed mere misunderstanding. In the name of its sacred code, the entire body of officers protested against this return of noise, against a not sufficiently binarized *tohu-wa-bohu*.

Command in war has to be digital precisely because war itself is noisy. To conquer the city of Troy, for Agamemnon's army, was no silent affair. However, as Villiers de l'Isle-Adam has so acutely remarked, the homeric rhapsodies, as opposed to phonographic devices, transmitted of all that fracas nothing but the very word of noise. Equally, the famous optical telegraph, as the *Oresteia* has described its passage from Asia Minor via the Sporadic islands to Agamemnon's capital, transmitted but a simple fire whose absence signalized the No, and whose presence the Yes, of Troy's conquest. These binary economics, marvelously suited to war as the very paradigm of zero-sum games, were somewhat obscured when, during the French revolution, optical telegraphy was technically reinstalled in order to transmit twenty-six letters, ten ciphers, and some special signs from Paris to the French armies and vice versa. Economics, however, triumphed again when optical telegraphy changed into electronics and when Friedrich Wilhelm Gerke in 1849 codified our modern telegrammar consisting only of dots and dashes.

Only since that time, the transmission of military commands ceased to be what it had been up to Napoleon's famous dispatches: a matter of oral, or at least, epistolary presence. There is no doubt that the Emperor, by means of a first general staff, channeled twenty letters per battle-hour to the sensationally autonomous corps and divisions of his Great Army. This frequency of information, however, made only numerical differences between Napoleon and *The Sufferings of Young Werther*, that other epistolary novel he so deeply admired.

In contrast, no modern *Oresteia* can compete anymore with telecommunications whose networks, channels, and codes cancel the millenary commerce between literature and strategy. Whereas traditional post systems at once transported letters, goods, and persons or, to put these entities into computer terminology, instructions, data, and addresses, modern strategy proceeds by their strict separation. When Field-Marshall Moltke invaded the French Empire in 1870, persons or soldiers were transported by railways, and instructions or orders by telegraphic networks which ran strictly parallel to these rails, whereas the old literary function of value or motivation was left to a newly invented postal device: the army post-card linking Prussian soldiers to their families.

Out of such technical separations, there arose a new concept of number that has since undermined the very bases of literature. Only three years after Gerke had introduced strictly binary signifiers into telegraphy, George Boole went so far as to conceive a formal digital logic. And although Boole's book-title identified it as the *Laws of Thought*, this formalism has since opened the very *possibility* of thought with switches, tubes, transistors, and finally, chips. Whereas the first historic binarism proposed by Leibniz was nothing but a simpler system of counting (on the basis of two instead of ten), Boolean algebra overcame enumeration by decision. Its symbols, devoid of any arithmetical value, assume strictly strategic ones. This is why the more silent digital signal processing appears, the more it covers the noise of war.

In 1898 Spain and the United States engaged in a two person zero-sum game. Islands such as Cuba and the Philippines changed

from old to modern colonial power simply because the telegraphi-
cally most advanced country had no trouble in winning what its general staff surnamed "the war of coal and cables." For at the same time
coal gave ships their kinetic energy, cables carried the information as
to where this energy had to be freighted. Since the United States had
intercepted all transatlantic cables, the Spanish fleet perished without a shot, simply by lack of energetic resources. The formal identity
between Boltzmann's entropic formula and Shannon's informational
one had been proved. Lawyers of the time now engaged in lengthy
debate about how to include totally immaterial blockades into the
traditional rights of war.

It was for precisely such reasons that Guglielmo Marconi, during
these very years, gave a practical and military form to Hertz's theoretical discovery of wireless telegraphy. The strategic risks of intercepted cables had to be eluded. Technical media don't arise out of
human needs, as their current interpretation in terms of bodily pros-
theses has it, they follow each other in a rhythm of escalating strategic answers. But alas, the new wireless medium of radio introduced
even greater risks of interception than telegraphic cables, as
Marconi's phonographically recorded, posthumous voice finally had
to "confess" via the channels of radio:

> I confess that when forty-two years ago I succeeded in making the first
> radio transmission at Pontecchio, I foresaw the possibility of sending
> electric waves to great distances but did not hold out hope of being
> able to obtain the great satisfaction which is being accorded to me
> today. In fact a major defect then was attributed to my invention, that of
> possible interception of messages transmitted. This defect preoccupied
> me so much that for many years my principle research was directed to
> its elimination. Nevertheless, this "defect" was utilized after about thirty
> years and has become radio, that means of reception which daily
> reaches more than 40,000 listeners.

Certainly, a name can be ascribed to those anonymous voices push-
ing Marconi to present them with a pure contradiction, that is, with
a radio system devoid of interception risks. Let's call them, in accordance with Eisenhower, the military-industrial complex. This complex, having endured the failure of Marconi's experiments, finally
contented itself with a difficult, but technically viable separation of
channels. On the one hand, the radio intercom systems introduced in

the trenches of 1917 lost their frequency-bandwidth and their emitting capacity. Thanks to newly issued postal decrees, there arose as a
left-over of army machinery a castrated civil broadcast system whose
definition up to this very day is its rather infrequent frequencies. The
lion's share remains with the military-industrial complex that, for
instance in the German Reich, tolerated civil competition only from
the day when the Deputy Post Secretary could promise the
Reichswehr a most recently developed machine capable of preventing
any civil or enemy interception of military radio signals. This
machine, on a worldwide scale, went by the name of Enigma.

For a partial solution to this enigma, one must return to the
trenches. World War I perfected technical storage information. The
immobilization of soldiers in their trenches during whole years only
followed that of moving pictures and moving sounds. Edison's two
inventions, the phonograph and the kinetoscope, broke the
immemorial monopoly of writing as a storage medium and following
Virilio, made possible technical warfare. At the same time, the development of typewriters broke the male hegemony in text production
and thus completed our modern trinity of the Real, the Imaginary
and the Symbolic, or (to put Lacan into more technical terms) the
trinity of sound recording, film dubbing, and dictated written orders.

Still, all these innovations of 1880 only registered data of a serial
and henceforth arbitrary materiality, be it optical, acoustic, or textual. As storage media, they still lacked an interconnection to transmission media such as radio and television. Consequently, there
arose a grave problem of how to mobilize the soldiers stored or
buried in the trenches. Especially on the English side, Field-Marshall
Harris's command system excelled in a total lack of telecommunications and feed-back loops. And when General Ludendorff, in order to
overcome this immobility, experimented with autonomous seconds-
in-command (who, by the way, would later on become the very leaders
of the Waffen-SS), his results proved modest even in the most
famous of cases. Lieutenant Ernst Jünger, one of Ludendorff's spe-
cially trained officers and poets, having glimpsed through the pow-
der smoke and trenches one of the essentially invisible enemy
soldiers, immediately confused him with his own double recorded by
a war movie. Consequently, what was far more important than military psychology and filmic persuasion was to implement technical

connections between storage media and transmission media. Early
on in World War I both sides developed tanks to make trails through
the enemy along which the infantry could then follow. For this purpose, tanks needed radio receivers and telecommanding. But, alas, it
was precisely their antennae that the ubiquitous barbed wires of
no-man's land tore off again and again. The Tactical Armored
Command had to regress from radiotelephony back to the carrier-
pigeons dear to the old Parisian communards.

Given these aporias and atavisms, the good news of lightning
war came down to new transmission media. It was frequency modu-
lated radio that, long before entertaining electronic rock music and
mass reception in the post-war period, guided three essentially
mobile weapon systems—the tanks, the submarines, and the dive
bombers of 1939. Lightning war, being a total mobilization by land,
sea, and air, would have been impossible without telecommand. Four
years before its outbreak, a certain Gimmler, engineer of the Heeres-
waffenamt, had successfully refuted the then current illusion that
very short waves, given their structurally optical propagation, were
useless in warfare. On the contrary, Gimmler's experiments (which
took place in exactly the mountains from which, a decade later, the
first autoguided missile would come) established the fact that electronic shadows cast by hills or mountains could not possibly hinder
the indispensable intercom between armored divisions and their
staffs. That's why General Guderian, Commander-in-Chief of a
German tank division, was well ahead of Colonel de Gaulle and other
colleagues. The Wehrmacht provided each single tank with FM
radio receivers that for three years proved to be decisive.

This material basis of lightning war has been rediscovered only
recently in an American monograph treating the very current issue of
Command in War. Its author writes: "Thus the credit for recognizing
the importance of the question, for the first successful attempts at its
solution, and for the first brilliant demonstration of how armored
command ought to operate belongs essentially to two men: General
Heinz Guderian—himself, not accidentally, an ex-signals officer
who entered World War I as a lieutenant in charge of a wireless station—and General Erich Fellgiebel, commanding officer, Signals
Service, German Wehrmacht. Between them, these men developed
the principles of radio command that, in somewhat modified and

technically more complex form, are still very much in use today. . . .
The critical importance of command in armored warfare cannot be
exaggerated and is equalled only by the lack of systematic attention
paid to it by most historians."

Unfortunately, a remaining lack of systematic attention infects
these very remarks. They ignore the fact that Guderian's innovations
would have been doomed to failure had not all this immensely
expanded radio traffic been operated by Enigma machines. To inter-
connect a whole army of about five million men, from the operational levels down to the tactical ones, by means of radio, was to raise
Marconi's risk to its maximum value. As had been the case with
World War I and its "virtually non-existent communications security," enemy interception could have easily reconstructed the very
structure of armies. Modern and only modern warfare coincides with
the organigrams of transmitted messages, with their distribution keys
and flow charts. Just like computers, it consists entirely of addresses,
data, and instructions or commands. This is why it passes essentially
through electronic networks. The lightning war, although or because
it depended on the most advanced transmission media, had to return
to the simple and most underrated among the storage media.
Systematically, it operated by means of typewriters that in contrast to
our everyday writer's boredom at least knew how to surprise their
users, that is, the intercom specialists of tanks and submarines. For
these machines didn't simply print, in a bi-univocal relationship, the
letters that had been typed. Instead, by means of five alphabetic
rotors and an electrical switch-board (whose start positions had to be
redefined every day), any input text was translated into two hundred
million mathematically possible and seemingly randomized outputs.
The name Enigma fit quite well.

From the first to the last day of the war, the German General
Staff put almost absolute trust in this device of perfectly mechanized
cryptography. Even in the most unlikely case that enemy cryptoan-
alysts succeeded in deciphering some sequences out of apparent
nonsense, these solutions would have come much too late in relation
to possible countermeasures. In technical wars, everything depends
on Real Time Analysis, the thousands of man hours needed for
Enigma's manual deciphering seemed to be a sufficient security
margin.

And still, the General Staff deluded itself. "The very fact that Enigma was a machine," *Command in War* explains, "made mechanical cryptoanalysis a possibility." Every machine controlled by algebraic rules can be beaten and overcome by its equal, provided that the enemy's machine operates on a superset of algorithms. Precisely such a technological advantage decided World War II, a war that otherwise, "might have gone on much longer, perhaps reaching an inconclusive result at best." But, as it happened, an army based on storage media and transmission media was beaten by computing media. Computers, nowadays a worldwide intelligence service offered to corporations, universities, writers, and postmodernity in general, nevertheless originated from an intelligence service in the strict military sense.

To make a long story short, World War II created a confrontation between two machines of different intelligence: on the one hand, there was Enigma enciphering a whole system of military telecommunications. On the other hand, there were an Oriental Goddess and eleven Colossi whose very names reflected their capacity to automatically decipher, after rather unproblematic interceptions, the system as such. Allied victory was guaranteed the day Britain's secret service installed the first operational computer in history. By chance or not.

For during the thirties, a homosexual young man had frequented the Sherborne public school without gaining official recognition, all his mathematical exploits notwithstanding. In the literate eyes of his teachers, his hands and copy books seemed much too stained. That is why young Alan Turing, instead of entering into our community of interpreters, preferred to start by constructing primitive typewriters and to end by conceiving, a few years later, the most primitive and most universal machine ever thought of. The Oriental Goddess and Colossi simply represented the first and partial realizations of Turing's Universal Discrete Machine. This young man had, by dismissing human and usually female secretaries, reduced the typewriter's discrete but not yet binary systems to its very principle. Finally devoid of alphabetic redundancies, a machine became identical with information.

Thus the circle of technical media was closed and history, that old continent of writing, brought to its end. The coupling of a storage medium and a transmission medium, of a typewriter and a radio network, finally resulted in a universal medium of computation, that is, a machine capable of registering, transmitting, and computing any data whatsoever without human intervention. As Turing has proved, the computerized calculation of recursive functions really exhausts the whole domain of computability.

Thus in a sense, the very history of human postal systems has come to an end. Data, addresses, and instructions, these three constitutive elements of every postal system, can handle each other by means of digital feedbacks such as if-then conditions and programmed loops. Since input data is always already transformed into a finite number of discrete states, there is no longer any need for human cutters as in film editing, or for tape recording-engineers as in analog sound processing. On the contrary, the very principle of automatized computation presupposes equally automatic operations of storage and of transmissions taking place in microseconds.

As you know, current Von Neumann-machines comprise in their very architecture, first, a memory for storage purposes, second, a bus for transmisson purposes and, third, by combining Leibniz and Boole, an arithmetical-logical unit for computing purposes.

This trinity of memory-stored data, bus-transmitted addresses, and central processing instructions constitutes a perfect postal system with physical dimensions, however, of only some three to five square-millimeters. Information has been transformed into matter and matter into information.

What remains open to question is the purpose of these purposes. In the academic beginning of his constructions, Turing intended to refute the decidability of mathematics as proposed by David Hilbert. By mechanizing computation as far as possible, he intentionally undermined the modern power of his equals, that is, of our intellectual community. Nothing, however, indicates that Turing, following Laplace's famous example, had looked for a new universal theory of nature. To his finite state machines, as opposed to physical and neurophysiological systems, he simply attributed the advantage of being predictable from start to end. Evidently, this feature hardly recommended them to applications in the analogous domains of physics or brains. Turing indeed voted for quite a different use. He wrote:

The field of cryptography will perhaps be the most rewarding. There is a
remarkably close parallel between the problems of the physicist and
those of the crytographer. The system on which a message is enciphered
corresponds to the laws of the universe, the intercepted messages to
the evidence available, the keys for a day or a message to important
constants which have to be determined. The correspondence is very
close, but the subject matter of cryptography is very easily dealt with by
discrete machinery, physics not so easily.

Thus Turing's cryptographic plain text established the not too
well known fact that computers follow no laws of nature, but the very
logic of decision-making, strategy, and information war. His appren-
tices, belonging not by chance, to the Post Office Research Station
at Dollis Hill, were able to bestow automatic cryptoanalysis on the
British secret service. Everything that on the enemy's side was programmable (that is, comprised in a network of addresses, data, and
instructions) was henceforth subject and bound to enter that network's identical reduplication.

After having deciphered, from 1943 on, about ninety per cent of
Germany's military telecommunications, the British Government
Code and Cipher school could dictate every suitable counter-measure.
However, by this transmission and propagation of secret information, it encountered a new and unique risk: the enemy (and possibly
also problematic allies such as the Russians) could have deduced from
the very precision of countermeasures the existence of cryptoanalytical computers. In this case Enigma's inestimable information source
would have dried up. Bletchley Park therefore went back to a stratagem almost as colossal as the Colossi themselves. In the last serious
battle of their history, the Anglo-American secret services built up an
immense simulation. Wars of persuasion culminated and ended in
persuading the enemy that traditional secret services and not computers had gathered the most vital information. Thus, the name of
man and the title of intelligence are pronounced, proclaimed, and
published only in order to better veil machines. "At some stage,"
wrote Alan Turing, "we should have to expect the machines to take
control."

Three weeks after Hiroshima, seven weeks after Potsdam,
President Truman issued a secret executive order in precisely this
sense. It classified every bit of information about computerized
information systems, their past as well as their future, their British

invention as well as their American serialization. The very fact that state-secrets are prey to computers became the greatest and most curious state-secret of our time. But with good reason. The British wires had scarcely ceased to interpret the German telecommunications, and their American counterparts the Japanese ones, when all of them received a new order to learn the Russian language and secret codes.

The success of Truman's secret executive order probably explains why, for thirty years, no history of computers ever mentioned their prototype, Bletchley Park's Colossus. It may even explain why Stalin, more or less blinded by the atomic lightning over Hiroshima and the autoguided missiles over Peenemünde, excommunicated cybernetics as one of the worst bourgeois deviations. As Turing's biographer put it: "The legacy of a total war, and the capture of a total communication system, could now be turned to the construction of a total machine."

"Post-war" means nothing else. Thanks to three secret agreements between the United Kingdom and the United States, the know-how of Bletchley Park was transferred to America. The same happened to the know-how of Peenemünde, where Werner von Braun, too, had dreamed of "digital computers." Having started by classifying computerized cryptoanalysis, Truman ended his presidency by issuing a top secret executive order. This still secret memorandum established the National Security Agency (NSA) as a natural heir to Bletchley Park. Following one of its few public statements, the NSA has accelerated computerization more than any other corporation or agency.

We talk, we write, we even try to persuade by means of discourse. However a whole global system composed of intercepting satellites and of cryptoanalytical computers performs all the storage, transmission, and computation needed to analyze about one out of a thousand messages that, at this very moment, passes across the telecommunications network of the earth. In a rather practical sense, NSA has universalized Turing's Universal Discrete Machine. Without intelligence services, the most central Pentagon subdepartment (whose beautiful acronym, C^3I, stands for Communications, Control, Command, Intelligence) would become blind and deaf in pursuing a task that coincides with the modern concept of war.

Technical media have to do neither with intellectuals nor with mass culture. They are strategies of the Real. Storage media were built for the trenches of World War I, transmission media for the lightning strikes of World War II, universal computing media for SDI: *chu d'un désastre obscur*, as Mallarmé would have it, fallen from an obscure disaster.

Or, as General Curtis D. Schleher put it in his *Introduction to Electronic Warfare:* "It is a universally accepted military principle that the victory in every future war will be on the side which can best control the electro-magnetical spectrum."

The World of the Symbolic—A World of the Machine

For Sepp

*A*ccording to Aristotle's commendable formula—*το ευσυνοπτον*—the beautiful is defined as that which the eye can easily embrace in its entirety and which can be surveyed as a whole.[1] The tragedy of King Oedipus may well arouse pity and fear, but according to *The Poetics* it is beautiful because it fulfills the temporalized optical requirement of having a beginning, a middle and an end.[2] Perception of its form is not resisted by boundlessness. Thus, long before Baumgarten's modern foundation of the concept and the subject matter of Aesthetics, and longer still before the term arose which will have guided my commentary, Aesthetics begins as 'pattern recognition.'*

The Aristotelian *το ευσυνοπτον* secretly carries over beyond the transcendental turning-point, possibly even as far as Nietzsche's Apollonianism. If in Kant, the Beautiful was distinguished, above all other notions, as that which was most advantageous to the imagination and understanding's joint enterprise of synthesizing facts or data (as Kant also said[3]), then the Beautiful continued to function primarily as an optical *gestalt* that would foster its own recognition as if by itself. By definition, the sublime was excluded from the Beautiful because of its boundless size (in the case of the mathematical sublime) or its endless strength (in the case of the dynamically sublime),[4] both of which resist any simple surveyability. Thus, from a simple mechanism of recognition, Kant created a mechanism of recognition to the second degree: henceforth, Aesthetics had mechanisms pertaining to its object, mechanisms which optimized the mechanism of recognition in general. In this

* [Tr.—The term 'pattern recognition' in English in the original text.]

context, an elaboration of the philosophical or at least techno-historical facts underscores that the recognition-mechanism—Kant's reflective judgment—could not be transferred to any mechanism, whether intellectual or material. Angels have no need to reflect on temporo-serial and spatio-discrete data; machines have no possibility of doing so.[5] The former skip over the problem; the latter over its solution. Consequently, in a very technical sense, Man has been the subject of Aesthetics.

This was reason enough to conduct or adjust a thought-experiment that proceeded from the hypothesis (ten years before Foucault) that Man did not survive the death of God by a single minute. The setting for the experiment is a mountainous region from which all human life, but not Aesthetics, has disappeared. "There are only waterfalls and springs left—lightning and thunder too," writes Lacan, in order to append the question of whether even without living beings, "the image [of these mountains] in the mirror, the image in the lake—do they still exist?".[6]

The answer is obviously positive if "still" designates all time t_1 at which the rays of light coming off an existing mountain are refracted on the water's surface and project a picture of the mountain, however virtual, into imaginary space. The answer is negative, however, if "still" designates all time t_2 at which the reflection of the lightning bolt endures only as long as the flash itself. Mirrors are a medium not for recording, but for transmitting nature. They perform only the function of $\alpha\iota\sigma\vartheta\eta\sigma\iota\zeta$ or perception, and at least in Lacan's inhuman model, this is already sufficient to cut through "the metaphysical . . . problem of consciousness" with a "Gordian" sword-stroke.[7] More precisely, in a "materialist definition" of consciousness any "surface" suffices where the refraction index biuniquely transfers individual points in the real to corresponding though virtual points in the image.[8] So-called Man, distinguished by his so-called consciousness, is unnecessary for this process because nature's mirrors can accommodate these types of representation just as well as the visual center in the occipital lobe of the brain.[9]

Lacan's aesthetic materialism has provoked opposition from the philosophers. To the question posed by the title of his book *Was ist Neostrukturalismus? [What is Neostructuralism?]*, Manfred Frank responds, "the dream of a machine without a subject," and goes on to present the following counter-argument: "Nothing in the play of visual reflections directly indicates that the mirror images sent back and forth exist for themselves as that which they are." On the contrary, any connection between the reflection and the object requires "a witness *for* whom it exists, or more exactly, exists *as* a reflection."[10] Moreover, Lacan must concede Man's necessary presence because his experiment ultimately re-invokes the humanity which had been expunged from the planet, in order to be able to demonstrate to those humans the possibility of machine consciousness.

The philosopher's objection has, however, two weaknesses. First of all, it remains open to question whether representations of bijection, which are only controlled logically by an algorithm, require additional witnesses in order to be what they are. Well before the advent of digital image processing, geometry and topology made do without this witness function. And secondly, Lacan returns to humanity at the end of the test in order to verify a different function which Frank's criticism for the most part overlooks: the storage of data. This is to say that any representation of the mountain "exists," according to Lacan, "for one very simple reason—at the high point of civilization we have attained, which far surpasses our illusions about consciousness, we have manufactured instruments which, without in any way being audacious, we can imagine to be sufficiently complicated to develop films themselves, put them away into little boxes, and store them in the fridge."[11] A photoelectric cell registers the flash of lightning and triggers the camera which records its reflection in the lake, until a humanity returning at time t_2 can witness the short-lived phenomenon of time t_1.

Philosophy teaches of an original "familiarity-with-ourselves," through which Man can both perceive representational relations as such and store a "continual process of iteration,"[12] so that all individuals become authors or Goethes narrating their own life stories. However, this philosophical teaching is precisely the point where psychoanalysis diverges from philosophy, by insisting that consciousness is only the imaginary interior view of media standards. Psychoanalysis contrasts the illusions of consciousness with a technically clean separation of functions. There are, first of all, media of transmission such as mirrors; secondly, storage media such as film;

and thirdly (to anticipate already), machines that manipulate words or figures themselves. So-called Man is not determined by attributes which philosophers confer on or suggest to people in order that they may better understand themselves; rather, He is determined by technical standards. Presumably then, every psychology or anthropology only subsequently spells out which functions of the general data processing are controlled by machines, that is, implemented in the real. Kant's "I think," which in Goethe's time had to accompany every reading or aesthetic judgment,[13] was within the true so long as no machine took over pattern recognition for him. A contemporary theory of consciousness which does not situate consciousness in the technical realm, as does Lacan, but has consciousness simultaneously transmit, store and calculate like a true behemoth without specifying the media or the technologies involved is merely an euphemism.

In contrast to philosophy, psychoanalysis was established during Freud's lifetime "on foundations similar to those of any other science,"[14] namely the strict separation of transmission and storage functions, so as not to fall prey to any "scientific self-misunderstanding."[15] The *Project of a Scientific Psychology* of 1895 made clear that consciousness and memory, transmission and storage, are mutually exclusive. If the φ-neurons of perception were not able to transmit data registered immediately and thereby expunge them so as to be available for subsequent data, there would be no possibility of responding to environments and their random series. If, on the other hand, ψ-neurons of the later so-called unconscious were not able to retain registered data and store it in unlimited amounts, there would be no fulfillment of the stipulation that "any psychological theory deserving consideration must provide an explanation of memory."[16] A Random Access Memory (RAM) and a Read Only Memory (ROM) are thus mutually in play because, according to Freud, "we cannot off-hand imagine an apparatus capable of such complicated functioning [wherein it is both influenced and also unaltered]."[17] This problem, which Freud's colleague Breuer incorporated into his formulation of the localized difference in brain-physiognomy between the "perceptual apparatus" and the "organ" where "memory-images"are stored,[18] remained critical until the *Mystic Writing Pad* of 1925.[19] Instead of attacking Lacan, whose experiment was obviously only a return to Freud, Manfred Frank should have attacked psychoanalysis itself, for a self-familiarity that must be immediately forgotten again by the φ-neurons, and a life-continuum that remains totally inaccessible in the ψ-neurons, eliminate any concept of the individual.

Freud's materialism reasoned only as far as the information machines of his era—no more, no less. Rather than continuing to dream of the Spirit as origin, he described a "psychic apparatus" (Freud's wonderful word choice) that implemented all available transmission and storage media, in other words, an apparatus just short of the technical medium of universal-calculation, or the computer.

The transmission medium in psychoanalytic treatment was a telephony which transformed sound or the patient's unconscious into electricity or conscious speech so that the unconscious could be transmitted, and then, through the synchronized vibrations of the attentive analyst, could be transformed back again into sound or the unconscious.[20] These are almost Freud's precise words. What he does not reveal, however, is that at Berggasse 19 in Vienna the telephone cable had (in 1895) only been laid in the family's living quarters and not in the consultation room, so that therapy as telephony was a wireless system, or more specifically, radio *avant la lettre*. The transmission medium of *The Interpretation of Dreams* was an optical, camera-like apparatus that converted latent dream thoughts into a system of conscious perception—and Lacan could easily decipher these virtual images as film.

Finally, to give due honor ultimately to Edison who invented both the kinetoscope and the phonograph, Freud (as did all physiologists of his time) conceived of pyschoanalytic data storage as functioning like the grooves which phonographs—instruments which, in contrast to Berliner's later Gramophone, could both play back *and* record—etch onto wax or tinfoil rolls. From 1880 on, having been freed from the archaic memory-model of the alphabet, Delbœuf and Guyau were teaching that "the Spirit is a collection of phonographic recordings."[21] This was supported not only by the *Bahnungen* [facilitations] or memory tracks in Freud's *Project*, but also by his descriptions of the talking cure itself. Although his case histories may not have been "absolutely—phonographically—exact," he nonetheless claimed that they possessed a remarkably "high degree of trustworthiness."[22] Furthermore, Freud's *Introductory Lectures on Psycho-*

Analysis were "word for word" presentations based on improvised drafts because according to his own testimony, he "still possessed the gift of a phonographic memory"[23] at age sixty. This is the degree to which the foundation of psychoanalysis was based on the end of the print monopoly and on the historical separation of different media. Telephone, film, phonograph and print (typewritten by Freud since the Spring of 1913) shaped the psychic apparatus.[24]

Only Lacan understood this. The first, and for that reason also the last, writer whose writings were simply called *Écrits*, whose seminars were called *Séminaires*, whose radio interview was called *Radiophonie*, and whose television broadcast was called *Télévision*, brought psychoanalysis to the level of high-tech. The plain media language of his chosen titles already contradicts their reception by German-speakers, who had "always" (with the exception of the lost *Wunderblock**) and only placed Lacan "in dialogue with philosophy,"[25] as if the print monopoly over data processing had not lost any of its power.

Hegel and Freud are separated (according to Lacan) by a technical invention: Watt's steam-engine centrifugal governor, the first negative feedback loop, and with that Mayer's Law of Constant Energy, the numerical basis of Freud's general economy of desire.[26] Similarly, Freud and Lacan are separated by the computer, Alan Turing's Universal Discrete Machine of 1936. Under high-tech conditions, therefore, psychoanalysis no longer constructs psychic apparatuses (if they are still psychic) merely out of storage and transmission media, but rather incorporates the entire technical triad of storage, transmission and computation. Nothing else is signified by Lacan's "methodological distinction"[27] of the imaginary, the real and the symbolic.

In all other German versions of Lacan, as we all know, one refers to reality [*Realen*] instead of the real [*Reelen*]. Thus, in order to clarify both the spelling of these *Technical Writings*** and the antonymous pair of terms real/imaginary, an excursion will be necessary into the history of that science which introduced them as a pair: modern mathematics.

---

* [Tr.—On the relation of the name *Wunderblock* to the German analytical discourse on Lacan, cf. Kittler, "Dracula's Legacy," n. 27, in this volume.]

** [Tr.—*Draculas Vermächtnis. Technische Schriften* is the full title of the collection of Kittler's essays in which the present essay appeared.]

"Neither the true nor the false roots are always real; sometimes they are imaginary; that is, while we can always conceive of as many roots for each equation as I have already assigned, yet there is not always a definite quantity corresponding to each root so conceived of. Thus, while we may conceive of the equation

$$x^3 - 6x^2 + 13x - 10 = 0$$

as having three roots, yet there is only one real root, 2, while the other two, however we may increase, diminish, or multiply them in accordance with the rules just laid down, remain always imaginary."[28]

That is the Cartesian *Geometry* of 1637. Descartes asserts here (though admittedly without the use yet of Gauss' proof) the fundamental law of algebra according to which a comparison to the n-th degree will have n solutions.[29] He first distinguishes these roots, in the speech of his day, as true and false, referring to either a positive or a negative sign before the radical; secondly, however, as real and imaginary, referring to either a positive or a negative sign under the radical. According to his definition, the example he provides of a comparison to the third degree has three solutions, only one of which, however, is real, whereas the other two, the complex numbers $2 + \sqrt{-1}$ and $2 - \sqrt{-1}$, were absolutely meaningless for the mathematics of his time. Descartes' innovation (going beyond Cardano) lies precisely in his giving a name to imaginary numbers like $\sqrt{-1}$, thus assuring mathematics that one could quite simply incorporate them into further computation. Just as in the *Meditations*, where thoughts in dreams are as indubitable as the act of thinking, the very "conception" of imaginary numbers is sufficient to their being used in mathematical operations, "without determining their values."[30] With that, however, Descartes' mathematical project, which through algebraic methods succeeded the ancient geometry of the compass and the ruler,[31] is temporarily brought to completion.

In 1936, Lacan, an avid reader of Descartes, may well have derived his term, the imaginary, primarily from Freud or more probably Jung's *Imago*. But as soon as he coupled it with the counter-term, the real, his connection to the Cartesian *Geometry* is clear. With explicit reference to the "theory of complex numbers," Lacan records the "imaginary function" of the phallus as $\sqrt{-1}$. Accordingly, "the phallus, that is, the image of the penis, is negativity in its place in the specular image," and, "as a part lacking in the desired image," is even the determination of a square root. However, this does not in any way prevent psychoanalysis, no more than it does modern mathematics, from further computation. Consequently, psychoanalysis is the only science which can conceive of, or rather formalize, the imaginary—"that is why [the erectile organ] is equivalent to the $\sqrt{-1}$ of the signification produced above, of the *jouissance* that it restores by the coefficient of its statement to the function of lack of signifier (-1)."[32] Mathematical psychoanalysis thus computes, apparently through squaring, beyond the imaginary value i arrived at in an intermediate step, until the final solution of i to the second power "restores" a real number. It is precisely these types of roots, however—and by no means the trigonometric functions employed by Euler, which Lacan, for his part, never applied—that were beyond the scope of Descartes' imaginary numbers. In full justification, therefore, Lacan, for once in direct contradiction with his mathematical advisor Jacques Riguet, could celebrate the radical sign itself:

> It is enough to note that by means of your 0 and 1, that is, the connotation of presence-absence, we are capable of representing everything which presents itself, everything which has been brought about by a determinate historical process, everything which has been developed in mathematics. We are in perfect agreement. All the properties of numbers are there, in these numbers written with binary numbers. Of course, that isn't how one discovers them. It took the invention of symbols, for instance, which made us take a giant step forward the day it was simply inscribed on a bit of paper. We were left for centuries with our mouths open when faced with equations of the second degree without being able to get it out, and it is through writing it down that an advance was made.[33]

This dispute with the proverbial ahistoricism of the mathematicians delivers not only a brief historical theory of the operators of mathematics, but also an example of the methodological distinction of the real, the symbolic and the imaginary.

Numbers are symbolic as long as they are, like signs in general, substitutable, that is, ultimately fully representable through the two binary numbers—under the condition, of course, that binary numbers already exist as an historical notation system. The same numbers are real, on the other hand, if their figures and operators require a specific and historically datable notation in similarly real media. Only media afford the real any guarantee of being "always in its place,"[34] and the radical sign, in particular, of finding this place "on a bit of paper."

Thus numerical roots are symbolic to the extent that a typographical symbol permits us to manipulate them mathematically, even without having to calculate their value. In the process, the symbols used never constitute anything but subsets of a principally finite set of operators. On the other hand, these same roots are real or imaginary to the extent that the calculation of their values yields numbers which are generally described as uncountable, or in other words, complex numbers.

A media theory which transfers Lacan's methodological distinction to information technologies does not distort it back into object categories, notwithstanding some criticism to that effect. That first of all, the medium of the symbolic is called the computer, or with Turing and Lacan, "the universal machine,"[35] follows directly from its conceptual coincidence with the natural numbers. That secondly, the medium of the imaginary must be optical follows not only from the primacy of *gestalt* recognition, but also, and more elegantly, from Cartesian geometry. To the eternal dismay of every computer graphics programmer who must eliminate unfriendly divisions and roots whenever possible because of operating time, the conditions for an object in three-dimensional space either reflecting other objects or allowing them to shine through or rather neither are determined solely by the question of whether the root of a scalar product of two vectors, the moment of direction and the perpendicular line on the object's surface, is real or imaginary.[36] Precisely these types of reflections and transparencies are referred to in Lacan's model experiment with a non-human medium, film. That thirdly, and finally, the medium of the real is to be found in analog storage devices is proven by every phonograph record. What is etched into its grooves can assume an infinite number of different numerical values but remains a function of a single real variable, time—at least so long as Stephen Hawking is merely keeping his counter-theory of imaginary time secret from the Pope, but has not yet proven it.[37]

Lacan also occupies himself with these assignments of the real, the imaginary and the symbolic to media. The mirror stage—his discovery of precisely the same year in which Alan Turing invented the universal discrete machine—is quite simply cinema. Lacan cited a film about infants (produced without his help) as the experimental proof of the imaginary's being the specifically human act of (mis)recognizing exact images.[38] On the one side we have the real of a prematurely born body, whose sensory neurons in the first months of life—none other than Flechsig, Schreber's psychiatrist, delivered the anatomical evidence to Lacan though he left it nameless—are myelogenetically still too immature (in Flechsig's words) to "associate visual perceptions with bodily sensations"[39] or (in Lacan's terms) not to have a fragmented body. On the other side of this fragmentation— a fragmentation similar to the 24 discrete film stills which comprise one second of a motion picture—we have a purely sensorial feedback of the mirror image which transmits optical illusions of unity to the infant, exactly as the film feed which appears to the eye as an imaginary continuum. Thus it follows that Manfred Frank's direct question whether "even mistaken consciousness is not also consciousness in general"[40] can remain open for the time being because Lacan is concerned with the control mechanism, not with perception. That this relation to the mirror image, however comprehensive or ενουνοπτου, does not yet allow for homeostasis is demonstrated to him by two robots (higher degrees of the inhuman automatic camera at the mountain lake) that stand in a mutual relation of positive feedback through optical sensors, until the circumstances of their shared system necessarily ends in disastrous oscillations—aporia of all imaginary, of all *gestalt* recognition. According to Lacan, only a sound recording device engaged between the two robots could stop these oscillations because of "the unconscious mathematical subjacency" of every discourse.[41]

The reason is clear. Like film, even the phonograph is an analog medium which, before the development of the compact disc, was not equipped with the 'no'-function. It does not, however, record an imaginary continuum as does the motion picture, but rather a real one: the voice with all the stochasticism of its oscillations or frequencies. In reference to Marey's chronograph of 1873, Lacan emphasizes what philosophers "always forget"—technical sound recording proves that language is "something material."[42] On these grounds, it is Edison's phonograph that first allows for the possibility of a methodical, distinct separation between the real and the symbolic, between phonetics and phonology, which is to say the possibility of structural linguistics itself.

Lacan demonstrates this split by referring to Claude Shannon, the famous wartime engineer at Bell Labs. Lacan's theory of "resonance" between the patient and the analyst is only an inversion of Shannon's redundance,[43] which haunts all amorous whisperings on the telephone. Neither information theory nor psychoanalysis has anything "to do with knowing whether what people tell each other makes any sense. Besides, what is said on the telephone, you must know from experience, never does. But one communicates, one recognises the modulation of a human voice, and as a result one has that appearance of understanding which comes with the fact that one recognises words one already knows."[44] Shannon could thus continue his work on optimizing the capacity of the medium's transmission wires—through band-pass filters, linear prediction coding, or even according to his own scanning theory by which discrete values per temporal unit are extracted from the analog continuity of telephone or gramophone vibrations—without worrying about sense or telephone love. The implication of this is that digital information is all of the information present in amorous telephone whisperings, whereas everything of the real falls under the category of noise. Lacan greets Shannon's technical slang word 'jam' as "one more symbol"—no more, no less—"It is the first time that confusion as such . . . appears as a fundamental concept."[45]

Structural psychoanalysis has every reason to adopt this stance. Only media technologies allow for the conception of a structure which itself emerges from stochastic disorder, instead of philosophically representing ontological or subjective orderings, which means to continue to write a metaphysics of genealogy.[46] Conversely, the ordering of the signifiers—that is, phonemes, letter-cases or typewriter keys[47]—is simply the other of 'jam.' According to Lacan, it is only due to the existence of the computer as universal machine that "we've gone beyond confusing symbolic intersubjectivity with cosmic intersubjectivity."[48] The symbolic, always transformed back into the God of the theologians or the philosophers in the reception of Lacan among German-speakers, is simply an encoding of the real in cardinal numbers. It is, *expressis verbis*, the world of the information machine.[49] In its primary stages, Shannon's machine calculated the probability of every single letter in the English language, and from these calculations produced a beautiful gibberish. It then went on to take into account the transition probabilities between two letters, that is, digraphs, and the gibberish began to sound a bit more like English. Finally, through the use of mechanical tetragrams (not to be confused with names of God) there arose that 'impression of comprehension' which so loves to hallucinate sense from nonsense.

Lacan's analysis of Poe works with precisely these types of transition probabilities, the major mathematical discovery of Markoff and Post, even if in Derrida's *Post Card* the Markoff-Post post does not appear to have been delivered. The input to the symbolic machine is a throw of the dice in the real because the French *dé*,* to the delight of Mallarmé and Lacan, is derived from the Latin *datum*.[50] And according to the calculation of transition probabilities of transition probabilities, etc., the output is chains or knots, oracles or fairy-sayings, because the French *fée*** is derived from the Latin *fatum*. Straightforward encoding transfers unlimited chance (the real) into a syntax with requirements and exemptions, that is, with laws. As a result, Poe's detective subjects, "grasped in their intersubjectivity," must follow the destiny of the symbolic "more docile than sheep."[51] They are indistinguishable from machines. Although the popular objection maintains that computers cannot think because they must always first be programmed, Lacan counters that human beings, who carry out the same operations as machines, think just as little for the same reason.[52]

As a rule of nature, this destiny would be scandal itself, but Lacan's theory, in distinction to Freud's psychoanalysis, is quite deliberately not a natural science. This is not because the theory concerns human beings, but rather because its unit of measure does not consist of the clocks which established the energy constants in Mayer and in Freud,[53] but of information machines such as dice, gates and digital calculators.[54] When Alan Turing's principle computer circuit of 1936 was being constructed in the course of World War II—a machine which would prove critical to winning the war because it

---

* [Tr.—French for 'dice.']
** [Tr.—French for 'fairy.']

cunningly decoded all of the secret radio transmissions of the Wehrmacht—Turing made the off-hand comment that computers do not answer the physicists' questions concerning nature nearly as "easily" or elegantly as they do the questions of the secret service concerning the enemy.[55] And when Shannon forged a machine English out of Markoff-chains, he did it in the service of American war-time cryptography.[56] Psychoanalysis also became a game of strategy from 1950 onwards, with Lacan's proposal that the conjectural sciences succeed the human sciences, which is to say, that in distinction to the natural sciences, chance rather than randomness is calculated.[57] In the place of a natural "science of what is found at the same place" and hence can be written down with real numbers, a science of the exchange of places as such emerged.[58] However, this discrete mathematics, for example between King and Queen or Minister and Detective in Poe, is war and it is destined to a computer simulation simply because digital calculators can process the yes/no of orders or prohibitions, wishes or fears, more elegantly than the curved lines of nature can.

In his lecture *Psychoanalysis and Cybernetics*, Lacan states the following:

> The one thing which cybernetics clearly highlights is the radical difference between the symbolic and the imaginary orders. A cybernetician recently admitted to me the extreme difficulty one has, whatever is said about it, in translating cybernetically the functions of *Gestalt*, that is the coaptation of good forms. And what is good form in living nature is bad form in the symbolic. [. . .] [O]ne encounters unprecedented difficulties, except in the most artificial manner, in getting one circle to correspond to another by means of a dialogue between two machines.[59]

This is a surprisingly explicit text in 1954, when human scientists had not yet responded to either the word 'pattern recognition' or Shannon's soup of digraphs. And in 1993,* it must be noted that 18 billion US-dollars from the treasury of the Japanese Office of Industrial Affairs have come somewhat closer to Aristotle's ευσυνοπτον or Lacan's good form. A digital signal processor— which, in contrast to the typical personal computer, is capable of

---

* [Tr.—Year in which German version of this essay was published.]

performing parallel multiplications in micro-seconds—probes the
mirror image of mountains or infants in strict accordance with
Shannon and calculates through discrete integration the affinity and
through discrete differentiation the contrast between image fields,
until out of the 'jam' of the real the diagram of a symbolic system of
equations emerges. And if the signal processor were to proceed further and remove image modulations caused by irregularities in the
mirror or ripples in the lake, that is, not only note them but cancel
them out, then Kant's reflective power of decision would finally be
automated—a machine can recognize figures and can distinguish
reflections from given patterns. Fifth generation calculators answer
Manfred Frank's question. (If not, then development will certainly
continue.)

But as the most objective Aesthetic, Hegel's Berlin lecture, could
have already taught us: pattern recognition is a prologue and is
quickly disposed of under the title of natural beauty. Problems of
gestalt recognition are only played out between an individual—which
according to Lacan could just as well be a dove or a chimpanzee—
and its environment. Where tragedy begins (also from the Lacan
lectures), pattern recognition, that is, design, is no longer of consequence. Consciousness is tied to the contingent presence of eyes or
ears, to analog media;[60] from the encoding of the real, on the other
hand, the location of the other necessarily emerges—a combinatorial
matrix of strategies. No one desires or fights (which is the same
thing) if others do not desire or fight. That infants, in contrast to
young chimpanzees, (mis)recognize their mirror image with identificatory exultation, only opens a gap that makes room for war, tragedy
and cybernetics.[61]

In this context, it is already clear that humanity could not have
invented information machines, but to the contrary, is their subject.
Lacan tells his seminar participants directly that they are today, to a
greater extent than they could ever imagine, the subjects of all types
of gadgets from the microscope to "radio-television."[62] If the real is
unconditionally in its place, while the symbolic is the exchange of
place itself,[63] then the exchange of place between the subject and the
specular *I* only opens up spaces of play, which, without implementation, would not stop not writing themselves. Media and information
machines, and culture as their independent variable, exist only when

something "function[s] in the real, independently of any subjectivity."[64] Tombstones, the oldest cultural symbols, remain with the corpse; dice remain on their side after the toss; only the door, or 'gate' in technical slang, permits symbols "to fly with their own wings,"[65] that is, to control presence and absence, high and low, 1 and 0, so that the one can react to the other—sequential circuit mechanism, digital feedback.

Lacan simply says "circuit,"[66] and does not hesitate in equating oscillation, the master clock of every computer system, with scansion, the rhythm of intersubjective or strategic time.[67] An inconspicuous but decisive step from the clock to circuit algebra, from natural to conjectural sciences, from Freud to Lacan. The enigmatic question of the *Project* concerning "an apparatus which would be capable of the complicated performance" of simultaneously transmitting and storing, of being both forgetting and memory, finds its answer at last. In circuit mechanisms, a third and universal function—the algorithm as the sum of logic and control[68]—comprehends the other two media functions. Computers release theory from the age-old constraint of having to conceive of storage as an engram—from cuneiform characters in sound through to sound-grooves in vinyl.

"Suppose," Lacan tells the participants of his seminar in Paris, "that I send a telegram from here to Le Mans, with the request that Le Mans send it back to Tours, from there to Sens, from there to Fontainebleau, and from there to Paris, and so on indefinitely. What's needed is that when I reach the tail of my message, the head should not yet have arrived back. The message must have time to turn around. It turns quickly, it doesn't stop turning, it turns around in circles.

It's funny, this thing turning back on itself. It's called feedback"[69] (and not, as should be noted, reflection).

It makes no difference whether these types of sliding registers are large as in the case of France, incarnate as in the family of the Rat-Man, or miniaturized as in silicon chips. Of primary importance is that information circulates as the presence/absence of absence/presence. And with sufficient storage capacity, that circulation is immortality in technical positivity. Two of Freud's riddles, the indestructibility of desire and the repetition of the death drive, are solved—without the biological miscalculation of instinct[70] or the metaphysics of writing.

That the unconscious is the discourse of the other is already repeated in the feuilletons. But that this discourse of the other is the discourse of the circuit[71] is cited by no one. And yet Lacan's entire teaching would remain mere theory without this clarification or technicality. It is not for nothing that Lacan forbid himself from talking about language with people who did not understand cybernetics.[72] Only when a theory is implemented in algorithms, graphs or knots (as in the later Lacan), is it possible that something stops not writing itself. Only when the Other, which is posited as a circuit mechanism or a set of signifiers, is "the pure subject of modern game theory, and as such perfectly accessible to the calculation of conjecture,"[73] does structural psychoanalysis become science. Because Lacan's wager, even more risky than that of Poe's Minister, literally reads:

> If there is such a thing as the Freudian unconscious, then we must say: if we understand the implications of the teaching of the experiences which he takes from the pathologies of everyday life, then it is not altogether unthinkable that a modern calculator might come to win the game of 'even and odd' beyond all customary proportions by disengaging the phrase that modulates the long-term choices of a subject without his knowing it.[74]

Thus the hermeneuticists with their divinations, as well as the analysts with their efforts at uncovering, can stand down. A computer which could win at dice, in Monte Carlo or anywhere else, would verify Lacan's dictum that the computer is more dangerous to mankind than the atom bomb.[75] Implemented in machines, the theory of risk—and psychoanalysis as conjectural science is nothing other—becomes the risk of theory.

As a result, it would not be difficult to demonstrate that Lacan's famous definition of human language which, in contrast to Frisch's 'wagging dance,'* simultaneously accounts for the subjectivity of the other in the act of address, is just as applicable to Cruise Missiles.[76] And the no less famous reproach that neo- or post-structuralism celebrates the death of the subject could be purged from the world because the remote-controlled subject of the weapon is located within it. According to Norbert Wiener's own testimony, the inven-

---

* [Tr.—'Wagging dance' refers to the communication code employed by bees.]

tion of cybernetics coincides with the automatically controlled weapons of World War II.[77] There is no post-modern; rather, only the or this modern post.[78]

Thus, according to Lacan's most concise statement on Aesthetics, there remain only three things for subjects who do not speak any formal languages: dance, jazz and libido.[79] At least for an inter-war period.

Translated by Stefanie Harris

*T*he present explosion of the signifying scene, which, as we know from Barry McGuire and A. F. N. Dahran, coincides with the so-called Western world, is instead an implosion. The bulk of written texts—including the paper I am actually reading to you— no longer exist in perceivable time and space, but in a computer memory's transistor cells. And since these cells, in the last three decades of Silicon Valley exploits, have shrunk to spatial extensions of less than one micrometer, our writing scene may well be defined by a self-similarity of letters over some six orders of decimal magnitude. This state of affairs does not only make a difference to history, in which, at its alphabetical beginning, a camel and its hebraic letter gamel were just two and a half orders of decimal magnitude apart. It also seems to hide the very act of writing.

As one knows without saying, we do not write anymore. The crazy kind of software engineering that was writing suffered from an incurable *confusion between use and mention*. Up to Hölderlin's time, a mere mention of lightning seems to have been sufficient evidence of its possible poetic use. Nowadays, after this lightning's metamorphosis into electricity, manmade writing passes instead through microscopically written inscriptions, which, in contrast to all historical writing tools, are able to read and write by themselves. The last historical act of writing may well have been the moment when, in the early seventies, the Intel engineers laid out some dozen square meters of blueprint paper (64 square meters in the case of the later 8086) in order to design the hardware architecture of their first integrated microprocessor. This manual layout of two thousand transistors and their interconnections was then miniaturized to the size of an actual chip and, by electro-optical machines, written into silicon layers. Finally, this 4004-microprocessor found its place in the new desk calculators of Intel's Japanese customer,[1] and our postmodern writing scene could begin. Actually, the hardware complexity of microprocessors simply discards such manual design techniques. In order to lay out the next computer generation, the engineers, instead of filling countless meters of blueprint paper, have recourse to Computer Aided Design, that is, to the geometrical or autorouting powers of the actual generation.

In constructing the first integrated microprocessor, however, Intel's Marcian E. Hoff had given an almost perfect demonstration of a Turing machine. After 1937, computing, whether done by men or by machines, can be formalized as a countable set of instructions operating on an infinitely long paper band and the discrete signs thereon. Turing's concept of such a paper machine,[2] whose operations consist only of writing and reading, proceeding and receding, has proven to be the mathematical equivalent of any computable function. Universal Turing machines, when fed the instructions of any other machine, can imitate it effectively. Thus, precisely because eventual differences between hardware implementations do not count anymore, the so-called Church-Turing hypothesis in its strongest or physical form is tantamount to declaring nature itself a universal Turing machine.

This claim in itself has had the effect of duplicating the implosion of hardware by an explosion of software. Programming languages have eroded the monopoly of ordinary language and grown into a new hierarchy of their own. This postmodern Tower of Babel reaches from simple operation codes whose linguistic extension is still a hardware configuration, passing through an assembler whose extension is this very opcode, up to high-level programming languages whose extension is that very assembler. In consequence, far-reaching chains of self-similarities in the sense defined by fractal theory organize the software as well as the hardware of every writing. What remains a problem is only recognizing these layers which, like modern media technologies in general, have been explicitly contrived to evade perception. We simply do not know what our writing does.

To wordprocess a text, that is, to become oneself a paper machine working on an IBM AT under Microsoft DOS, one must first of all buy some commercial files. Unless these files show the file extension names of EXE or of COM, wordprocessing under DOS could never start. The reason is that only COM- and EXE-files entertain a peculiar relation to their proper names. On the one hand, they bear grandiloquent names like WordPerfect, on the other hand, more or less cryptic, because nonvocalized, acronyms like WP. The full name, alas, serves only the advertising strategies of software manufacturers, since DOS as a microprocessor operating system cannot read file names longer than eight letters. That is why the unpronounceable acronym WP, this posthistoric revocation of a fundamental Greek innovation, is not only necessary, but amply sufficient for postmodern wordprocessing. In fact, it seems to bring back truly magical power. WP does what it says. Executable computer files encompass, by contrast not only to WordPerfect but also to big but empty Old European words such as the Mind or the Word, all the routines and data necessary to their self-constitution. Surely, tapping the letter sequence WP and Enter on an AT keyboard does not make the Word perfect, but this simple writing act starts the actual execution of WordPerfect. Such are the triumphs of software.

The accompanying paperware cannot but multiply these magic powers. Written to bridge the gap between formal and everyday languages, electronics and literature, the usual software manuals introduce the program in question as a linguistic agent ruling with near omnipotence over the computer system's resources, address spaces, and other hardware parameters: WP, when called with command line argument X, would change the monitor screen from color A to B, start in mode C, return finally to D, etc. ad infinitum.

In fact, however, these actions of agent WP are virtual ones, since each of them (as the saying goes) has to run under DOS. It is the operating system and, more precisely, its command shell that scans the keyboard for eight-bit file names on the input line, transforms some relative addresses of an eventually retrieved file into absolute ones, loads this new version from external mass memory to the necessary random access space, and finally or temporarily passes execution to the opcode lines of a slave named WordPerfect.

The same argument would hold for DOS, which, in the final analysis, resolves into an extension of the basic input and output system called BIOS. Not only no program, but also no underlying microprocessor system could ever start without the rather incredible autobooting faculty of some elementary functions that, for safety's sake, are burnt into silicon and thus form part of the hardware. Any transformation of matter from entropy to information, from a million sleeping transistors into differences between electronic potentials, necessarily presupposes a material event called reset.

In principle, this kind of descent from software to hardware, from higher to lower levels of observation, could be continued over more and more orders of magnitude. All code operations, despite such metaphoric faculties as call or return, come down to absolutely local string manipulations, that is, I am afraid, *to signifiers of voltage differences*. Formalization in Hilbert's sense does away with theory itself, insofar as "the theory is no longer a system of meaningful propositions, but one of sentences as sequences of words, which are in turn sequences of letters. We can tell [say] by reference to the form alone which combinations of the words are sentences, which sentences are axioms, and which sentences follow as immediate consequences of others."[3]

When meanings come down to sentences, sentences to words, and words to letters, there is no software at all. Rather, there would be no software if computer systems were not surrounded by an environment of everyday languages. This environment, however, ever since a famous and twofold Greek invention, has consisted of letters and coins, of books and bucks.[4] For these good economical reasons, nobody seems to have inherited the humility of Alan Turing, who, in the stone age of computing, preferred to read his machine's outprint in hexadecimal numbers rather than in decimal numbers.[5] On the contrary, the so-called philosophy of the so-called computer community tends systematically to obscure hardware with software, electronic signifiers with interfaces between formal and everyday languages. In all philanthropic sincerity, high-level programming manuals caution against the psychopathological risks of writing assembler code.[6] In all friendliness, "BIOS services" are currently defined as designed to "hide the details of controlling the underlying hardware from your program."[7] Consequently, in a perfect gradualism, DOS services would hide the BIOS, WordPerfect the operating system, and so on and so on until, very recently, two fundamental changes in computer design (or DoD politics) have brought this system of secrecy to closure. First, on an intentionally superficial level, perfect graphic user interfaces, since they dispense with writing itself, hide a whole machine from its users. Second, on the microscopic level of hardware, so-called protection software has been implemented in order to prevent "untrusted programs" or "untrusted users" from any access to the operating system's kernel and input/output channels.[8]

This ongoing triumph of software is a strange reversal of Turing's proof that there can be no mathematically computable problem a simple machine could not solve. Instead, the physical Church-Turing hypothesis, by identifying physical hardware with the algorithms forged for its computation, has finally gotten rid of hardware itself. As a result, software has successfully occupied the empty place and profited from its obscurity. The ever-growing hierarchy of high-level programming languages works exactly the same way as one-way functions in recent mathematical cryptography. Such functions, when used in their straightforward form, can be computed in reasonable time, for instance, in a time growing only in polynomial expressions with the function's complexity. The time needed for its inverse form, however (that is, for reconstructing from the function's output its presupposed input), would grow at exponential and therefore unviable rates. One-way functions, in other words, hide an algorithm from its result. For software, this cryptographic effect offers a convenient way to bypass the fact that by virtue of Turing's proof the concept of mental property as applied to algorithms has become meaningless. Precisely because software does not exist as a machine-independent faculty, software as a commercial or American medium insists on its status as property all the more. Every license, every dongle, every trademark registered for WP, as well as for WordPerfect, proves the functionality of one-way functions. In this country, notwithstanding all mathematical tradition, even a copyright claim for algorithms has recently succeeded. And, finally, IBM has done research on a mathematical formula for measuring the distance in complexity between an algorithm and its output. Whereas in the good old days of Shannon's mathematical theory of information, the maximum in information coincided strangely with maximal unpredictability, or noise,[9] the new IBM measure, called logical

depth, has been defined as follows: "The value of a message ...
appears to reside not in its information (its absolutely unpredictable
parts), nor in its obvious redundancy (verbatim repetitions, unequal
digit frequencies), but rather in what may be called its buried redundancy—parts predictable only with difficulty, things the receiver
could in principle have figured out without being told, but only at
considerable cost in money, time, or computation. In other words,
the value of a message is the amount of mathematical or other work
plausibly done by its originator, which the receiver is saved from having to repeat."[10] Thus, logical depth in its mathematical rigor could
advantageously replace all the old, everyday language definitions of
originality, authorship, and copyright in their necessary inexactness,
were it not for the fact that precisely this algorithm intended to compute the cost of algorithms in general is Turing-uncomputable
itself.[11]

Under these tragic conditions, criminal law, at least in Germany,
has recently abandoned the very concept of software as mental property; instead, it defines software as necessarily a material thing. The
high court's reasoning, according to which no computer program
could ever run without the corresponding electrical charges in silicon
circuitry,[12] can illustrate the fact that the virtual undecidability
between software and hardware by no means follows, as systems the-
orists would probably like to believe, from a simple variation of
observation on points. On the contrary, there are good grounds to
assume the indispensability and, consequently, the priority of hardware in general.

Only in Turing's paper *On Computable Numbers with an
Application to the Entscheidungsproblem* does there exist a machine with
unbounded resources in space and time, with an infinite supply of
raw paper and no constraints on computation speed. All physically
feasible machines, in contrast, are limited by these parameters in
their very code. The inability of Microsoft DOS to tell more than the
first eight letters of a file name such as WordPerfect gives just a trivial
or obsolete illustration of a problem that has provoked not only
increasing incompatibilities between the different generations of
eight-bit, sixteen-bit, and thirty-two-bit microprocessors, but also a
near impossibility of digitalizing the body of real numbers formerly
known as nature.[13]

According to Brosl Hasslacher of Los Alamos National Laboratory:

> This means [that] we use digital computers whose architecture is given to us in the form of a physical piece of machinery, with all its artificial constraints. We must reduce a continuous algorithmic description to one codable on a device whose fundamental operations are countable, and we do this by various forms of chopping up into pieces, usually called discretization . . . The compiler then further reduces this model to a binary form determined largely by machine constraints.
>
> The outcome is a discrete and synthetic microworld image of the original problem, whose structure is arbitrarily fixed by a differencing scheme and computational architecture chosen at random. The only remnant of the continuum is the use of radix arithmetic, which has the property of weighing bits unequally, and for nonlinear systems is the source of spurious singularities.
>
> This is what we actually do when we compute up a model of the physical world with physical devices. This is not the idealized and serene process that we imagine when usually arguing about the fundamental structures of computation, and very far from Turing machines.[14]

Thus, instead of pursuing the physical Church-Turing hypothesis and "injecting an algorithmic behavior into the behavior of the physical world for which there is no evidence,"[15] one has rather to compute what has been called "the price of programmability" itself. This all-important property of being programmable has, in all evidence, nothing to do with software; it is an exclusive feature of hardwares, more or less suited as they are to house some notation system. When Claude Shannon, in 1937, proved in what is probably the most consequential M.A. thesis ever written that simple telegraph switching relays can implement, by means of their different interconnections, the whole of Boolean algebra,[16] such a physical notation system was established. And when the integrated circuit, developed in the 1970s out of Shockley's transistor, combined on one and the same chip silicon as a controllable resistor with its own oxide as an almost perfect isolator, the programmability of matter could finally "take control," just as Turing had predicted.[17] Software, if it existed, would be just a billion-dollar deal based on the cheapest elements on earth. For in their combination on chip, silicon and its oxide provide perfect hardware architectures. That is to say, millions of basic elements work under almost the same physical conditions, especially as regards the most critical, namely, temperature-dependent degradations, and yet electrically all of them are highly isolated from each other. Only this paradoxical relation between two physical parameters, thermal continuity and electrical discretization on chip, allows integrated circuits to be not only finite-state machines like so many other devices on earth, but to approximate that Universal Discrete Machine into which its inventor's name has long disappeared.

This structural difference can easily be illustrated. "A combination lock," for instance, "is a finite automaton, but it is not ordinarily decomposable into a base set of elementary-type components that can be reconfigured to simulate an arbitrary physical system. As a consequence it is not structually programmable, and in this case it is effectively programmable only in the limited sense that its state can be set for achieving a limited class of behaviors." On the contrary, "a digital computer used to simulate a combination lock is structurally programmable since the behavior is achieved by synthesizing it from a canonical set of primitive switching components."[18]

Switching components, however, be they telegraph relays, tubes, or, finally, microtransistor cells, pay a prize for their very composability. Confronted as they are with a continuous environment of weather, waves, and wars, digital computers can cope with this real number avalanche only by adding element to element. However, the growth rate of possible interconnections between these elements, that is, of the computing power as such, has proven to have as its upper bound a square root function. In other words, it cannot even "keep up with polynomial growth rates in problem size."[19] Thus, the very isolation between digital or discrete elements accounts for a drawback in connectivity that otherwise, "according to current force laws" as well as to the basics of combinatorial logics, would be bounded only by a maximum equalling the square number of all elements involved.[20]

Precisely this maximal connectivity, on the other, physical side, defines nonprogrammable systems, be they waves or beings. That is why these systems show polynomial growth rates in complexity and, consequently, why only computations done on nonprogrammable machines could keep up with them. In all evidence, this hypothetical, but all too necessary, type of machine would constitute sheer hardware, a physical device working amidst physical devices and subject to the same bounded resources. Software in the usual sense of an ever-feasible abstraction would not exist any longer. The procedures of these machines, though still open to an algorithmic notation, should have to work essentially on a material substrate whose very connectivity would allow for cellular reconfigurations. And even though this "substrate can also be described in algorithmic terms, by means of simulation," its "characterization is of such immense importance for the effectiveness . . . and so closely connected with choice of hardware," that programming it will have little to do any longer with approximated Turing machines.[21]

In what I have tried to describe as badly needed machines that are probably not too far in the future (and drawing quite heavily on recent computer science), certain Dubrovnik observers' eyes might be tempted to recognize, under evolutionary disguises or not, the familiar face of man. Maybe. At the same time, however, our equally familiar silicon hardware obeys many of the requisites for such highly connected, nonprogrammable systems. Between its million transistor cells, some million to the power of two interactions always already take place. There is electron diffusion; there is quantum-mechanical tunneling all over the chip.[22] Technically, however, these interactions are still treated in terms of system limitations, physical side effects, and so on. To minimize all the noise that it would be impossible to eliminate is the price we pay for structurally programmable machines. The inverse strategy of maximizing noise would not only find the way back from IBM to Shannon, it may well be the only way to enter that body of real numbers originally known as chaos.

PROTECTED MODE

*T*he air-to-surface battle of 1991 demonstrated once again that among postmodern strategies of appearance, none is as effective as the simulation that there really is software. Until the proof to the contrary on the field of combat—where computers unambiguously revealed themselves as hardware for the destruction of Iraqi hardware (as durable goods are still called in everyday English)—advertising brochures and media conferences spread the fairytale of a development of software that would become increasingly more innocuous and user-friendly, more spiritual and intelligent, until one day in the not so distant future it would effectively lead to German idealism—that is, it would become human.

And that is why software, the billion-dollar enterprise out of one of the cheapest elements on Earth, makes every attempt to prevent the aforenamed humans from ever even coming into contact with the corresponding hardware. With Word 5.0 on a no-name AT 386 and (as one so nicely says) under the operating system Microsoft DOS 3.3, one can write entire essays on precisely these three entities without even suspecting the strategy of appearance. For one writes—the 'under' says it already—as a subject or underling of the Microsoft Corporation.

This worm's-eye view did not always prevail. In the good old days when microprocessor pins were still big enough for simple soldering irons, even literary critics could do whatever they wished with Intel's 8086 Processor. Even standard chips, which at that time still required one hundred thirty-three cycles for the multiplication of a single whole number, could be raised to the processing speed of primitive signal processors through a variety of strategies: not differentiating between RAM and ROM, misusing both of the stack registers as universal registers, avoiding any interrupts, employing the wait-state for other than its intended purpose, and so on. The silicon chip, which was as stupid as the hobbyist and user, could accommodate all of this because the Von Neumann architecture recognizes no difference between commands and data. In order to get a program to run, the user had to first forget everything pertaining to mathematical elegance or a closed solution that still haunted his mind from his school-days. He even forgot his ten fingers, and translated all decimal numbers that would play a part in the program into monotonous columns of binary digits. As a result, he forgot the immediacy of the task as such and pored over data sheets in order to translate the commands IN, OUT, etc. (already formulated in English, of course), into their op-codes. This is an activity that only Alan Mathison Turing—when he finally had his universal discrete machine of 1936 at his technical disposition one World War later—is said to have preferred over all mnemonic aids and higher programming languages.[1] But once this expulsion of spirit and language was completed, the machine's stupidity equalled that of its user.

To be sure, this so-called machine language ran a million times faster than the pencil with which the user had pieced together the zeros and ones from Intel's data sheets. To be sure, the flip-flops whose infinitely repeated pattern covers the silicon chip took up a million times less space than on paper. But with that, the differences between computers and paper machines, as Turing had renamed humanity,[2] were also already fully accounted for.

Those good old times are gone forever. In the meantime, through the use of keywords like user-interface, user-friendliness or even data protection, the industry has damned humanity to remain human. Possible mutations of this humanity into paper machines are obstructed by multiple malicious tricks. First of all, Microsoft's user data sheets switched over to designating the Assembler grammalogue as the maximum demand or machine approximation that would be granted, meaning that op-codes would no longer be made public.[3] Secondly, the pertinent industry publications "assure us that even under the best circumstances, one would quickly go crazy from programming in machine language."[4] Thirdly, and lastly, these same publications already consider it criminal "to write a procedure for the calculation of sine in Assembler, of all things."[5]

At the risk of having already gone crazy long ago, the only thing one can deduce from all of this is that software has obviously gained in user-friendliness as it more closely approximates the cryptological ideal of the one-way function.[6] The higher and more effortless the programming languages, the more insurmountable the gap between those languages and a hardware that still continues to do all of the work. This is a trend that probably cannot be adequately explained either through technical advances or through the formalities of a theory of models, but rather, like all cryptology, has strategic functions. While on the one hand it remains possible in principle to write user-software or cryptograms with a knowledge of codes or algorithms, on the other and user-friendly concealed hand it is by now impossible to decipher the product specifications of the finished product or even to change these specifications. The users fall victim to a malicious mathematical trick that Hartley, one-time head of Bell Labs, is said to have already instituted while in the slump of old-age—the fact that one can no longer examine the operands of many of the operations.[7] The sum hides the addends, the product the factors, and so forth.

This mathematical trick is ideally suited to software. In an era that has long since abandoned the phantoms of creators or authors, but which through copyright passionately holds on to such historical ghosts for strong financial reasons, the trick becomes a goldmine. In any case, the subjects of the Microsoft Corporation did not simply fall from the sky, but first had to be produced like all of their media-historical predecessors—the readers of books, film audiences and TV viewers. The only problem now is how their subjugation can be hidden from the subjects in order that they fall in step with the global triumphal march.

In the domain of the politics of knowledge, the answer follows a proven recipe for the success of modern democracies, while in the technical arena it has changed the hardware of the microprocessors themselves. As concerns the politics of knowledge, perhaps only Siemens' engineers can tell it like it is, as Klaus-Dieter Thies did in the *80186-Handbuch*:

> Today's modern 16-bit micro-processors assume in increasing amounts tasks that are assigned to classic mini-computers in the typical application range. Thus in multi-user systems, it is necessary that the programs and data of individual users are isolated, just as the operating

system must be protected against user software. In order to give every
individual user the possibility of implementing his software
independently of the number of other users, and in order to give him the
impression that the computer is only there for him, it is essential to
allocate the CPU to the individual programs through multi-tasking, which,
however, can only remain hidden from the user if the CPU is extremely
powerful.[8]

Thus, according to this Siemens version—which also circulates at
IBM-Germany—Intel did not propel the operating-frequencies of
the 80286 and the 80386 to levels between 12 and 33 megahertz in
order that they correspond to the demands of professional users or
even to the Pentagon's specifications for electronic warfare,[9] but
rather in order to entangle civilian users in an opaque simulation.
Multitasking should then, like the hedgehog in the fairy tale, delude
the user into believing that only a single hedgehog or process is run-
ning, and, above all, that this race or process only benefits a single
rabbit or user.* This is the same tune by which the novels and poetry
of Goethe's time promised their male, and before that their female,
readers that the texts were uniquely addressed to them; it is the same
tune by which modern politics presents itself to the public as its
absolute antithesis—that is, individuals.

In contrast with traditional simulations which all had an absolute
limit in the power or impotence of everyday language, today's electronic simulation—according to which every microprocessor should
only be there for a single user—also employs hardware. From the
80286 on, Intel's processors are equipped with a Protected Mode

* [Tr.—The story of the Hare and the Hedgehog (*Der Hase und Der Igel*) is
taken from Grimm's fairy tales. A hare and a hedgehog argue who is the fastest
runner and decide to wager a piece of gold and a bottle of brandy over a foot race.
The hedgehog secretly tells his wife to hide in a furrow at the end of the field which
is to serve as the race track. The hare and the male hedgehog start the race together,
but just as the hare is approaching the finish line, the hedgehog's wife pops up and
calls out, "I'm already here!" The hare insists on a rematch in the other direction.
This time the female hedgehog begins the race with him, and as the hare approaches
the finish line, her husband pops up and calls out, "I'm already here!" The hare
demands still more races to prove his speed, only to be beaten each time by the
hedgehog(s). The hare finally drops dead in the middle of the seventy-fourth race,
and the hedgehog and his wife take their prizes and return home. (*The Grimms'
German Folk Tales*, "The Hare and the Hedgehog," trans. Francis P. Magoun, Jr. and
Alexander H. Krappe (Carbondale: Southern Illinois UP, 1960) 604–7.)]

that (in the words of the Siemens engineer) protects the operating system from the users, and through this protection, first allows the users to be deceived. What began as the simple capability of switching between the supervisor and the user stack in Motorola's 68000[10]—naturally, a secret rival system—is extended to system-wide procedure in the separation of Real Mode and Protected Mode. Different command sets, different address possibilities, different register sets, even different command execution times, henceforth separate the wheat from the chaff, the system design from the users. Thus it is precisely in the silicon on which the prophets based all their hopes for a microprocessed democracy of the future that the elementary dichotomy of modern media technologies again returns. A German civil radio network, for example, was permitted from the day when the postal service of the Reich could credibly promise the armed forces that the consumer radios of 1923, which were capable of any possible transmission, would never be able to disrupt military-industrial radio communication because an automatic encoding machine—which Turing's proto-computer would only put out of action in World War II—had just been invented.

The innovation of Intel's Protected Mode consists only in having transferred this logic from the military-industrial realm into that of information itself. The distinction between the two operating levels is not only quantitative—as for example among the varying ranges of operating temperatures for commercial, industrial and military silicon chips (in this indicative ranking)—but more importantly, qualitative because the CPU itself works with priorities, prohibitions, privileges and handicaps of which it constantly keeps a record, though only in Protected Mode of course. That such controls, which themselves require time, are not exactly conducive to the general goal of increasing data output goes without saying. In Protected Mode, the same interrupt requires up to eight times more cycles than in Real Mode, but evidently a high technology can only be passed on to end users and "non-trustworthy" programs (as Intel calls them) under these circumstances, even if and precisely because the signal processing, the military-industrial dimension of computers,[11] is slowed down by bureaucratic data processing. Although there may no longer be any written prohibitory signs that guarantee a power gap, the binary system itself encodes the distinction between commands and data, what the system permits and what, conversely, is prohibited to user programs. John von Neumann's classic architecture, which made absolutely no distinction between commands and data—unnecessary in an era when all existing computers were still state-secrets—disappears under four consecutively numbered privilege levels. It is for good ironical reason that the only incorruptible German publication in the area of computer applications wrote: "Even if all the talk is of privileges, higher privileged code segments, privilege violations and the like, you are not reading the political manifesto of a former official of the SED,* but rather the explanation of the security concept of the 80386!"[12]

Political manifestos, as the name already indicates, were performed in the dominant sphere of everyday language; for that reason, the privileges with which they took offense are, at least since November, 1989, meaningless. On the other hand, the privilege levels of Intel's so-called 'flagship'—this Cocom-List** transferred to the very heart of the binary system—contributed, even more so than the innundation of Eastern Europe with television, only to the liquidation of politically based privileges. A short essay by Carl Schmitt, *Gespräch über die Macht und den Zugang zum Machthaber [A Conversation on Power and Access to the Dictator]*, culminated in the thesis that power is reducible to its conditions of access: the antechamber, the office or, more recently, the front office consisting of typewriter, telephone and secretary.[13] With this authority and through this authority, conversations could in fact still be conducted; however, technically implemented privilege levels draw their power precisely from mute efficacy. In order to take advantage of his memory reserves beyond DOS in a sort of posthistorical metaphysics, the 80386-user installs one of the available user-friendly utilities, loads the debugger with a built-in program that still ran yesterday without any problem, and discovers that the new

---

* [Tr.—Sozialistische Einheitspartei Deutschlands: United Socialist Party of Germany; political party of the former GDR.]

** [Tr.—'Cocom' is the abbreviation for the Coordinating Committee for East-West-Trade-Policy. The 'Cocom-List' is an embargo list drawn up by the majority of NATO members and Japan, which specifies those goods and technologies which because of their strategic military sensitivity are prohibited export to East-block countries.]

installation not only manages memory as promised, but concurrently, and without any warning, has locked all privileged commands.[14] As Mick Jagger already so pointedly formulated it, instead of what he wants, the user always only gets what he needs (according to the industry standard, that is).

As a result, a double shadows the analysis of power systems, that immense assignment that was Foucault's legacy. To begin with, one should attempt to abandon the usual practice of conceiving of power as a function of so-called society, and, conversely, attempt to construct sociology from the chip's architectures. For the present at least, it is a reasonable assumption to analyze the privilege levels of a microprocessor as the reality of precisely that bureaucracy that ordered its design and called for its mass application.[15] It is no coincidence that the separation between supervisor level and user level at Motorola, and Protected Mode and Real Mode at Intel, came about in the same years when the United States of America embarked on the construction of an impermeable two-class system. (One recognizes the Embedded Controller in every improved hotel door-lock in New York.) It is no coincidence that in the 80386, it is precisely the input and output commands that are protected by the highest privilege level—in an empire in which the public views the rest of the world only through the haze of television news, even the thought of foreign policy is a privilege of the government. This is probably also the reason why the latest varieties of systems theory simply deny, at the highest theoretical level, the finding that information systems control input and output. When all is said and done, this would also be a good reason for computer scientists from other countries—that is, somewhere between Japan and Europe—to oppose the US bureaucracy submerged in silicon with other possible bureaucracies. Whether there are better ones is beside the point because they would in any case also have to be bureaucracies; but a competition between different systems and different bureaucracies would as such already allow the subjects of MS-DOS to breathe a little easier.

Of course, as long as the celebration of the triumph of IBM-compatibility continues, the demand is for strategy, more so than sociology. With its move out of front offices and everyday language into the micrometer realm, power has also changed the processes and the working surfaces. The unequivocal 'no' of an access denied is no longer a given in binary code, simply because the entire hierarchical standard of self-similar program levels—from the highest programming language down to elementary machine code[16]—rests completely flat on the material. In silicon itself there can be, to borrow from Lacan, no other of the other,[17] which is also to say, no protection from the protection. Furthermore, the hidden segment registers that keep a record of all access rights of all programs of a system, must be accessible in order to work. Legible traces even remain when the CPU sets these registers to zero[18] in the case of privilege violations that occur despite all possible and explicit commands. At the level of the machine, then, protection mechanisms have no absolutely protected hiding-place. Because microprocessors must despite everything remain usable to users, that is, communicate with them, Intel's Protected Mode describes a classic power dilemma.

According to the *Programmer's Reference Manual*, even tasks of the operating system are not permitted to enjoy the privilege of freely accessing tasks of a lower privilege level. Because the traffic over the stack runs symmetrically or on a democratic basis—that is, the caller must PUSH the same number of bytes as the program that has been called POPS—the lower privileged task could attempt to maintain control after its completion, and smuggle itself up to the level of the higher task through a technically simulated program return. For that reason, the Intel engineers considered it safer to employ the Boolean concept of gates and to convert to a bureaucratic control of access.

What such prohibitions conclusively demonstrate, however, is only the impossibility of perfect access control. In the good old microprocessor days when the difference between system and application itself resided in the silicon into which it was literally burned— the system in ROM, the application in RAM—there was nothing to assail it. Once the difference has been rendered programmable, however, it is already vulnerable to all sorts of circumventions.

Intel's *Programmer's Reference Manual* repeats approximately 170 times—at each individual 80386 command—the warning that Interrupt 13 is triggered in Real Mode as soon as any part of the command operator exceeds the actual 20-bit address field. In other words (but still those of the company itself), in Real Mode the 80386 would only run as a faster AT.[19] In the case of contraventions, a draconian sentence is invoked—"all violations of privilege that do not cause a more specific exception" trigger a monstrosity with the name of "General Protection Exception."[20] But neither the 170 repetitions in the manual nor their countless transcriptions in a computer book market—which for its part seems to offer only partial mechanical translations under the names of fictitious authors—make this warning any more true. A single subordinate clause in the manual discloses that any address boundaries in Real Mode are no more and no less than presuppositions programmed into the system start-up. This sentence disappears, of course, from all translations, summaries, popularizations and user handbooks, simply to conceal from the subjects of Microsoft its logical reversal— namely, that presuppositions are easily changed.[21] Instead of the deliberately low default value that the CPU automatically loads into the hidden sections of its segment register at every reversion to Real Mode, programs could also set completely different values. Every 386-AT goes into all four of the possible operating modes with 100 lines of code—into Protected Modes with 32- or 16-bit segment width, but also into Real Modes with the corresponding segment width. As a result, the Real Mode with 32-bit segments could produce the most compact and thereby fastest code by far, although there is no mention in the data sheets and manuals of its being even a possibility,[22] to say nothing of real existing operating systems of the 80386.

One hundred lines of Assembler, but only of Assembler, solve the problem of a postmodern metaphysics. At the risk of going crazy, they lead through MS-DOS beyond MS-DOS. Along with the infamous sound barrier at which the operating memory in DOS remains limited to a ridiculous mega-byte, all of the advantages for which Windows is praised dwindle to nothing. In a drastic paradox, it is precisely the most antiquated of all operating systems that provides the trap door out of the operating system. Intel's built-in blockades—which engage immediately in more complex operating systems such as UNIX, and subsequently even pick out those hundred program lines as illegal commands and refuse them—are powerless against stupidity.

Thus a machine can simultaneously do less and more than its data sheets admit. It is not only this aforesaid trick that expands the addressable storage capacity from one mega-byte to four giga-bytes—a 4,000 percent increase—but in addition, the 80386 has at least two "undocumented commands" that the data sheet intentionally keeps secret,[23] and in the 32-bit Real Mode, at least one operation that it disregards without any intention whatsoever. Such chaos does not reign at the elevated level of information science, where the computability of Finite State Machines and their ability to predict is argued over in general, but rather at the modest level of the engineer's empiricism. Only because, as Morgenstern said, "nothing can be that is not allowed to be," mere presuppositions are sold to the users as absolutes. In similar fashion, the Reichs-post at one time was careful to insure that only detector equipment and no tube equipment would be sold to civilian radio consumers of the early '20s—if this were not the case, the listeners would have been able to transmit and thereby disrupt military-industrial radio traffic.

In other words, information science appears to be confronted with internal information obstacles. Information science must refer to the actual domain of code, even if the theory could generate completely different models (and should). And despite the will and belief of the code's developers, decodings are just as possible as they are rare. Long after the end of the print monopoly and authorship, the phantom of humanity apparently makes sure that mere opinions or even assertions of protection will continue to be recorded, as opposed to actually cracking the codes. A systems program must be created precisely to this end—to be used by programmers, to begin with, but in principle for machines as well. Just as it is possible, and in the meantime also realizable, for programs generated by chance to compete with each other according to purely Darwinian rules, the empirical control characteristics of the machines would first have to be deciphered and then contrasted with their data sheets.

At least to the literary critic, it appears that this, as it were, military-strategic field of information science has a big future before it. Specifically, it could proceed on a strictly technical plane according to methods similar to those which Foucault's discourse analysis proposed for utterances and texts. Rather than investigating the meaning of a sign-chain as interpretation or investigating the rules of a sign-chain as grammar, discourse analysis is quite simply concerned with sign-chains inasfar as they exist and do not, on the contrary, not exist. Whether meanings are merely a pedagogical-philosophical fiction, and whether grammar rules comprehend completely and are completely comprehensible, is beside the point. But that the two words 'grammar' and 'rule' are connected in a single verbal expression is and remains a fact.

Johannes Lohmann, the renowned language scholar and Indo-Germanist, already proposed thirty years ago that one look for the historical condition of possibility of programming languages in the simple fact that they exist in English, and furthermore that they exist only in English verbs such as 'Read' and 'Write,' that is, verbs which in distinction to the Latin *amo amas amat* and so forth have shed all conjugation forms. According to Lohmann, these context-free word blocks may well stem from the historically unique confusion of Norman and Saxon in old England, but that is no hindrance to their being translated into context-free mnemonics and ultimately into computer op-code. As everyone knows, the endless litany of 'read' and 'write,' 'move' and 'load' is called Assembler.

A discourse analysis whose elements are obviously not only words but also codes, would, of course, level the sacred distinction between everyday languages and formal languages. In light of the wonderful "orthogonality" that, for example, Motorola's processor series flaunts since the 68000, that would be heresy. The history of Protected Mode as a half-compatible, half-incompatible extrapolation of good old standards could, however, teach us that codes are subject to the same opacity as everyday languages. As everyone knows, in the 8086 there were more than a few commands that were synonymous with other commands and that were only obviated through operating speed. It made a significant temporal difference whether a universal register or an accumulator wrote its contents into memory. However, Intel's new generation de-optimized precisely this speed advantage, while still permitting the synonymous commands to survive for compatibility reasons. Thus the code has achieved a redundancy that everyday language already boasted in Frege's wonderful example of "evening star" and "morning star."

As history has shown, this redundancy can only increase if machine codes are to remain compatible over the generations. In contrast to everyday languages—and especially to German where there are neither (to deliver concurrently two autonomous examples) restrictions on the length of a word [Wortlängenbegrenzungen] nor restrictions on the length of word combinations [Wortkombinationslängenbegrenzungen]—all elements of a command set are of a finite length and for that reason also of a countable quantity. As a result, there would be no more room for the extended commands of the 80386, for example, if there were no authorization for over-length. Under these circumstances, the codes begin to grow wild, no matter how economical or orthogonal their first design may have been. The silver chip-surface, concurrently the model and the main field of application of all topological optimizations, loses its mathematical transparence—it becomes a Babylonian tower in which the ruins of towers that have already been demolished remain built-in. Protected Mode as both the enemy and co-existent partner of a Real Mode that has already been superceded technically for some time is computer history *on chip*. And David Hilbert's dreamlike program to clear out the opacity of everyday language once and for all through formalization is undone not only at the clear, axiomatic level of Gödel or Turing, but already by the empiricism of the engineers. Codes with compatibility problems begin to grow wild and to adopt the same opacity of everyday languages that have made people their subjects for thousands of years. The wonderful term source code becomes literal truth.

To be sure, a discourse analysis can neither tame nor debug such wild growth. But it is quite possibly more efficient simply to count on its happening. Turing's old idea of allowing the machines themselves to roll out their code may well have already secretly come true. Precisely because "the complex function of highly integrated circuits (aside from memory-ICs) can no longer, as in the case of a simple, logical connection, be checked by testing all of the possible input signal combinations,"[24] tests that are independent of the producer are in order. Resistances—recently raised to a system by US patent law—should not prevent the publication of unedited test results, patches and detour techniques, of which there is no comment in the official documentation. That would be information about information science, whether for peace or not.

Hugo von Hofmannsthal once ascribed the ability to read "what has never been written" to the "wonderful being" called Man. Similar crypto-analyses must become universal and mechanical in the chaos of codes that begins with the world-historical dismissal of everyday language in favor of a universal discrete machine.

Translated by Stefanie Harris

N O T E S

Preface by Saul Ostrow

1. Among these are "Media and Drugs in Pynchon's Second World War,"
    which is translated here by Stefanie Harris but has also been translated by
    Michael Wutz and Geoffrey Winthrop-Young and is included in *Materialities
    of Twentieth-Century Narrative* (Cornell University Press, 1997) edited by
    Joseph Tabbi (University of Illinois, Chicago) and Michael Wurtz (Weber
    State University).
2. *C Theory, Post-Modern Culture, et al.*
3. *October* #41 (Summer 1987); pubished here in its entirety.
4. Of these, only *Discourse Networks 1800/1900* is available in English. Published
    by Stanford University Press, 1990 (trans. Michael Metteer with Chris
    Cullens).

Introduction by John Johnston

1. Friedrich Kittler, *Grammophon Film Typewriter* (Berlin: Bosemann, 1986). A
    translation of the first chapter, entitled "Gramophone, Film, Typewriter,"
    was published in *October* #41 (1987); it is republished here, with a new
    translation of the book's preface.
2. Friedrich Kittler and Laurence Rickels, "Spooky Electricity," *Artforum*
    (December 1992), 67.
3. Friedrich Kittler, "Benn's Poetry—'A Hit in the Charts': Song Under
    Conditions of Media Technologies," *SubStance* 61 (1990), 11.
4. As Kittler asserts in "A Discourse on Discourse," *Stanford Literary Review* 3,
    no. 1 (Spring 1986), 159: "The data processing of a given society can be
    reconstructed by analyzing its artistic media. Being less formal than its
    systems of knowledge, those media display and propagate the elementary
    regulations that culturalize the natives of that society. Before anything can be
    known, there must be rules or signs for identifying things as signs or data;
    there must be rules defining which persons or devices will be acceptable as
    source, as emitter, as channel, and as receiver of information. [Claude]
    Shannon's four functions are historically variable, in other words: they have
    to be instituted."
5. Kittler, "A Discourse on Discourse," 163.

6. Friedrich Kittler, *Discourse Networks 1800/1900*, trans. Michael Metteer with Chris Cullens (Stanford: Stanford University Press, 1990), 305. Published originally in German as *Aufschreibesysteme 1800/1900* in 1985 by Wilhelm Fink Verlag. All subsequent citations will be from the American edition, with page numbers inserted directly into the text, following the abbreviation DN.

7. See Marshall McLuhan, *Understanding Media* (New York: McGraw-Hill, 1964), and Paul Virilio, *War and Cinema: The Logistics of Perception* (London and New York: Verso, 1989).

8. See, for example, Kevin Kelly, *Out of Control* (New York: Addison Wesley, 1994) and N. Katherine Hayles, "Vie artificielle et culture litteraire," in *Théorie, Littérature, enseignement* 12 (1994), 69–90.

9. In his foreword to *Discourse Networks 1800/1900*, David E. Wellbery points out several ways in which poststructuralism serves as the "operating equipment, the hardware" (viii) for Kittler's book.

10. See Samuel Weber, "Introduction" to Daniel Paul Schreber, *Memoirs of My Nervous Illness* (Cambridge: Harvard University Press, 1988).

11. Sigmund Freud, "Psycho-analytic Notes on an Autobiographical Account of a Case of Paranoia." In *The Standard Edition of the Complete Psychological Works of Sigmund Freud*, vol. 12, ed. and trans. James Strachey, (London: Hogarth Press, 1953–74).

12. See Michel Foucault, *The Archaeology of Knowledge and the Discourse on Language*, trans. A. M. Sheridan Smith (New York: Pantheon, 1972).

13. For the details, see *Discourse Networks 1800/1900*, 31ff.

14. In his very useful foreword to *Discourse Networks 1800/1900*, David E. Wellbery describes the "Republic of Scholars" (that is, the previous discourse network) as follows: "We are dealing here with the system of learning that developed in early modern Europe in the wake of printing, a system in which knowledge was defined in terms of authority and erudition, in which the doctrine of rhetoric governed discursive production, in which patterns of communication followed the lines of social stratification, in which books circulated in a process of limitless citation, variation and translation, in which universities were not yet state institutions and the learned constituted a special (often itinerant) class with unique privileges, and in which the concept of literature embraced virtually all of what was written" (*DN*, xviii).

15. See Friedrich Kittler, "The Mechanized Philosopher" in *Looking After Nietzsche*, ed. Laurence A. Rickels (Albany: State University of New York Press, 1990), 195–207.

16. Wellbery makes this point in his foreword to *Discourse Networks 1800/1900* before offering an analysis of Kittler's style.

17. Martin Heidegger, *Parmenides* (Bloomington: Indiana University Press, 1992).

18. Martin Heidegger, *Holzwege* (Frankfurt am Main: Klostermann, 1950), 272.

19. The passage is quoted by Jonathan Crary in *Techniques of the Observer* (Cambridge: MIT Press).

20. Crary, 94.

21. Michel Foucault, *Discipline and Punish*, trans. Alan Sheridan (New York: Pantheon, 1979), 194.

22. See also *War in the Age of Intelligent Machines* (New York: Zone books, 1991), wherein Manuel De Landa traces the efforts on the part of the military to get human beings "out of the loop."

23. Jacques Derrida, "Freud and the Scene of Writing," in *Writing and Difference*, trans. Alan Bass (Chicago: University of Chicago Press, 1978). Page numbers for quotations will be inserted directly into the text, following the abbreviation WO.

24. See Bernard Stiegler, *La technique et le temps, Vol. 2. La désorientation* (Paris: Galilee, 1996), for a further development of this Derridean problematic.

25. Friedrich Kittler, "The World of the Symbolic—A World of the Machine," in this edition.

26. Jacques Lacan, *Le Séminaire, Livre II: Le moi dans la théorie de Freud et dans le technique de la psychanalyse* (Paris: Editions de Seuil, 1978).

27. The Turing Machine, or rather Turing's concept of such a machine, is an attempt to address the question of whether there are (or can be) general formalized procedures or algorithms for solving all mathematical and logical problems. It is usually said to date from 1936, the publication date of Turing's paper "On computable numbers, with an application to the *Entscheidungsproblem*." The first general idea of such a machine is usually traced back to Leibniz's notion of a *characteristica universalis*, or logical calculus. For a lucid exposition of the nature and function of the Turing Machine, see Roger Penrose's "Algorithms and Turing Machines," in *The Emperor's New Mind* (New York and Oxford: Oxford University Press, 1989), 30–73.

28. Kittler makes this point in "Spooky Electricity," 67.

29. In *A Thousand Plateaus*, trans. Brian Massumi (Minneapolis: University of Minnesota Press, 1987), Gilles Deleuze and Félix Guattari define the "machinic phylum" as "materiality, natural or artificial, and both simultaneously; it is matter in movement, in flux, in variation, matter as a conveyor of singularities and traits of expression" (409). The new machinic phylum referred to is the one made possible by silicon, and out of which emerge new kinds of human-machine assemblages.

Preface to Gramophone, Film, Typewriter

1. Gottfried Benn, April 10, 1941, *Briefe. Erster Band: Briefe an F.W. Oelze*, eds. Harald Steinhagen and Jürgen Schröder (Wiesbaden: 1977–1980), 267.

2. On the precision of Benn's "Take stock of the situation! [Erkenne die Lage!]" cf. Roman Schnur, "Im Bauche des Leviathan. Bemerkungen zum politischen Inhalt der Briefe Gottfried Benns an F.W. Oelze in der NS-Zeit," *Auf dem Weg zur Menschenwürde and Gerechtigkeit. Festschrift Hans R. Klecatsky*, eds. Ludwig Adamovich and Peter Pernthaler, Vol. 2 (Wien: 1980), 911-28, where it also becomes clear that the poet's maxim which immediately follows—"Reckon with your defects and rely on your resources, not your slogans!"—only rewrites problems with the distribution of German raw materials during the war (Benn, *Der Ptolemäer*, excerpt in *Prose, Essays, Poems*, ed. Volkmar Sander, trans. Joel Agee (New York: Continuum, 1987), 70.

3. Cf. Rolf Schwendter, *Zur Geschichte der Zukunft. Zukunftsforschung and Sozialismus* (Frankfurt/M.: 1982).

4. Cf. Thorsten Lorenz, "Die deutsche Stummfilmdebatte 1907–1929," diss., Freiburg/Br., 1985, 19.

5. Martin Heidegger, *Holzwege* (Frankfurt/M.: 1950), 272.
6. Adolf Hitler, January 1945, in Percy Ernst Schramm, ed., *Das Kriegstagebuch des Oberkommandos der Wehrmacht (Wehrmachtführungsstab) 1940–45*, project eds. Helmuth Grener und Percy Ernst Schramm, Vol. IV (Herrsching: 1982) 1652. Cf. also Hitler, May 30, 1942, in Henry Picker, *Hitlers Tischgespräche im Führerhauptquartier*, 3rd ed. (Stuttgart: 1976), 491. (The text includes previously unpublished testimony by Adolf Hitler, photos, eye witness reports, and the following commentary by the author: HITLER, AS HE REALLY WAS.) The Heraclitus-fragment, the infinitely true and "very serious maxim of a great military philosopher," appears here. But as Ernst Jünger noted, only world wars mount innovation as such, rather than continuing to fight by "constant means" (Jünger, *Das Wäldchen 125. Eine Chronik aus den Grabenkämpfen 1918*, 2nd ed. (Berlin: 1926), 125).
7. Cf. Thomas Pynchon, *Gravity's Rainbow* (New York: Viking, 1973), 520ff.

Gramophone, Film, Typewriter

1. Karl Haushofer—who, "though not the author of the technical term *geopolitics*," was nevertheless "its main representative in its German version"—prophesized: "After the war, the Americans are going to appropriate a more or less wide strip of the European west and south coasts, and simultaneously annex England, thus fulfilling Cecil Rhodes's ideal from the opposite coast. They will thereby act in accordance with the age-old ambition of every naval power to gain control over the opposite coast(s) in order completely to dominate the ocean in between. The opposite coast is at least the entire east coast of the Atlantic, and—in order to round off the domination over the 'seven seas'—possibly also the entire west coast of the Pacific. In so doing, America wants to connect the outer crescent to the "axis" (Karl Haushofer, "Nostris ex ossibus. Gedanken eines Optimisten" [1944], in Hans-Adolf Jacobsen, *Karl Haushofer, Leben und Werk*, Boppard, Rhein, 1979, vol II, pp. 635, 639).
2. In West Germany, in contrast to the U.S., telephone and telegraph services are subject to the federal postal service (translator's note).
3. Wilhelm Hoffmann, "Vom Wesen des Funkspiels" (1933), in Gerhard Hay, ed., *Literatur und Rundfunk 1923–1933*, Hildesheim, 1975, 374.
4. Norbert Bolz, "Die Schrift des Films," in *Diskursanalysen I: Medien*, Wiesbaden, 1986, 34.
5. Otto Abraham and Erich Moritz von Hornbostel, "Über die Bedeutung des Phonographen für vergleichende Musikwissenschaft," *Zeitschrift für Ethnologie*, no. 36 (1904), 229.
6. *Geschichte*, the German word for history, means both "story" and "history" (translator's note).
7. See Rüdiger Campe, "Prontol Telefonate und Telefonstimmen," in *Diskursanalysen I: Medien*, Wiesbaden, 1986, 70ff.
8. Michel Foucault, *Schriften zur Literatur*, Munich, 1974, 101.
9. J. W. Goethe, *Wilhelm Meisters Wanderjahre!* (1829), *Sämtliche Werke*, Jubiläums-Ausgabe, Eduard von der Hellen, ed., Stuttgart and Berlin, 1904, vol. XXXVIII, 270.

10. J. W. Goethe, *Die Farbenlehre* (1810), *Sämtliche Werke*, vol. XXXX. p. 148.
     (The German word for legend, *Sage*, derives from *sagen*, "to say"—translator)

11. See Walter J. Ong, *Orality and Literacy: The Technologizing of the World*,
     London and New York, 1982, 27, and, more clearly, 3.

12. See the second book of Moses, 24:12 to 34:28.

13. *Koran*, 96, V. 1–6.

14. L. W. Winter, ed., *Der Koran. Das Heilige Buch des Islam*, Munich, 1959, 6.

15. See Aleida and Jan Assman, eds., *Schrift und Gedächtnis. Archäologie der
     literarischen Kommunikation I*, Munich, 1983, 268.

16. Friedrich Nietzsche, *Geschichte der griechischen Literatur* (1874), *Sämtliche
     Werke*, Musarion-Ausgabe, Munich, 1922–29, vol. V. 213.

17. J. W. Goethe, *Aus meinen Leben. Dichtung und Wahrheit* (1811–14), *Sämtliche
     Werke*, vol. XXII, 279.

18. Botho Strauss, *Die Widmung, Eine Erzählung*, Munich, 1977, 21ff.

19. G. W. F Hegel, *Phänomenologie des Geistes* (1807), *Gesammelte Werke*,
     Hamburg, 1968ff., vol. 8, 42. Kittler uses the neologism *alphabetisiert* (literally
     "alphabeticized") to refer to a literate individual. German has no precise word
     meaning "literate," whereas it does have the noun *Analphabet* which means
     "illiterate"—ed.

20. Friedrich von Hardenberg (Novalis), *Das allgemeine Brouillon* (1798–99),
     Schriften, Paul Kluckliohn and Richard Samuel, eds., Stuttgart, Berlin,
     Cologne, Mainz, 1960–75, vol. III, 377.

21. Friedrich Schlegel, *Über die Philosophie* (1799), *Kritische Ausgabe*, Ernst Behler,
     ed., Munich, Paderborn, Vienna, 1958ff., vol. VIII, 42.

22. See Friedrich Kittler, *Aufschreibesysteme 1800/1900*, Munich, 1985,
     115–130.

23. J. W. Goethe, *Zureignung* (1797), *Sämtliche Werke*, vol. XIII, pp. 3ff. For the
     reasons why even a fully alphabetized literature simulated orality, see Heinz
     Schlaffer, introduction to Jack Goody, Ian Watt, and Kathleen Gough.
     Entstehung und Folgen der Schriftkultur, Frankfurt/Main, 1986, 20–22.

24. J. W. Goethe, *Die Leiden des jungen Werther*, (1774), *Sämtliche Werke*, vol.
     XVI, 137.

25. Walter Benjamin, *Goethes Wahlverwandtschaften* (1924–25), *Gesammelte
     Schriften*, Rolf Tiedemann and Hermann Schweppenhäuser, eds.,
     Frankfurt/Main, 1972–85. vol. I, part I, 200.

26. J. W. Goethe, *Die Wahlverwandtschaften* (1809). *Sämtliche Werke*, vol. XXI,
     302.

27. Bettina Brentano, *Goethes Briefwechsel mit einem Kinde* (1835), *Bettina von Arnim.
     Werke und Briefe*, Gustav Konrad, ed., Frechen, 1959–63, vol. II, 222.

28. Chris Marker, *Sans Soleil. Unsichtbare Sonne. Vollständiger Text zum
     gleichnamigen Film-Essay*, Hamburg, 1983, 23ff.

29. See Gilles Deleuze, "Pierre Klossowski ou les corps-language," *Critique*, no.
     21 (1965), 32.

30. See André Leroi-Gourhan as quoted in Jacques Derrida, *Of Grammatology*,
     trans. Gayatri Chakravorty Spivak, Baltimore, 1976.

31. E. T. A. Hoffmann, *Der Sandmann* (1816), *Späte Werke*, Walter Müller-
     Seidel, ed., Munich, 1960, 343.

32. See Nadar, "My Life as a Photographer," *October*, no. 5 (Summer 1978),
     7–28.

33. Rudolf Arnheim, "Systematik der frühen kinematographischen Erfindungen" (1933) in Helmut H. Dieterichs, ed., *Kritiken und Aufsätze zum Film*, Munich, 1977, 27.

34. Jacques Lacan, *Le séminaire, livre II: Le moi dans la théorie de Freud et dans la technique de la psychanalyse*, Paris, 1978.

35. Thomas Edison, quoted in Roland Gelatt, *The Fabulous Phonograph 1877–1977: From Edison to Stereo*, New York, 1977, 29. Phonograph recordings of last words presuppose that "physiological time *is not reversible*" and that "in the realm of rhythm and time there is absolutely no symmetry" (Ernst Mach, *Beiträge zur Analyse der Empfindungen*, Jena, 1886, 108).

36. See John Brooks, "The First and Only Century of Telephone Literature," in Ithiel de Sola Pool, ed., *The Social Impact of the Telephone*, Cambridge, Massachusetts, 1977, 213ff.

37. Walther Rathenau, *Gesammelte Schriften*, Berlin, 1918–29, vol. IV, 347. Two examples of professional deformation among the dead of Necropolis: "A writer is not content with his epitaph. An employee of the telephone company rings in short and long intervals, signaling, in a kind of Morse code, a criticism of his successor." King Alexander, the protagonist of Bronnen's *Ostpolzug*, says all there is to say about telephonitis and Hades while, according to the stage directions, the telephone is ringing: "Oh, you black beast, growing on fatty brown stems, you flower of untimeliness, you rabbit of dark rooms! Your voice is our beyond, and it has displaced heaven" (Arnolt Bronnen, *Ostpolzug* (1926), *Stücke*, Hans Mayer, ed., Kronberg, 1977, vol. I, 133.

38. Indeed, the song "Example #22" montages the announcements and sound of "Beispiels Nr. 22" ("Hier spricht Edgar" [Hildegard Schäfer, *Stimmen aus einer anderen Welt*, Freiburg, 1983. 11]), which must have wandered on a paranormal cassette-to-book from Freiburg to the U.S.

39. See Jacques Lacan, *Ecrits: A Selection*, trans. Alan Sheridan, New York, 1977, 184.

40. Schäfer, 3.

41. *Ibid.*, 2.

42. See Jacques Lacan: *Ecrits*, Paris, 1966.

43. See Don E. Gordon, *Electronic Warfare: Element of Strategy and Multiplier of Combat Power*, New York, 1981, *passim*.

44. Peter Watson, *War on the Mind: The Military Uses and Abuses of Psychology*. New York, 1978.

45. See Alfred Walze, "Auf den Spuren von Christopher Latham Sholes. Ein Besuch in Milwaukee, der Geburtsstätte der ersten brauchbaren Schreibmaschine," *Deutsche Stenografenzeitung*, 1980, 133.

46. See Niklas Luhmann, "Das Problem der Epochenbildung und die Evolutionstheorie," in Hans Ulrich Gumbrecht and Ulla Link-Heer, eds., *Epochenschwellen und Epochenstrukturen im Diskurs der Literatur- und Sprachhistorie*. Frankfurt/Main, 1985, 20–22.

47. Martin Heidegger, *Parmenides* (1942–43), *Gesamtausgabe*, Manfred S. Frings, ed., Frankfurt, Main. 1982, part 2, vol. 54, 127. The professionalism of this assertion is confirmed by Eric Klockenberg, *Rationalisierung der Schreibmaschine und ihre Bedienung*, Berlin, 1926, 3.

48. Gottfried Keller, *Die missbrauchten Liebesbriefe* (1865), in *Die Leute von Seldwyla. Gesammelte Gedichte*, Munich, 1961, 376.

49. See Stéphane Mallarmé, *La littérature. Doctrine* (1893), *Oeuvres complétes*, Henri Mondor and G. Jean-Aubry, eds., Paris, 1945, 850.

50. Lacan, *Le séminaire, livre II.*

51. Jacques Lacan, "The mirror stage as formative of the function of the I," in *Ecrits: A Selection*, 1–7.

52. Jacques Lacan, *Le séminaire, livre XX: Encore*, Paris, 1975, 53, 73.

53. See Jacques Lacan, "The Seminar on 'The Purloined Letter,' " *Yale French Studies*, no. 48 (1973).

54. Friedrich Nietzsche, *Unzeitgemässe Betrachtungen* (1873–76), *Werke*, Kritische Gesamtausgabe, Giorgio Colli and Mazzino Montinari, eds., Berlin, 1967 ff., vol. 3, part I, 278.

55. See Alan Turing, "Computing Machinery and Intelligence," *Mind: A Quarterly Review of Psychology and Philosophy*, no. 59 (1950); see also Andrew Hodges, *Alan Turing: The Enigma*, New York, 1983, 415–417.

56. Hodges, 279.

57. *Ibid.*, 30.

58. *Ibid.*, 14.

59. Quoted in Hodges, 387.

60. See Konrad Zuse, *Der Computer, Mein Lebenswerk*, Berlin 1984, 41: "Decisive thought, June 19, 1937. There are elementary operations to which all computing and thinking operations can be reduced. A primitive type of mechanical brain consists of a storage system, a dialing system, and a simple apparatus which can treat conditional chains of two or three links. With this form of brain it has to be theoretically possible to solve all puzzles that can be mechanically dealt with, regardless of the time required. More complex brains are merely a matter of the faster accomplishment of those processes."

Dracula's Legacy

1. The *koan* or *kung-an*, employed by certain Buddhist sects, is a paradoxical question meant to bring students to the realization that all conceptual thinking is futile. It is thus comparable to the tying of knots that cannot be untied (translator's note).

2. Until 1964, Lacan gave his lectures at the psychiatric hospital *Saint Anne* in Paris. See Juliet Mitchell and Jacqueline Rose, eds., *Feminine Sexuality: Jacques Lacan and the école freudienne* (London: Macmillan, 1982) 160 (translator's note).

3. See: J. Lacan, "Radiophonie," *Scilicet*, 2/3 (1970), 94–95.

4. English in original (translator's note).

5. Qtd. in Oliver Reed and Walter L. Welsh, *From Tin Foil to Stereo: Evolution of the Phonograph* (Indianapolis, 1959), 12.

6. Concerning "re-lecture," see: Jacques Lacan, *Le séminaire, livre XX: Encore?* (Paris: Éditions du Seuil, 1975), 30.

7. Lacan, *Encore*, 34.
   Kittler, for the most part, quotes Lacan in German translation. Many of these passages are not yet available in English, and, unless otherwise noted, I have translated them myself (translator's note).

8. See: Freud, *Vorlesungen zur Einführung in die Psychoanalyse*, vol. 11 of *Gesammelte Schriften* (London, 1944–68), 157–58.

9. See: Lacan, *Encore*, 15.

10. Lacan, *Encore*, 116.
11. Anna Freud, *Das Ich und die Abwehrmechanismen* (Munich, n.d.), 8.
12. Lacan, *Encore*, 125. Ever since my nose has made its way into Stoker's novel, Jann Matlock and Friedhelm Rong know what it has to thank them for.
13. Lacan, *Encore*, 29–30. See also: 83.
14. Lacan, *Encore*, 77.
15. See: Lacan, *Encore*, 53.
16. Lacan, *Télévision* (Paris: Éditions du Seuil, 1973), 10.
    I refer to the English translation "Television" by Denis Hollier, Rosalind Krauss, and Annette Michelson in: *October 40* (1987), 8 (translator's note).
17. Lacan, *Encore*, 76.
18. See: Lacan, *Encore*, 34, as well as 51: "En fin de compte, il n'y a que ça, le lien social. Je le désigne du terme de discours parce qu'il n'y a d'autre moyen de le désigner dès qu'on s'est aperçu que le lien social ne s'instature que de s'ancrer dans la façon dont le langage se situe et s'imprime, se situe sur ce qui grouille, à savoir l'être parlant."
19. Lacan, *Encore*, 11.
20. See: Lacan, *Encore*, 83.
21. Lacan, *Encore*, 77.
    This passage has been quoted here according to Rose's translation in Mitchell and Rose, 154. For the term *jouissance*, Kittler uses the German *Lust* (pleasure). For an explanation of the significance of this term in Lacan's thought, see Mitchell and Rose, 137–38 (translator's note).
22. Lacan, *Encore*, 33–34.
23. Lacan, *Encore*, 35.
24. All quotations from the novel come from: Bram Stoker, *Dracula: a Mystery Story*, (New York: W.R. Caldwell, 1897). I have provided page numbers following quotations based on this edition (translator's note).
25. See: Lacan, "Radiophonie," 97.
26. See: Lacan, "L'Etourdit," *Scilicet* 4 (1973), 9.
27. See Freud's "Notiz über den 'Wunderblock' " (1925), ("A Note upon the 'Mystic Writing Pad'." A journal published in West Berlin, *Der Wunderblock: Zeitschrift für Psychoanalyse*, derives its name from this article. As the journal has been greatly concerned with Lacan, *Wunderblock* is the "name" for the German analytic discourse on Lacan (translator's note).
28. See: Nina Auerbach, "Magi and Maidens: The Romance of the Victorian Freud," *Critical Inquiry*, 8 (1981): 290.
29. See: Arminius Vámbéry, *The Story of my Struggles: The Memoirs of Arminius Vámbéry* (London, 1904) 2, 480–83.
30. Historical data from: Raymont T. McNally and Radu Florescu. *In Search of Dracula: A True History of Dracula and Vampyre Legends* (New York: New York Graphic Society, 1972).
31. See: C. F. Bentley. "The Monster in the Bedroom: Sexual Symbolism in Bram Stoker's *Dracula*," *Literature and Psychology* 22 (1972), 28.
32. This data on Vámbéry is taken from his second autobiography, *Geschichte meiner Kämpfe (History of my Struggles)*.
33. See: McNally and Florescu, *In Search of Dracula* 178.
34. Qtd. in Daniel Farson, *The Man Who Wrote Dracula: A Biography of Bram Stoker* (London: M. Joseph, 1975), 124.

35. The German translation (Bram Stoker, *Dracula: Ein Vampirroman*. Munich 1967), which I quote from generally, has the attraction of here translating "kill" with "*überbieten*" (outdo) and "power" with "*Reiz*" (attraction). This is the autonimical way in which one produces entertainment literature.

36. Concerning this pack, and the fact that an ill-informed Freud generally reduced it to one (father) wolf, see Gilles Deleuze and Félix Guattari, *Mille plateaux: Capitalisme et schizophrénie II* (Paris, 1980), 42.

37. See: Bentley, 28.

38. Lacan, *Encore*, 33.

39. For reasons of structure, an incorrect dating by Stoker has been corrected here: In the novel the lawyer Hawkins does not die until September 18, the day after Harker's return.

40. This is the opinion of Richard Wasson, "The Politics of Dracula," *English Literature in Transition* 9 (1966), 25. At least the clever title of this article allows one Stoker interpreter to escape the endless talk of sex and crime in the novel. Whether vampires are more likely to be anally or orally sadistic, whether Stoker's wife was frigid, and whether or not his morals are Victorian—this and nothing else concerns interpreters.

41. See Lacan, *Encore*, 67–69.

42. For details see: Bruce Bliven, *The Wonderful Writing Machine* (New York, 1954), 3–16, 71–79.

43. See: A. Conan Doyle, *The Complete Sherlock Holmes* (New York, 1930), 322 "The Adventure of the Copper Beeches," and 517 "The Adventure of the Dancing Man."

44. Auerbach, 289.

45. Freud, *Aus den Anfängen der Psychoanalyse: Briefe an Wilhelm Fliess. Abhandlungen und Notizen aus den Jahren 1887–1902* (London, 1950), 187. For translation see: Eric Mosbacher and James Strachey, trans. *The Origins of Psycho-Analysis: Letters to Wilhelm Fliess. Drafts and Notes 1887–1902* by Sigmund Freud (New York: Basic Books, 1954), 215 (translator's note).

46. See: Lacan, *Encore* 69. Concerning intra-uterine phantasms based on the vampire myths of films, see also: Roger Dadoun, "Der Fetischismus im Horrorfilm," *Objekte des Fetischismus*, ed. Jean-Betrand Pontalis (Frankfurt am Main, 1972), 354–60.
   Kittler here again uses the word *Lust* for what I give as "pleasure." Lacan, in the reference given, uses *jouissance* (translator's note).

47. McNally and Florescu, *In Search of Dracula*, 162, are the only critics who point this out.

48. Lacan, "L' Etourdit," 30–31.

49. See, for example: Daniel Ferrier, *Die Functionen des Gehirnes, Autoisirte, deutsche Ausgabe* (Braunschweig, 1897), 285–325. Most likely this Ferrier (in the original English) was Stoker's source of "brain-knowledge," and not the metaphysician James Frederick Ferrier, as claimed by Leonard Wolf, ed., *The Annotated Dracula*, by Bram Stoker (New York: Clarkson N. Potter, 1975), 74.

50. Georg Hirth, *Aufgaben der Kunstphysiologie*, 2nd ed. (Munich, 1897), 38.

51. Lacan, "Radiophonie," 89.

52. Freud, *Bruchstück einer Hysterie-Analyse*, vol. 5 of *Gesammelte Schriften*, 167.

53. One can compare this therapy with Azam's proud conclusion: "Aujourd'hui, ces idées, qui autrefois étaient le proie du charlatanisme et de la crédulité,

sont devenues une science: la Physiologie des fonctions intellectuelles, ou la Psycho-Physiologie." From: Eugène Azam, *Hypnotisme et double conscience: Origine de leur étude et divers travaux sur des sujets analogues* (Paris, 1893) VII.

54. For details see: Azam, *Hypnotisme et double conscience*, 37–118. It is of interest to note that on the same page on which he mentions lycanthropy and vampirism (78), Azam also develops his theory of a total (and this means lucid) somnambulism, which could also apply to Lucy's existence as an Un-Dead.

55. Freud, *Vorlesungen zur Einführung in die Psychoanalyse* 11, 157.

56. Lacan, "Radiophonie", 61.

57. Anonymous, "Schreiben mit der Maschine," *Vom Fels zum Meer: Spemann's Illustrirte Zeitschrift für das Deutsche Haus* (1889), col. 863.

58. See: Marshall McLuhan, *Die magischen Kanäle* (Düsseldorf, 1968), 283.

59. Erich Brandes, *Betrachtungen über das weibliche Geschlecht und dessen Ausbildung in dem geselligen Leben* (Hannover, 1802) 1, 53.

60. Wasson, *The Politics of Dracula*, 26.

61. Ferrier, *Die Functionen des Gehirnes*, 306.

62. Ferrier, *Die Functionen des Gehirnes*, xiv.

63. "Nachts auf Reisen Wellen schlagen hören und sich sagen, daβ sie immertun," is how Benn's poem "Was schlimm ist" ("What is terrible") puts it. ("To hear waves beating at night on a journey, and to say to yourself that they always do this.")

64. See: Lacan, *Télévision*, 26.
    For an English translation see: Denis Hollier, 18 (translator's note).

65. See: Azam, *Hypnotisme et double conscience*, 79.

66. Rudolph Lothar, "Die Sprechmaschine: Ein technisch aesthetischer Versuch," *Das blaue Heft* 5 (1924), 49. "Sprechmaschine" was the generic name for phonographs and gramophones (as these were once protected trademarks).

67. See: William Stevenson, *A Man Called Intrepid. The Secret War* (New York, 1977), 16–17.

68. Lacan. *Télévision*, 47. (The text says "TV" instead of "radio.").

69. Phyllis A. Roth, "Sexualität der Frau in Bram Stokers *Dracula*," *Psychoanalyse und das Unheimliche: Essays aus der amerikanischen Literaturkritik*, ed. Claire Kahane (Bonn: Verlag H. Grundmann, 1981), 264.

70. Lacan, *Télévision*, 40.
    Oscar Wilde, *The Annotated Oscar Wilde: Poems, Fiction, Plays, Lectures, Essays, and Letters*, ed. H. Montgomery Hyde (New York: Clarkson N Potter, 1982), 325.

71. See: Lacan, *Encore*, 71
    For an English translation, see: Mitchell and Rose, 147 (translator's note).

72. Rainer Maria Rilke, *Die Aufzeichnungen des Malte Launds Brigge, Sämtliche Werke*, ed. Ernst Zinn (Wiesbaden, 1955–66) 6, 776.

73. Freud, *Aus den Anfängen der Psychoanalyse*, 186–87.
    The translation is from Mosbacher and Strachey, 215–16 (translator's note).

74. Roth, "Sexualität der Frau," 254.

75. Lacan, *Télévision*, 53–54.
    The translation comes from Hollier, 36 (translator's note).

76. See: Wolf, *The Annotated Dracula*, 350.

77. See: Hugo Münsterberg, *The Photoplay: A Psychological Study* (New York, 1916).

78. See: James B. Twitchell, *The Living Dead: A Study of the Vampire in Romantic Literature* (Durham NC: Duke UP, 1981), 139.

79. Gilles Deleuze and Félix Guattari, *Anti-Ödipus Kapitalismus und Schizophrenie 1* (Frankfurt/M, 1974), 268.
   The translation of the passage is based on, but deviates somewhat from: Robert Hurley, Mark Seem, and Helen R. Lane, trans., *Anti-Oedipus: Capitalism and Schizophrenia*, by Gilles Deleuze and Félix Guattari (Minneapolis: Univ. of Minnesota Press, 1983), 209 (translator's note).

Romanticism—Psychoanalysis—Film

1. Adelbert von Chamisso, "Erscheinung," *Gesammelte Werke in vier Bänder*, Bd. II (Stuttgart: 1828/undated), 13–15.

2. Cf. Sigmund Freud, "The 'Uncanny,' " *The Standard Edition of the Complete Psychological Works of Sigmund Freud*, Vol. XVII, ed. and trans. James Strachey (London: Hogarth, 1955), 219–226. By exploring the word in its literal sense, Freud follows in the footsteps of his predecessor. Ernst Jentsch, who the countless Freud exegetes of today no longer read, of course, does not generally consider "the spirit of language" a "particularly strong psychologist," but must attribute the Germans with "a quite fortuitous construction" in the "word 'unheimlich.' " (Jentsch, "Zur Psychologie des Unheimlichen," *Psychiatrisch-neurologische Wochenschrift* (22: 1906), 195.)

3. Otto Rank, *The Double: A Psychoanalytic Study*, trans. and ed. Harry Tucker, Jr. (Chapel Hill: University of North Carolina Press, 1971), 35–7.

4. Rank, 76–7.

5. Rank, 69. Cf. Friedrich Kittler, " 'Das Phantom unseres Ichs' und die Literaturpsychologie," *Urszenen. Literaturwissenschaft als Diskursanalyse und Diskurskritik*, eds. F.A. Kittler, Horst Turk (Frankfurt/M: 1977), 139–66.

6. Freud's acumen had already led him to indicate the exception in Goethe's famous self-encounter at the departure of Sesenheim and Francis Brion: A garment whose "color was the gray of a pike"—a garment that the double wore in 1771 and that Goethe would first wear in 1779 at the next visit— describes "the costume of officialdom" of a successful bureaucrat who composes official records first and poems second. Cf. Rank 39 and 40, n.10. On the historical background conditions of Goethe's double (modern nuclear family and narcissism), see also Jacques Lacan, "Der Individualmythos des Neurotikers," *Der Wunderblock* (5/6: 1980) 61–8.

7. Rank 39. Primary source for this information was Paul Auguste Sollier, *Les phénomènes d'autoscopie* (Paris: 1913).

8. Johann Wolfgang von Goethe, *Wilhelm Meister's Apprenticeship*, ed. and trans. Eric A. Blackall, *Goethe's Collected Works*, Vol. 9 (New York: Suhrkamp, 1989), 103.

9. Friedrich Wilhelm Riemer, *Mitteilungen über Goethe*, ed. Arthur Pollmer (Leipzig: 1841/1921), 261.

10. Goethe, 112.

11. Daniel Jenisch, *Ueber die hervorstechendsten Eigenthümlichkeiten von Meisters Lehrjahren; oder, über das, wodurch dieser Roman ein Werk von Göthen's Hand ist. Ein ästhetisch-moralischer Versuch* (Berlin: 1797), 14. Even according to

Friedrich Schlegel, "although the characters in this novel are, through their manner of representation, similar to the portrait[!], they are in their being more or less universal and allegorical" ("Über Goethe's Meister," *Kritische Friedrich-Schlegel-Ausgabe*, Vol. II, ed., Ernst Behler (Paderborn: 1798/1958ff.), 143).

12. Jenisch, 14ff. On writing and reading techniques of identification in general, cf. Friedrich Kittler, "Über die Sozialisation Wilhelm Meisters," *Dichtung als Sozialisationsspiel*, eds., Gerhard Kaiser, F.A. Kittler (Göttingen: 1978), 99–114.

13. Cf. Schlegel, 136 and 141ff.

14. Fragment of 1809. In: Novalis, *Schriften*, eds. Paul Kluckhohn and Richard Samuel, Bd.III (Stuttgart: 1960–75), 377.

15. Alfred de Musset, "La nuit de décembre," *Œuvres complètes*, ed. Philippe van Tieghem (Paris: 1835/1963), 153.
[Musset, "The December Night," *The Complete Writings of Alfred de Musset*, Vol. II, trans. George Santayana, Emily Shaw Forman, Maire Agathe Clarke (New York: Edwin C. Hill, 1907), 336:

> A schoolboy, I my vigils kept
> One night, while my companion slept;
> Into the lonely room forlorn
> There came and sat a little lad,
> Poor, and in sombre garments clad,
> As like me as my brother born.]

16. Freud 248, n.1.

17. Stéphane Mallarmé, "Sur le beau et l'utile," *Œuvres Complètes* (Librarie Gallimard, 1945) 880. The act of rowing in Mallarmé's prose-poem, *Le nénuphar blanc*, is a pre-technical realization of this camera ride (Mallarmé, 1945, 283–6). On cinema and automobile driving in general, cf. also, Paul Virilio, *L'insécurité du territoire* (Paris: 1976), 251–7.

18. Mallarmé, "Sur le livre illustré," 1945, 878.

19. Georg Büchner, "Leonce und Lena," *Sämtliche Werke und Briefe*, Bd. I, ed. Werner R. Lehmann (Hamburg: 1838/1967–71), 140. Police warrants seem to go back to the time of high absolutism. That Büchner parodies them from experience is revealed in his own warrant:
"Warrant. By his leaving the country, the herewith designated Georg Büchner, medical student from Darmstadt, has denied himself legal examination of his indicated participation in the offence of traitor to the state. We entreat the national and international public to arrest the same on sight and to deliver him in custody to the place indicated below. Darmstadt, June 13, 1835. Hessian Court Tribunal of the Province of Oberhessen, Examining Magistrate, Tribunal Counsellor Georgi. Personal description. Age: 21 years; Height: 6 feet, 9 inches, new Hessian measure; Hair: blond; Brow: very arched; Eyebrows: blond; Eyes: gray; Nose: strong; Mouth: small; Beard: blond; Chin: round; Face: oval; Facial color: robust; Posture: strong, slim; Special characteristics: near-sighted." Supplement to *Frankfurter Journal*, No. 166, Thursday, June 18, 1835. Facsimile in: Georg Büchner, *Leben, Werk, Zeit. Ausstellung zum 150. Jahrestag des »Hessischen Landboten«*. Katalog (Marburg: 1985), 203.

20. Cf. details in Carlo Ginzburg, "Clues: Morelli, Freud, and Sherlock Holmes," *The Sign of Three: Dupin, Holmes, Peirce,* eds. Umberto Eco and Thomas A. Sebeok (Bloomington: Indiana UP, 1983), 81–118.
21. Jentsch, 205.
22. Cf. Walter Görlitz, *Kleine Geschichte des deutschen Generalstabes* (Berlin: 1967), 194ff. Ludendorff's words are cited in: *Hätte ich das Kino Die Schriftsteller und der Stummfilm: eine Ausstellung des Deutschen Literaturarchivs im Schiller-Nationalmuseum. Marbach a. N. vom 24. April bis 31. Oktober 1976,* eds., Ludwig Greve, Margot Pehle, Heidi Westhoff (München: 1976), 75.
23. Cf. Michael Herr, *Dispatches* (New York: Knopf, 1978).
24. Cf. Henri Bergson, *L'évolution créatrice,* 26th ed. (Paris: 1907/1923), 330ff.
25. Cf. Michel Foucault, *The History of Sexuality. Volume 1: An Introduction,* trans. Robert Hurley (New York: Vintage, 1990), 56 n.
26. Cf. Jean Martin Charcot, *Œuvres complétètes,* Vol. I (Paris: 1880–93).
27. Information on Albert Londe (1858–1917) from Hrayr Terzian, "La fotografia psichiatrica," *Nascita della fotografia psichiatrica,* ed. Franco Cagnetta (Venice: 1981), 39. Information on his hysteria-'films' from Joël Farges, "L'image d'un corps," *Communications. Psychanalyse et cinéma* (23: 1975), 89.
28. Rank, 3ff.
29. Rank, 65, n.69.
30. Tzvetan Todorov, *The Fantastic: A Structural Approach to a Literary Genre,* trans. Richard Howard (Ithaca: Cornell UP, 1975), 160–1.
31. Hugo Münsterberg, *The Photoplay: A Psychological Study.* Republished as *The Film. A Psychological Study. The Silent Photoplay in 1916,* ed. Richard Griffith (New York: 1970) 15: "Rich artistic effects have been secured, and while on the stage every fairy play is clumsy and hardly able to create an illusion, in the film we really see the man transformed into a beast and the flower into a girl. There is no limit to the trick pictures which the skill of the experts invent. [. . .] Every dream becomes real." Münsterberg's thesis can be unequivocally verified in precisely the literature that, since 1895, the film replaced. In the manifestly Romantic novel, Hardenberg's *Heinrich von Ofterdingen,* the hero dreams, as is well-known, of a blue flower. "He wanted finally to approach her, when she suddenly began to move and to change; the leaves became brighter and pressed themselves close to the growing stalk, the flower bowed towards him and the petals revealed an extended blue collar in which a tender face was suspended." (Novalis, Bd. I, 197.)
32. Rank 7.
33. Cited in Greve/Pehle/Westhoff, 110. On *The Student of Prague* as the filming of film itself, cf. also, Jean Baudrillard, *Symbolic Exchange and Death.*
34. Discussion of Gerhart Hauptmann's film, *Phantom* (1922), cited in Greve/Pehle/Westhoff, 172.
35. Paul Lindau's "Schauspiel in vier Akten," from which the film was produced and which I, by necessity, cite, uses photography as a metaphor for film. Cf. Paul Lindau, *Der Andere* (Leipzig: 1893/ca. 1906), 22 and 81. Lindau, one of the first users of the typewriter amongst Germany's authors, was also an early reader of Freud. Cf. Ernest Jones, *Sigmund Freud, Leben und Werk,* eds. Lionel Trilling, Steven Marcus (Frankfurt/M.: 1969), 182.
36. Paul Wegener, *Die künstlerischen Möglichkeiten des Films* (1916); cited in Kai Möller, *Paul Wegener. Sein Leben und seine Rollen* (1954), 111.

37. Georg Seeβlen and Claudius Weil, *Kino des Phantastischen. Geschichte und Mythologie des Horror-Films* (Reinbek: 1978), 48.
38. Cf. Friedrich Kittler, "Weltatem. Über Wagners Medientechnologie," *Diskursanalysen, Bd. I: Medien,* eds. F.A. Kittler, Manfred Schneider, Samuel Weber (Opladen: 1987), 94–107.
39. Edgar Morin, *Le cinéma; ou, L'homme imaginaire, essai d'anthropologie sociologique* (Paris: 1956), 139.
40. Gustav Meyrink, *Der Golem. Ein Roman* (Leipzig: 1915), 1–4.
41. Cf. Henri Bergson, 1907/1923, 330ff.; and on this, Gilles Deleuze, *Cinema 1: The Movement-Image,* trans. Hugh Tomlinson and Barbara Habberjam (Minneapolis: U Minnesota P, 1986).
42. Meyrink, 25 (with thanks to Michael Müller/Freiburg).
43. Cf. Daniel Paul Schreber, *Denkwürdigkeiten eines Nervenkranken,* ed. Samuel M. Weber (Berlin: 1903/1973) 145 and 161. The context proves sufficiently that identify-less and serial groups of Doubles are also commuters for Schreber.
44. Cf. Hugo Münsterberg, *Grundzüge der Psychotechnik* (Leipzig: 1914)—seven hundred sixty-seven equally great as forgotten pages.
45. Münsterberg, 1916/1970, 31–48.
46. Cf. Jones, 350.
47. Biographical information on Münsterberg from Richard Griffith's Introduction to *Photoplay*-reprint (Münsterberg 1916/1970).

Media and Drugs in Pynchon's Second World War

1. *Frankfurter Allgemeine Zeitung* 3 Nov. 1983, 12.
2. Regarding the strategy of the autobahns since World War I, cf. Friedrich Kittler, "Autobahnen. Kulturrevolution," *Zeitschrift für angewandte Diskurstheorie* (5: 1984), 42–4.
3. Cf. Erik Bergaust, *Werner von Braun: Ein unglaubliches Leben* (Düsseldorf, Wien: Econ., 1976), 111.
4. Regarding World War II and post-war fantasy, cf. Pink Floyd, *The Final Cut: A Requiem for the Post War Dream* (London: EMI, 1983), side 1.
5. Thomas Pynchon, *Gravity's Rainbow* (New York: Viking, 1973), 39. Page numbers for all further references to this work will be noted in parenthesis.
6. For the recollections of Werner von Braun, cf. Bernd Ruland, *Werner von Braun. Mein Leben für die Raumfahrt* (Offenburg: Burda, 1969), 141; and the understandable deviations in Walter Dornberger, *V-2—Der Schuβ ins Weltall: Geschichte einer groβen Erfindung* (Eβlingen: Bechtle, 1953), 120.
7. Ruland, 268.
8. Regarding Nordhausen, the largest publicly-known underground factory, cf. Manfred Borneman, *Geheimprojekt Mittelbau: Die Geschichte der deutschen V-Waffen-Werke* (München: 1971).
9. Regarding the birth of computers from the spirit of espionage, see Friedrich Kittler, "Das Gespenst im Computer. Alan Turing und die moderne Kriegsmaschine," *Überblick* (8: 1984) 9, 46ff. At the date of publication of *Gravity's Rainbow,* the fact still lay dormant in the secret archives that at the British Bletchley Park, information machines were already replacing agents as early as 1942.

10. Here follows the wording of *Zahmen Xenions* [*Tame Xenion*], in which the introduction of general war duty is determined neither militarily nor ideologically, but rather discourse-analytically. Johann Wolfgang Goethe, *Sämtliche Werke. Jubiläums-Ausgabe*, ed. Eduard von der Hellen, vol. IV (Stuttgart: Cotta, 1904–5), 131:

> Hatte sonst einer ein Unglück getragen,
> So durft' er es wohl dem andern klagen;
> Mußte sich einer im Felde quälen,
> Hatt' er im Alter was zu erzählen.
> Jetzt sind sie allgemein, die Plagen,
> Der einzelne darf sich nicht beklagen;
> Im Felde darf nun niemand fehlen—
> Wer soll denn hören, wenn sie erzählen?

[Before, if one experienced misfortune, he could always blame it on the others; if one underwent agony in the field, he had something to tell in his old age. Now the torment is general and the individual cannot complain; no one can be missing from the field—who then shall listen when they narrate?]

11. Regarding absolute enmity, total mobilization and Kleist's "Partisandichtung," cf. Carl Schmitt, *Theorie der Partisanen. Zwischenbemerkung zum Begriff des Politischen* (Offenburg: Burda, 1963).

12. Cf. Paul Fussell, *The Great War and European Memory* (New York: Oxford UP, 1975).

13. Cf. Ernst Jünger, *Der Kampf als inneres Erlebnis* (Berlin: Mittler, 1922, 92, 98); World War I as "strangler of our literature" ["Würger unserer Literatur"].

14. Cf. Jünger 12, 28, 50, 107ff.

15. In the case of the V-2, its delay amounted to 16 seconds, cf. Ruland, 221.

16. Friedrich Kamper, *Atlantis—vorgeschichtliche Katastrophe, nachgeschichtliche Dekonstruktion* (Paris: Publisher's manuscript, 1984).

17. Cf. William Stevenson, *A Man Called Intrepid: The Secret War* (New York: Simon & Schuster, 1977); also, the deficient monograph on IG Farben by Joseph Borkin, *Die unheilige Allianz der I.G. Farben: Eine interessengemeinschaft im Dritten Reich* (Frankfurt/M.: Campus, 1979).

18. Regarding Flaubert's *Tentation de Saint-Antoine* [*The Temptation of Saint Anthony*], cf. Michel Foucault, *Schriften zur Literatur* (München: Nymphenburger, 1974), 157–77.

19. Cf. Sigmund Freud, *Gesammelte Werke, chronologisch geordnet*, ed. Anna Freud et al., vol. X (London, Frankfurt/M.: Fischer, 1946–68), 302.

20. Cf. Charles William Morris, *Foundations of the Theory of Signs* (Chicago: U of Chicago P, 1972), 67ff.

21. Regarding Staver, cf. Ruland 249. Further name games between fact and fiction: Höhler, the architect of the Nordhausen central plant (Bornemann 23), appears as Ölsch (Pynchon 298–302); Enzian, the code name of a Peenemünder rocket project (Ruland 261), appears as the name of a leader of a fictitious Herero SS combat unit. Finally, "Max" and "Moritz," the two engineers at the launch of the manned V-2 (Pynchon 757–8), cite von Braun's A2 of November, 1934 (Ruland 89ff.). Readers are encouraged to look for more. . . .

22. Cf. Claude E. Shannon and Warren Weaver, *Mathematische Grundlagen für Informationstheorie* (München, Wien: 1976), 22.

23. Regarding Speer's theory that the design of all architecture must incorporate its eventual "value as ruins," cf. Paul Virilio, *War and Cinema*, trans. Patrick Camiller (London, New York: Verso, 1989), 55.

24. Cf. Ellie Howe, *Die schwarze Propaganda. Ein Insider-Bericht über die geheimsten Operationen des britischen Geheimdienstes im Zweiten Weltkrieg* (München: Beck, 1983).

25. After seeing this film of a rocket flight to the moon, one of Pynchon's characters theorizes: "Real flight and dreams of flight go together" (159). Regarding UFA (Universum Film AG) and Prof. Oberth's first liquid-fuel rocket project, cf. Ruland, 57–67. Regarding *Frau im Mond* and, consequently, the power of film, Virilio, 58–9: "The film came out on 30 September 1929, but without the intended publicity of a real rocket launch from the beach of Horst in Pomerania to an altitude of forty kilometres. By 1932 jet technology, being developed at Dornberger's newly opened Kummersdorf West Research Centre, was set to become one of the major military secrets of the Third Reich, and the German authorities of the time seized Lang's film on the grounds that it was *too close to reality*. A decade later, on 7 July 1943, von Braun and Dornberger presented Hitler with film of the real launch of the A4 [= V-2] rocket. The Führer was in a bitter mood: 'Why was it I could not believe in the success of your work? If we'd had these rockets in 1939 we'd never have had this war.'" There exists no clearer proof for the power of film: Hitler the cineaste, who was bored by all demonstrations of the real V-2 (cf. Dornberger 73–7, 99–101), was convinced through film.

26. Cf. Virilio 11, regarding Marey's chrono-photographic gun.

27. Compare the confessions of the head of this department, Reginald V. Jones, *Most Secret War* (London: Hamish Hamilton, 1978).

28. Function and picture of this gun, cf. Siegfried Giedion, *Mechanization Takes Command: A Contribution to Anonymous History* (New York: Oxford UP, 1948), 21ff.

29. For details, cf. Friedrich Kittler, "Romanticism-Psychoanalysis-Film," in this volume.

30. Cf. Virilio, 81.

31. Cf. Dornberger, 259.

32. Regarding Kammler's building activity (also for Nordhausen) from the Chief Economic Administration Office of the SS, cf. Enno Georg, *Die wirtschaftlichen Unternehmungen der SS* (Stuttgart: DVA, 1963) 37ff.; and Bornemann 43, 82ff., 125. For his resumé through 1932 (Eastern Boundary Defense, Rosbach Storm Troopers, Danzig Housing Development Office, Employment Ministry of the Reich, etc.), cf. Hans Kammler, *Zur Bewertung von Geländerschliessungen für die grossstädtliche Besiedlung* (Hannover: Diss.ing., 1932). If readers can oblige with any further information. . . .

33. Cf. Ruland 170, where, incidentally, no mention is made of Kammler's motives. In Pynchon's case, on the other hand, one knows from *Gravity's Rainbow* that he also asks of his readers: "Is that who you are, that vaguely criminal face on your ID card, its soul snatched by the government camera as the guillotine shutter fell?" (134).

34. As a model for the conversation between Weissmann and Pökler, read the long dialogue between Dornberger and Dr. Steinhoff, the electrician at Peenemünde, in Dornberger, 147–9.

35. Cf. Dornberger 286: "Kammler did not want to believe in the forthcoming collapse. He raced from the fronts in Holland and in the Rheinland, to Thüringen and Berlin. He was underway day and night. Always there and back. Meetings were called at one in the morning somewhere in the Harz, or we met at midnight somewhere on the autobahn, in order to return again to our work after a short briefing and quick exchange of opinion. An inhuman nervous tension held our breath in check. We were irritated, nervous, over-worked. We didn't take any of his words at face-value. Once, when things weren't going fast enough for him, Kammler woke his accompanying officer with a blast from his gun before travelling further."

36. Cf. Ruland 282ff: "Because the SS-General Kammler, Hitler's special proxy of the V-weapons, could not be found [after the war], London wanted to put Dornberger on trial in his place. No one knew at the time what had happened to Kammler. Certainty only arises several years later: On May 4, 1945, Kammler arrived with an airplane in Prague. On May 9, he defended a bunker with 21 SS-soldiers against 600 Czech partisans. Triumphantly, Kammler emerged from the bunker and fired with his gun on the attacking Czechs. Some months precedent to this date, Kammler's adjutant, Storm Trooper leader Starck, had received the order, under no circumstances to allow his leader to fall into the hands of enemies. Rather, he was to follow him from 10 paces—'shooting distance.' Here, in this hopeless situation, Starck fired a bullet from his gun into the back of the SS-General's head."

The World of the Symbolic—A World of the Machine

1. Cf. Aristotle, *The Poetics*, 1451 a 4.
2. Cf. Aristotle, 1450 b 22–31.
3. Immanuel Kant, *Kritik der Reinen Vernunft [Critique of Pure Reason]*, A 239. Regarding this point and more generally, Bernhard Dotzler, "Die Revolution der Denkart und das Denken der Maschine: Kant und Turing," *Diskursanalysen 1: Medien*, eds. Friedrich A. Kittler, Manfred Schneider, Samuel Weber (Opladen, 1987), 150–163.
4. Cf. Immanuel Kant, *Kritik der Urteilskraft [Critique of Judgment]*, B 79ff.
5. Cf. Kant, *Kritik der Urteilskraft*, B 16.
6. Jacques Lacan, *The Seminar of Jacques Lacan. Book II: The Ego in Freud's Theory and in the Technique of Psychoanalysis 1954–1955*, ed. Jacques-Alain Miller, trans. Sylvana Tomaselli (New York: W.W. Norton & Company, 1988), 46.
7. Lacan, *Seminar II*, 46.
8. Jacques Lacan, "Remarques sur le rapport de Daniel Lagache," *Écrits* (Paris: 1966) 679.
9. Cf. Lacan, "Remarques sur le rapport . . .," 66ff.
10. Manfred Frank, *Was ist Neostrukturalismus?* (Frankfurt/M.: 1983), 398.
11. Lacan, *Seminar II*, 46.
12. Frank, 358 and 538.
13. Cf. Friedrich Kittler, "Das Subjekt als Beamter," *Die Frage nach dem Subject*, eds. Manfred Frank, Gérard Raulet and William van Reijen (Frankfurt/M.: 1988), 403–5.

14. Sigmund Freud, *An Outline of Psychoanalysis*, in *The Standard Edition of the Complete Works of Sigmund Freud*, Vol. XXIII, ed. and trans. James Strachey et al., with Anna Freud (London: Hogarth, 1964), 196.

15. Jürgen Habermas, *Knowledge and Human Interests*, trans. Jeremy J. Shapiro (Boston: Beacon, 1971), 214ff.

16. Sigmund Freud, *The Origins of Psychoanalysis. Letters to Wilhelm Fliess, Drafts and Notes: 1887–1902*, eds. Maria Bonaparte, Anna Freud and Ernst Kris, trans. Eric Mosbacher and James Strachey, (New York: Basic Books, 1954), 359.

17. Freud, *The Origins of Psychoanalysis*, 360.

18. Josef Breuer, *Studies on Hysteria*, in Freud, *The Origins of Psychoanalysis*, 363, n.1.

19. Cf. Jacques Derrida, "Freud and the Scene of Writing," *Writing and Difference*, trans. Alan Bass (Chicago: U Chicago P, 1978), 196–231.

20. Sigmund Freud, *Recommendations to Physicians Practicing Psycho-Analysis*, in Freud, *Standard Edition*, Vol. XII, 115ff.

21. Jean Marie Guyau, *La mémoire et la phonographe* (1880).

22. Sigmund Freud, *Fragment of an Analysis of a Case of Hysteria*, in Freud, *Standard Edition*, Vol. XII, 10.

23. Sigmund Freud, *New Introductory Lectures on Psychoanalysis*, in Freud, *Standard Edition*, Vol. XXII, 5.

24. Freud acquired a typewriter in his house in 1913. Cf. Ernest Jones, *The Life and Work of Sigmund Freud*, Vol. II (New York: Basic Books, 1955), 98.

25. Frank, 394.

26. Lacan, *Seminar II*, 74ff. (It is true that Lacan dates Watt's centrifugal governor, which actually went into operation in 1784, after Jena, Auerstedt and the "Phenomenology of Spirit.").

27. Jacques Lacan, *Écrits* (Paris: 1966), 720.

28. René Descartes, *The Geometry*, trans. David Eugene Smith and Marcia L. Latham, in *Great Books of the Western World*, vol. 28, ed. Mortimer J. Adler (Chicago: Encyclopaedia Britannica, 1952/1990), 564.

29. Descartes, 560.

30. Descartes, 562.

31. Cf. Descartes, 526ff.

32. Jacqes Lacan, *Écrits: A Selection*, trans. Alan Sheridan (New York: W. W. Norton & Company, 1977), 318 ff.

33. Lacan, *Seminar II*, 285.

34. Jacques Lacan, "Seminar on 'The Purloined Letter,' " trans. Jeffrey Martin, in *The Purloined Poe: Lacan, Derrida & Psychoanalytic Reading*, eds. John P. Muller and William J. Richardson (Baltimore: The Johns Hopkins UP, 1988), 40. On the difference between the mathematical self-sufficiency of the symbolic and the physical measurement of the real, cf. Bernhard Riemann, "On the Hypotheses Which Lie at the Foundations of Geometry," trans. Prof. Henry S. White, *Source Book in Mathematics*, 1st ed., ed. David Eugene Smith (New York: McGraw-Hill, 1854/1929) 424: "The question of the validity of the postulates of geometry in the indefinitely small is involved in the question concerning the ultimate basis of relations of size in space. In connection with this question, which may well be assigned to the philosophy of space, the above remark is applicable, namely that while in a discrete manifold the principle of metric relations is implicit in the notion of this manifold, it must come from somewhere else in the case of a continuous manifold. Either then

the actual things forming the groundwork of a space must constitute a
discrete manifold, or else the basis of metric relations must be sought for
outside that actuality, in colligating forces that operate upon it."

35. Lacan, *Seminar II*, 284.
36. Cf. Andrew S. Glassner, "Surface Physics for Ray Tracing," *An Introduction to Ray Tracing*, ed. Andrew S. Glassner (London: 1989), 130–137.
37. Cf. Stephen W. Hawking, *A Brief History of Time* (Toronto: Bantam, 1988) 134, 143ff.
38. Lacan, *Écrits* (Paris).
39. Paul Flechsig, *Über die Associationscentren des menschlichen Gehirns. Dritter Internationaler Congress für Psychologie in München vom 4. bis 7. August 1896* (München: 1897) 58. As if in formulation of Lacan's theorem of *corps morcelé*, Flechsig says the following: "The newborn, the infant, probably has a great number of *distinct consciousness circles*. Initially, every sensory sphere represents a distinct, independent organ which absorbs sensations of a particular quality, processes them to a greater or lesser degree, that is cathects them, transmits them to the locomotor system of the corresponding sensory instrument, practices perhaps the movements of the same, and the like. In the beginning, therefore, the undeveloped areas of the cerebral lobes lying between the individual sensory centers appear as isolators, like the ocean surfaces which separate the continents of the Earth." One should compare Frank's elegiac discussion of Lacan, the infant, and the mother (Frank, 383) with Flechsig's precision as a physiologist.
40. Frank, 399.
41. Lacan, *Seminar II*, 54.
42. Lacan, *Seminar II*, 82.
43. Lacan, *Écrits*, 86ff.
44. Lacan, *Seminar II*, 82.
45. Lacan, *Seminar II*, 83.
46. Cf. Lacan, *Écrits* (Paris), 658.
47. Cf. Lacan *Écrits*, 153: Because language consists of differentially determined elements, "one sees that an essential element of the spoken word itself was predestined to flow into the mobile characters which, in a jumble of lower-case Didots or Garamonds, render validly present what we call the 'letter,' namely, the essentially localized structure of the signifier."
48. Lacan, *Seminar II*, 47.
49. Lacan, *Seminar II*, 47.
50. Lacan, "Seminar on E.A. Poe's 'The Purloined Letter,' " *Écrits* (Paris), 61.
51. Lacan, "Seminar on 'The Purloined Letter,' " *The Purloined Poe*, 43.
52. Lacan, "Seminar on E.A. Poe's 'The Purloined Letter,' " *Écrits* (Paris) 60; cf. Lacan, *Seminar II*, 304.
53. Lacan, *Seminar II*, 298.
54. Lacan, *Seminar II*, 300.
55. Alan Turing, *Intelligent Machines* (1969).
56. Cf. Friedrich-Wilhelm Hagemeyer, *Die Entstehung von Informationskonzepten in der Nachrichtentechnik. Eine Fallstudie zur Theoriebildung in der Technik in Industrie-und Kriegsforschung.* (Diss. phil. FU Berlin, 1979).
57. Cf. Lacan, *Seminar II*, 298–300.
58. Lacan, *Seminar II*, 299.

59. Lacan, *Seminar II*, 306.
60. Cf. Lacan, *Seminar II*, 48.
61. Cf. Lacan, "Seminar on E.A. Poe's 'The Purloined Letter,' " *Écrits* (Paris), 53.
62. Jacques Lacan, *Seminar XX: Encore* (Paris: 1975), 76.
63. Cf. Lacan, *Seminar II*, 297–300.
64. Lacan, *Seminar II*, 300.
65. Lacan, *Seminar II*, 300.
66. Lacan, *Seminar II*, 77–90.
67. Lacan, *Seminar II*, 302.
68. Cf. Robert A. Kowalski, "Algorithm = Logic + Control," *Communications of the Association for Computing Machinery* (2: 1979), 424–436.
69. Lacan, *Seminar II*, 88.
70. Lacan, "Seminar on E.A. Poe's 'The Purloined Letter,' " *Écrits* (Paris), 42.
71. Lacan, *Seminar II*, 89.
72. Lacan, *Seminar II*, 83.
73. Lacan, *Écrits*, 304.
74. Lacan, "Seminar on E.A. Poe's 'The Purloined Letter,' " *Écrits* (Paris), 59.
75. Cf. Lacan, *Seminar II*, 88.
76. Cf. Friedrich Kittler, *Grammophon Film Typewriter* (Berlin: Brinkmann & Bose, 1986), 372ff.
77. Cf. Norbert Wiener, *Cybernetics: or Control and Communication in the Animal and the Machine*, 2nd ed. (Cambridge: MIT Press, 1948/1961), 28.
78. Niklas Luhmann, oral.
79. Cf. Lacan, *Seminar II*, 72.

There Is No Software

1. See Klaus Schrödl, Quantensprung, DOS 12/1990: 102f.
2. See Alan M. Turing, *On Computable Numbers, with an Application to the Entscheidungsproblems*, Proceedings of the London Mathematical Society, 2nd ser. 42 (1937), 249.
3. Stephen C. Kleene, quoted by Robert Rosen, "Effective Processes and Natural Law," in Rolf Herken, ed., *The Universal Turing Machine: A Half-Century Survey* (Oxford: Oxford University Press, 1988), 527.
4. See Johannes Lohmann, "Die Geburt der Tragödie aus dem Geiste der Musik," Archiv für Musikwissenschaft (1980), 174.
5. See Andrew Hodges, *Alan Turing: The Enigma* (New York: Simon and Schuster, 1983), 399.
6. See *TOOL Praxis: Assembler-Programmierung auf dem PC*, 1st ed. (Würzburg: Vogel, 1989), 9.
7. Nabajyoti Barkalati, *The Waite Group's Macroassembler Bible* (Carmel, Indiana: Howard H. Sams, 1989), 528.
8. See Friedrich Kittler, "Protected Mode," in this volume.
9. See Friedrich Kittler, "Signal-Rausch-Abstand," in Hans Ulrich Gumbrecht and Karl Ludwig Pfeiffer, eds., *Materialität der Kommunikation* (Frankfurt a. M.: Suhramps 1988), 343–45.
10. Charles H. Bennett, "Logical Depth and Physical Complexity," in Herken, ed., 230.
11. With thanks to Oswald Wiener/Yukon.

12. *The German says* Vgl. M. Michael König, 1991, Sachlich sehen. Probleme bei der Überlassung von Software. C't, Heft 3, 5. 73. (Bundesgerichtshofentscheidung vorn 2.5, 1985, Az. IZB 8/84, NIW-RR 1986, 219). Programs are defined as "Verkörperungen der geistigen Leistung damit aber Sachen" ("embodiments of intellectual achievement, but in material things").

13. I am at a loss to understand how Turing's famous paper could, in its first line, "briefly describe the 'computable numbers' as the real numbers whose expressions as a decimal are calculable by finite means" (Turing, *On Computable Numbers,* 230), then proceed to define the set of computable numbers as countable and, finally, to call Pi, taken as "the limit of a computably convergent sequence," a computable number (256).

14. Brossl Hasslacher, "Algorithms in the World of Bounded Resources," in Herken, ed., 421f.

15. Hasslacher, 420.

16. See Friedrich-Wilhelm Hagemeyer, "Die Entstehung von Informationskonzepter der Nachrichtentechnik. Eine Fallstudie zur Theoriebildung in der Technik Industrie und Kriegsforschung," Ph.D. dissertation, Free University, Berlin, 1979, 432.

17. See Alan Turning "Intelligent Machinery: A Heretical Theory," in Sarah Turing, *Alan M. Turing* (Cambridge: W. Heffer, 1959), 134.

18. Michael Conrad, "The Price of Programmability," in Herken, ed., 289.

19. Conrad, 293.

20. Conrad, 290.

21. Conrad, 304.

22. See Conrad ,303f.

Protected Mode

1. Cf. Andrew Hodges, *Alan Turing: The Enigma* (New York: Simon and Schuster, 1983), 399.

2. Cf. Alan M. Turing, "On Computable Numbers, with an Application to the Entscheidungsproblem," *Proceedings of the London Mathematical Society* (42: Jan. 1937), 230–265.

3. Cf. Microsoft Corporation, *Macro Assembler 5.1, Reference* (1987) 115: "This section provides an alphabetic reference to instructions of the 8087, 80287, and 80387 coprocessors. The format is the same as for the processor instructions except that encodings are not provided."

4. TOOL Praxis, *Assembler-Programming auf dem PC. Ausgabe 1* (1989: Würzburg), 9.

5. TOOL Praxis, 39.

6. Regarding one-way functions in mathematics and cryptology, cf. Patrick Horster, *Kryptologie: eine Anwendung der Zahlentheorie und Komplexitätatheorie* (Mannheim-Wien-Zürich: 1982/1985), 23–27.

7. Personal communication of Hartley to Friedrich-Wilhelm Hagemeyer, Berlin.

8. Klaus-Dieter Thies, *Das 80186-Handbuch* (Düsseldorf-Berkeley-Paris: 1986), 319.

9. For details of the Pentagon specification pamphlet, cf. D. Curtis Schleher, *Introduction to Electronic Warfare* (Norwood/MA: 1986).

10. Cf. Gerry Kane, *68000 Microprocessor Book* (Berkeley: 1981), 8ff.
11. Cf. Michael Löwe, "VHSIC: Ultraschnelle Schaltkreise frisch vom Band ins Pentagon," *Militarisierte Informatik*, eds. Joachim Bickenbach, Reinhard Keil-Slawik, Michael Löwe and Rudolf Wilhelm (Münster: 1985), 64.
12. Harald Albrecht, *MSDOS in a box. Teil 1* (1990), 258.
13. Cf. Carl Schmitt, *Gespräch über die Macht und den Zugang zum Machthaber* (Pfullingen: 1954).
14. This occurred with a QEMM 386 from Quarterdeck during an attempt to execute the commands LGDT and SGDT within CODEVIEW.
15. For evidence from an authorized source, namely the Intel Corporation, cf. Sharad Gandhi, "Die Intel Architektur & RISC," in *Pentium-Prozessor. Die nächste Generation der Intel Architecktur*, eds. Johann Wiesböck, Bernhard Wopperer, Gerold Wurthmann (Haar: 1993), 80: "The primary benefit of a faster CPU, which the RISC-Processors previously had, will in time become more of a secondary quality. Let me put forward an analogy. The core of the CPU behaves like an entrepeneur who starts a new, innovative company. If the company is small, it flourishes according to the ideas and inspirations of the entrepeneur. With increasing size, the company's success will be increasingly determined through peripheral functions such as sales, marketing, publicity, finances, accounting, and so on, functions which usually have no connection to the company's product. Large companies compete with each other on the basis of their peripheral functions. In the future, the performance share of the (mathematical) core will continue to decrease." This is a strangely ambiguous estimation of success which would also permit totally different endings and thoughts on still newer innovative companies. If on the chip surface of the Pentium-Processor, only 8% in calculating performance is opposed to 92% in self-representation of the company (Ghandi 79), then high-technology comes dangerously close to the ratio between brain and body weight in dinosaurs.
16. Cf. Arne Schäpers, *Turbo Pascal 5.0* (Bonn-Reading/MA-Menlo Park/CA-New York-Don Mills-Wokingham-Amsterdam-Sydney-Singapore-Tokyo-Madrid-San Juan: 1989), 1: " 'The processor's address space is organized through the architecture of the system into areas of RAM and ROM, whereby the RAM becomes subdivided into the operating system into storage blocks for the recording of programs. One program consists of individual segments, a portion of which contain procedures and functions which for their part can locally define further routines.' One is almost reminded of a painting by Escher (or even more to the spirit of the age, by Apfelmännchen)."
17. Cf. Jacques Lacan, *Écrits*, trans. Alan Sheridan (New York: W.W. Norton & Company, 1977), 316.
18. Cf. Intel Corporation, *80386 Programmer's Reference Manual*, Chap. 17 (Santa Clara/CA: 1986), 145: "The DS, ES, FS, and GS segment registers can be set to 0 by the RET instruction during an interlevel transfer. If these registers refer to segments that cannot be used by the new privilege level, they are set to 0 to prevent unauthorized access from the new privilege level." In the code segment GS, such sledge-hammer protection tactics are eliminated in order not to block the entire system.
19. Cf. Intel Corporation, Chap. 14, 1.
20. Intel Corporation, Chap. 9, 16.

21. Cf. Harald Albrecht, *Grenzenlos. Vier Gigabyte im Real Mode der 80386 adressieren*, Vol. 1 (1990), 212: "In the 80386, the segment boundary of 64 K-Bytes is not as firmly set as it appears, for example, in Intel's documentation over the 386 DX. If one persistently follows the necessary steps for the return of the 80386 out of Protected Mode into Real Mode, then suddenly the entire address space of the 4 G-Bytes of Real Mode is opened up (whereby the smirk of the Motorola fans noticeably diminishes in width)." The following is with extensive thanks to this really inspired suggestion.

22. One exception is made, though tellingly without any commentary, in Klaus-Dieter Thies, *PC XT AT Numerik Buch. Hochgenaue Gleitpunkt-Arithmetik mit 8087 . . . 80287 . . . 80387 . . . Nutzung mathematischer Bibliotheksfunktionen in 'Assembler' und 'C,' "* (München: 1989), 638. Edmund Strauss, on the other hand, though he (according to the Preface of the 80386 architect, Robert Childs) "has seen the full range of system issues and devised many practical solutions during his work for Intel," completes the work of art by keeping silent about the non-documented room for play, over the course of an entire authoritative handbook. Cf. Edmund Strauss, *80386 Technical Reference. The guide for getting the most from Intel's 80386* (New York: 1987).

23. Cf. Andrew Stiller, *Bitter für 32-Bitter*, Heft 8 (1990) 202. For details on the command LOADALL (including the dubious assertion that only the 80286 accepts it), cf. Norbert Juffa and Peter Siering, *Wege über die Mauer. Loadall—Extended Memory in Real Mode des 80286*, Heft 11 (1990), 362–6.

24. Löwe, 70.

Essays by Friedrich A. Kittler reprinted in this book orginally appeared in the following publications:

"Gramophone, Film, Typewriter"
    as Preface to *Grammophon Film Typewriter*, 3–6. Berlin: Brinkmann & Bose, 1985.
    English translation by Stefanie Harris; and
    as Introduction to *Grammophon Film Typewriter*, 7–33.
    English translation in *October* 41 (Summer 1987): 101–18.
    Reprinted by permission.

    Both translations are published with the permission of Stanford University Press,
    publishers of the forthcoming *Grammophon Film Typewriter* by Friedrich Kittler,
    tr. Winthrop-Young and Wutz (1998).

"Dracula's Legacy"
    under the title "Draculas Vermächtnis" in *Draculas Vermächtnis: Technische
    Schriften*, 11–57. Leipzig: Reclam Verlag, 1993.
    English translation in *Stanford Humanities Review* 1 (1989): 143–73.
    Reprinted by permission.

"Romanticism—Psychoanalysis—Film: A History of the Double"
    under the title "Romantik—Psychoanalyse—Film: eine Doppelgängergeschichte" in
    Draculas Vermächtnis: Technische Schriften, 81–104.
    Reprinted by permission.

"Media and Drugs in Pynchon's Second World War"
    under the title "Medien und Drogen in Pynchons Zweitem Weltkrieg" in *Die
    Unvollendete Vernunft. Moderne versus Postmoderne*, ed. Diemar Kamper and
    Willem van Reijen, 240–59. Frankfurt am Main: Suhrkamp Verlag, 1987.
    © Suhrkamp Verlag 1987.
    Reprinted by permission.

"Media Wars: Trenches, Lightning, Stars"
    English translation in *1-800* (Fall 1989): 5–9.
    Reprinted by permission.

"The World of the Symbolic—A World of the Machine"
    under the title "Die Welt des Symbolischen—eine Welt der Maschine" in
    Draculas Vermächtnis: Technische Schriften, 58–80.
    Reprinted by permission.

"There is No Software"
    under the title "Es gibt keine Software" in *Draculas Vermächtnis: Technische
    Schriften*, 225–44.
    English translation in *Stanford Humanities Review* 1 (1989): 81–90.
    Reprinted by permission.

"Protected Mode"
    in *Draculas Vermächtnis: Technische Schriften*, 208–24.
    Reprinted by permission.